INESSENTIAL SOLIDARITY

Pittsburgh Series in Composition, Literacy, and Culture

DAVID BARTHOLOMAE AND JEAN FERGUSON CARR, Editors

INESSENTIAL SOLIDARITY

RHETORIC AND FOREIGNER RELATIONS

Diane Davis

UNIVERSITY OF PITTSBURGH PRESS

Published by the University of Pittsburgh Press, Pittsburgh, Pa., 15260
Copyright © 2010, University of Pittsburgh Press
All rights reserved
Manufactured in the United States of America
Printed on acid-free paper
10 9 8 7 6 5 4 3 2 1

Library of Congress Cataloging-in-Publication Data

Davis, D. Diane (Debra Diane), 1963–
   Inessential solidarity : rhetoric and foreigner relations / Diane Davis.
      p. cm. — (Pittsburgh series in composition, literacy, and culture)
   Includes bibliographical references and index.
   ISBN 978-0-8229-6122-2 (pbk. : alk. paper)
   1. English language—Rhetoric. 2. Language and culture. 3. Critical
theory. I. Title.
   PE1408.D2384 2010
   808'.042—dc22   2010020950

To Mom and Dad—
for your enduring courage and your gigantic hearts

Contents

Acknowledgments

I am very grateful to the students in my seminars over the last few years, for their insights and enthusiasm, their humor and tenacity, which kept me on my toes—thanks especially to Jennifer Edbauer Rice, Kevin Johnson, Johanna Hartelius, Jamie Wright, James Brown, and Trevor Hoag. I am deeply indebted to colleagues who offered me feedback on this work, talking me through small sections and/or responding to one or more chapters: Michelle Ballif, Michael Bernard-Donals, Timothy Crusius, Christopher Fynsk, Joshua Gunn, Werner Hamacher, Michael Hyde, Steven Mailloux, John Muckelbauer, Jean-Luc Nancy, Jeffrey Nealon, Avital Ronell, Wolfgang Schirmarcher, Fred Ulfers, and Victor J. Vitanza. I owe Michelle a spa day for her speedy and constant responsiveness: thank you. Chapter one owes itself entirely to Avital, as it was written in response to a comment she scribbled in the margins of a very early draft of what is now chapter two: "too fast." And chapter three owes itself to Steve, as it was written in response, finally, to a challenge he issued over his beer in downtown Austin in 2002. Thank you all for your inspiration, your guidance, your generosity, and your friendship.

I'd like to thank my wonderful colleagues at the University of Texas at Austin for challenging, supporting, and entertaining me over the last several years, for offering me a sheltering space in which to write, teach, and play. And I want to express my gratitude to Milan and Vera Kundera, who graciously granted me permission to cite a long and crucial passage from *Immortality*.

I don't have to tell you, the ones for whom I write, that the demand of writing can really wear a Dasein down, or that precious moments of lollygagging-with can play as vital a role in the production of a work as any text on the works cited page. So, I want to thank my dear friends Michelle, Victor, Avital, Cynthia Haynes, Rebecca Sabounchi, Roxanne Mountford, Brette Lea, and Lisa Neumann Minnick for consistently generating lightness, often under a weight; my amazing guys, Paul Mowery and Mojo Mowery Davis, not only for their patience and understanding, but for frequently peeling me away from my desk with the most unique and persuasive of appeals; and my parents, Guy and Jeanne McNeely for their love, encouragement, and unwavering faith in me.

Portions of this book have appeared in various forms: Chapter one was originally published in *Rhetoric Society Quarterly* as "Identification: Burke and Freud on Who You Are," 38.2 (2008): 123–47. An early version of chapter three appeared in *Philosophy and Rhetoric* as "Addressing Alerity: Rhetoric, Hermeneutics, and the Non-Appropriative Relation," 38.3 (2005): 191–212. And a very early version of the "P. S. on Humanism" was published in a special issue of *JAC: A Journal of Composition Theory* devoted to the work of Emmanuel Levinas as "Greetings: On Levinas and the Wagging Tail," 29.1 (2009): 711–48. I am grateful to the editors for their permission to revise and reprint this material.

Abbreviations

The following abbreviations have been used in the text for frequently cited sources. Full documentation is provided in the list of works cited.

A	Jacques Derrida. *Adieu to Emmanuel Levinas.*
BIC	Jean-Luc Nancy. "Of Being-in-Common."
BT	Martin Heidegger. *Being and Time.*
CW	Avital Ronell. *Crack Wars: Literature Addiction Mania.*
D	Jean-François Lyotard. *The Differend: Phrases in Dispute.*
DF	Emmanuel Levinas. *Difficult Freedom: Essays on Judaism.*
EE	Emmanuel Levinas. *Existence and Existents.*
EI	Emmanuel Levinas. *Ethics and Infinity.*
ET	Mikkel Borch-Jacobsen. *The Emotional Tie: Psychoanalysis, Mimesis, and Affect.*
FS	Mikkel Borch-Jacobsen. *The Freudian Subject.*
GP	Sigmund Freud. *Group Psychology and the Analysis of the Ego.*
IC	Maurice Blanchot. *The Infinite Conversation.*
IOC	Jean-Luc Nancy. *The Inoperative Community.*
IR	Emmanuel Levinas. *Is It Righteous to Be?*
OCF	Jacques Derrida. *On Cosmopolitanism and Forgiveness.*
OH	Jacques Derrida and Anne Dufourmantelle. *Of Hospitality.*
OTB	Emmanuel Levinas. *Otherwise than Being: Or, Beyond Essence.*
OTWL	Martin Heidegger. *On the Way to Language.*
RH	Steven Mailloux. *Reception Histories: Rhetoric, Pragmatism, and American Cultural Politics.*
RM	Kenneth Burke. *A Rhetoric of Motives.*
RR	Paul de Man. *The Rhetoric of Romanticism.*
S	Avital Ronell. *Stupidity.*
SL	Maurice Blanchot. *The Space of Literature.*
TI	Emmanuel Levinas. *Totality and Infinity: An Essay on Exteriority.*
TO	Emmanuel Levinas. *Time and the Other.*
WCT	Martin Heidegger. *What Is Called Thinking?*
WD	Maurice Blanchot. *The Writing of the Disaster.*

INESSENTIAL SOLIDARITY

A Rhetoric of Responsibility

But communication would be impossible
if it should have to begin in the ego, a free subject,
to whom every other would only be a limitation that invites war,
domination, precaution and information.

Emmanuel Levinas, *Otherwise than Being*

The unconditionality of being hostage is
not the limit case of solidarity, but the condition for all solidarity.

Emmanuel Levinas, *Otherwise than Being*

In *A Rhetoric of Motives*, Kenneth Burke makes a point that perhaps goes without saying in rhetorical studies today: belonging is fundamentally rhetorical (27–28). That insight will serve as the thesis of this present work, but with a twist. According to Burke, belonging is not fixed ontologically by a shared essence but is instead a function of rhetorical identification, which is itself an effect of shared symbol systems. Scholars in rhetorical studies generally accept this elemental insight: what is common among those who "belong together" does not constitute an essence. What is common among the members of a nation, an ethnic group, a gang, or even a family operates not ontologically but symbolically—"blood" every bit as much as "native soil," "cultural history," and "turf colors." Nonetheless, inasmuch as what is common is identified as a *condition* for belonging, inasmuch as it symbolizes a bond or property that is shared by otherwise *discrete* "individuals," it is both retroactively essentialized and grounded in the presumption of a prior essence. The field remains mostly unaware of or unconcerned with an intersection of rhetoric and solidarity that neither references a preexisting essence of the individual (organism) nor installs, as a product of human work, an essence of the community (of the "common").[1]

In the pages that follow, the primary goal will be to expose a sort of commonality oblivious to borders (a *débordement*) that precedes and exceeds symbolic identification and therefore any prerequisite for belonging; or, put another way: the goal is to expose an originary (or preoriginary) rhetoricity—an affect*ability* or persuad*ability*—that is the condition for symbolic action. I get how this may sound, but I'm not going mystical or even particularly abstract on you here. By definition, communication can take place only among existents who are given over to an "outside," exposed, open to the other's affection and effraction. And this "community," without essence or project, this foreign(er) *relation* irreducible to symbolic prereqs, will be the primary focus of our investigation. Let me say provisionally that what's at stake in this exposition of exposedness is the affirmation of a "rhetorical power," as Steven Mailloux might put it, that is not the effect of representation (conscious or unconscious). As anyone who has irrepressibly tapped her foot to an unfamiliar tune will acknowledge, "persuasion" frequently succeeds without presenting itself to cognitive scrutiny. The fact that this extra-symbolic rhetoricity remains irreducible to epistemological frame-ups makes it no less powerful, no less fundamental, no less significant to rhetorical studies.

By pulling into focus this always prior rhetoricity that is the condition for what is called the "art" of rhetoric, I intend neither to drown "little rhetoric" in the sea of "big rhetoric" nor to subordinate rhetorical practice to rhetorical theory. I hope, rather, to begin to articulate a different sort of task for rhetorical studies, a theoretical task indissociable from its practical implementation. The task: to examine the implications of this always prior relation to the foreign(er) without which no meaning-making or determinate (symbolic) relation would be possible. I hope, that is, to nudge rhetorical studies beyond the epistemological concerns that have for so long circumscribed our theories of persuasion toward the examination of a more fundamental affectability, persuadability, responsivity. What would it mean for rhetorical practice, theory, and analysis if we were to acknowledge that communication in the most simplistic sense—as symbolic exchange—does not first of all lead to solidarity or "community" but instead remains utterly dependent upon a sharing and a response-ability that precede it? What would it mean for the field's focus if it could be shown that rhetoric's operations exceed not simply the representations of the intentional subject but the "subject of representation" as such, the symbol using animal who knows itself as and through its representations? What theoretical and analytical practices might emerge if it were admitted that rhetorical identification, for example, is at work prior to and in excess of symbolic meaning, prior even to the symbolic distinction between self and other? Or if it could be demonstrated that rhetoric is not, therefore, indissociable from hermeneutics? What would it mean for our theories of social change or for public sphere studies if it could be shown that the speaking subject is the product neither of self-determination nor of structural overdetermination but instead emerges, each time, according to a relationality and responsivity irreducible to dramatistic mappings? My aim is not once and for all to answer these questions; it is only to provoke them, to hold them open, to begin a conversation with you that is long overdue.

In a certain way, this book joins a vast array of other works in the field devoted to examining rhetoric's relation with relationality itself. As Walter Jost and Michael Hyde put it in their introduction to *Rhetoric and Hermeneutics in Our Time*, rhetoric is "a practice that by its very nature is *other-oriented*" (29). Indeed, the practice of rhetoric is frequently celebrated for its capacity to create cohesive social bonds, to incite unification where there would otherwise be fragmentation and violence; it is praised for inviting identification through the exchange of shared meaning and values, and for its ability to provoke social change by moving audiences to action or to attitude, either through direct argumentation or, more subtly, through epideictic's display.[2] The flip side to this optimistic take on the role that rhetoric plays in the building and sustaining of social bonds is also frequently explored: the problems of the scapegoat and, more generally, of congregation via segregation.[3] And I have no desire to quibble with any of this or to produce a polemic. I do, however, propose that there is another, prior intersection of rhetoric and solidarity that the field has left virtually unexamined and that could have a profound effect on both its self-understanding and its scholarly practices. For there to be any sharing of symbolic meaning, any construction of a common enemy or collective goal, any effective use of persuasive discourse at all, a more originary rhetoricity must already be operating, a consitutive persuadability and responsivity that testifies, first of all, to a fundamental structure of exposure. If rhetorical practices work by managing to have an effect on others, then an always prior openness to the other's affection is its first requirement: the "art" of rhetoric can be effective only among affectable existents, who are by definition something other than distinct individuals or self-determining agents, and whose relations necessarily precede and exceed symbolic intervention.[4] We are talking here about an intersection of rhetoric and solidarity that would be the condition not only for symbolic action but for the symbol-using animal itself.

Being-With

An obscene amount of political, ethical, and scholarly energy has been invested in "the individual," that indivisible atom, absolutely detached and for-itself, which is situated at the origin of the origin. And yet, "one cannot make the world with simple atoms," Jean-Luc Nancy reminds us. "There has to be a *clinamen*. There has to be an inclination or an inclining from one toward the other, of one by another, or from one to the other. Community is at least the *clinamen* of the 'individual.'" Rephrased for our purposes: solidarity is at least the rhetoricity of the affect as such, the "individual's" irreparable openness to affection/alteration. But "there is no theory, ethics, politics, or metaphysics of the individual that is capable of envisaging this *clinamen*, this declination or decline of the individual within community." What individualism can't quite assimilate is that "the atom is a world" (*IOC* 3–4). Despite the breathlessness of the presentation, this is what Heidegger demonstrates in *Being and Time*: that there is no being that is not already being-with, no Dasein that is not already *Mitsein* or *Mit-da-sein*. Nancy tracks the unplumbed (and perhaps unplumbable) implications of the insight, pointing out that "the 'mit' does not modify the 'sein,' (as if being could already sustain itself in some way, as if being *were itself*, that is as if being *were* or *existed* absolutely)"; but further still, he continues, "the 'mit' does not even qualify the 'Dasein,' but . . . constitutes it essentially." This means that "the *there*" of Da-sein "is not a grounding for existence," Nancy insists, "but rather its taking *place*, its arrival, its coming—which also means its difference, its withdrawal, its excess, its 'exscription'" (*BIC* 2).

Though Heidegger's split-second explication of the originariness of being-with is elliptical, it nonetheless issues an irrevocable challenge to pre-Heideggerian approaches to ontology: if the "with" is already operative essentially, constitutively, then contamination is originary and ontology's project is busted before it begins. There is no longer any way to pose its defining question, a question of uncontaminated essence: "what is X?" There is no immanent or intrinsic being, no essence in itself that would therefore be capable of presenting itself as such. What Heidegger gives us to think is that prior to the symbolic exchange of any particular content—prior also, then, to the symbolic distinction between self and other—the "I" is already a kind of "we," the singularity is already a collective. Being is not simply posed; it is exposed. "The logic of the 'with,'" Nancy explains, "is the singular logic of an inside-outside," the existential equivalent of a Klein jar or Möbius strip (*BIC* 6). This originary "collective," then—which

Nancy will elsewhere, disappointingly, call "fraternity"[5]—consists not in a shared essence or common being (or even a common purpose or interest or practice or value) but in a sharing out (*partáge*) of being itself. The solidarity from which any sense of the "individual" would have to be extracted takes place as being-*in*-common, precisely to the extent that it is not "common being." "Henceforth," Nancy writes, "the question should be the community of being, and not the being of community. Or if you prefer: the community of existence, and not the essence of community" (*BIC* 1).

Behind and beyond the theme of the individual, Nancy proposes, "lurks the question of singularity. What is *a* body, *a* face, *a* voice, *a* death, *a* writing—not indivisible but singular?" Singularity does not have the indivisible and so identifiable nature or structure of the individual; rather, singularity "takes place at the level of the *clinamen*, which is unidentifiable" (*IOC* 6–7).[6] Singularity, then, is not simply an upgraded or more theoretically sophisticated synonym for the individual. Nor—and here Nancy breaks with the early Heidegger—does the singular being emerge through a process of "singularization," as if it rose up "against the background of a chaotic, undifferentiated identity of beings"—that is, against the background of what Heidegger calls "the 'they'" (*IOC* 27).[7] Rather "'singularity' would designate precisely that which, each time, forms a point of exposure, traces an intersection of limits on which there is exposure. To be exposed," Nancy continues, "is to be on the limit where, at the same time, there is both inside and outside, and neither inside nor outside." Singularity is exposedness itself, an "in oneself" that *is* only by virtue of partition: "both division and distribution." This limit, in joining what it also separates, is the site of an "extreme *abandonment* in which all property . . . is first of all given over to the outside (but not to the outside of an inside . . .)." This makes the singularity "a generalized ectopia of all 'proper' places," an inside that is "brought about essentially by a 'cleaving' or by a 'schism.'" Singularity is what it is only inasmuch as it is exposed on and as its limit (*BIC* 7, 8).

In contemporary physics, a singularity indicates a particular anomaly that escapes all known laws of physics (the big bang is a famous example) but that is not simply observable because it resides inside a black hole, which sucks everything inward, including light, and remains hidden beyond an event horizon. A naked singularity, on the other hand, is described as an anomaly that occurs (theoretically) without an event horizon; it therefore would be an observable yet still wildly ungraspable "event." Nancy's sociopolitical use of the term "singularity" is aligned with naked singularity, as both would be observable (exposed) but not for that reason simply containable or assimilable. The singular being is not enclosed in a form and cannot appear or even exist alone; singularity is by definition shared. As exposedness, says Nancy, the singular being "appears as finitude itself: at the end (or at the beginning) with the contact of the skin (or the heart) of another singular being, at the confines of the same singularity, that is, as such, always other, always shared, always exposed" (*IOC* 28).[8]

Significantly, this "appearing (*apparaître*) is not an appearance (*apparence*); it is on the contrary the at once glorious and destitute appearing (*paraître*) of being-finite itself," Nancy writes (*IOC* 28). The dichotomous energy separating finitude from infinity is here dissolved: "finitude is the truth of which the infinite is the sense," as Nancy puts it elsewhere (*Sense of the World* 29). Infinity is inherent in finitude, which is not about absolute boundaries but about being-on-the-limit, *as* the limit: being as threshold. "It would be foolish to imagine that finitude designates an absolute limit," Avital Ronell explains. "An absolute limit—if it were possible to imagine such a thing—would be a boundary without an outside, without a foreign, neighboring land, an edge without an outer dimension" (*Finitude's Score* 5). But there is no essence or in-itselfness of finitude; it is only inasmuch as it is shared. "Finitude itself *is* nothing," Nancy writes; it is not an essence and so cannot operate as a ground or show up as a substance. But it does appear: "it presents itself, it exposes itself, and thus it *exists* as communication . . . finitude co-appears or *compears* (*com-paraît*) and can only *compear*: in this formulation we would need to hear that finite being always presents itself 'together,' hence severally" (*IOC* 28).[9]

The communication to which Nancy refers is not a bond but consists *in* this exposition and compearance. For "compearance is of a more originary order than that of a bond. It does not set itself up, it does not establish itself, it does not emerge among already given subjects (objects). It consists in the appearance of the *between* as such: you *and* I (between us)." Communication as exposition and compearance has nothing to do with the transfer of messages or the desire for consensus or recognition. It has nothing to do with rules or strategies or communicative competence. Before any of that, before all else, "in 'communication' what takes place is an exposition: finite existent exposed to finite existent, co-appearing before it and with it" (*IOC* xl). Nancy offers a formula for compearance and suggests that we learn to read it in all "possible combinations: 'you (are/and/is) (entirely other than) I' ('*toi [e(s)t] [tout autre que] moi*'). Or again, more simply: *you shares me* ('*toi partage moi*')" (*IOC* 29). Singular beings are given in this communication and as this communication, together, but "without a bond *and* without communion" (29). Community consists in this communication that neither appropriates nor fuses; it consists in the fact that singularity is exposed to an inappropriable outside that constitutes it, affects and alters it, prior to and in excess of symbolic intervention.

Ex-centrically structured, the singular being exists as an outside-inside, or an inside-outside. As such it has "access to what is *proper* to existence, and therefore of course to the proper of *one's own* existence," Nancy writes, "only through an 'expropriation' whose exemplary reality is that of 'my' face always exposed to others, always turned toward an other and faced by him or her, never facing myself." And this, Nancy proposes, "is the archi-original impossibility of Narcissus that opens straight away onto the possibility of the political" (*IOC* xxxvii). But this exposition does not constitute an essence:

> [T]he thinking of community as essence—is in effect the closure of the political. Such a thinking constitutes a closure because it assigns to the community a *common being*, whereas community is a matter of something quite different, namely of existence inasmuch as it is *in* common but without letting itself be absorbed into a common substance. Being *in* common has nothing to do with communion, with fusion into a body, into a unique and ultimate identity that would no longer be exposed. Being *in* common means, to the contrary, *no longer having, in any form, in any empirical or ideal place, such a substantial identity, and sharing this* (narcissistic) *"lack of identity."* This is what philosophy calls "finitude." . . . Finitude, the infinite lack of an infinite identity, if we can risk such a formulation, is what makes community. (*IOC* xxxviii)

Preceding symbolic identification, exposedness is relationality as such; it is constitutive of being, which is always and only in the mode of exposition and not essence: "Being 'is' the 'in' that divides and joins, that 'partitions and shares,' the limit where partitioning and sharing are exposed" (*BIC* 8).

But it is precisely this "in" that disappears whenever what is in-common is passed off as an essence that can be represented, an immanence that simply appears or presents itself as such; wherever fascistic fusions enable a communion of the One to establish itself, to individually or collectively close in on itself, all community and communication have been effaced. To understand community "as a work or through its works would presuppose that the common being, as such, be objectifiable and producible (in sites, persons, buildings, discourses, institutions, symbols: in short, in subjects)." It would be to presuppose the immanence of what is common, and therefore the capacity to represent it or even to constitute it through some form of epideictic display. But community is not the work of singular beings; it cannot be built and is not a project or product: "One does not produce it, one experiences or one is constituted by it as the experience of finitude" (*IOC* 31).

It is this experience of community that Nancy tries to spotlight: "I am trying to indicate, at its limit, an experience—not, perhaps, an experience that we have, *but an experience that makes us be.*" Inasmuch as this experience resists conceptualization and exceeds our thought, it "tries our thinking," and for this reason, it "demands our thought" (*IOC* 26). The Heideggerian insight is worth reiterating: thinking calls as and through the failure of hermeneutic appropriation. Thinking is not the same as knowing, and the challenge today, the social, ethical, and political challenge is to learn to think the sharing of community without effacing precisely this sharing by conceptualizing it, turning it into an object to be grasped and put to work. How to think a community, without essence or project, shaped by the eruption of an inappropriable outside, "a community," as Ronell has so beautifully put it, "shattered and way past the mirror stage of self-recuperation" (*Finitude's Score* 2)? In place of conceptualization and appropriation, Nancy calls for *exposition,* the exposition of exposedness: "[w]e must expose ourselves to what has gone unheard in community" (*IOC* 26).

Community is not a work and doesn't belong to the domain of work, but a strict reading of Nancy indicates that it is not simply "worklessness," either. According to him, it is instead simultaneously a gift and a *task*: "Community is given to us—or we are given and abandoned to the community: a gift to be renewed and communicated, it is not a work to be done or produced. But it is a task, which is different—an infinite task at the heart of finitude" (*IOC* 35). The task inherent in this gift, then, is to renew it and to communicate it but without turning it into a "work," without essentializing or substantializing it. The task given to "us," in the name of solidarity, is to expose exposedness, "to expose the unexposable *in,*" as Nancy puts it (*BIC* 10). This exposition takes place in writing and through writing—broadly speaking, "writing" as any performance of the inscription, aural, visual, and so on—a sharing that testifies to the shattering limit by "touching" it. Still, Nancy hastens to add: "that does not entail the conclusion that all we have to do is to say it to expose it" (*BIC* 9). The exposition depends on a writing (a saying) that undermines and interrupts language's awesome powers of representation.

Nancy's call "to expose the unexposable *in*" came through to me as an assignment that I could not refuse—I did try for a while—an undeniable charge to which this present work attempts to respond. The one who writes is first of all called to write, put "on assignment," as Ronell likes to say, so that one is always writing in response to the Other and because there are others. An encapsulated interiority would have no need or desire to write; writing, no matter what it says, testifies to exposedness, to vulnerability—to responsivity. What's at stake in communicating this exposedness is not community, which is already given: "we cannot not compear" (*IOC* 35). What's at stake, rather, is communal sensibility, a supplement of responsivity for which, it seems to me, "being-with" alone cannot adequately account. My receptors are rhetorically tuned, so in this case the charge that announced itself to me was not only to expose exposedness (which I think really should have been enough) but to demonstrate that the *exposure* to exposedness issues a rhetorical imperative, an obligation to respond that is the condition for symbolic exchange.

Being-For

"To begin with," Nancy writes, "the logic of being-with corresponds to nothing other than what we could call the banal phenomenology of unorganized groups of people." Singularities are like passengers in the same train compartment, he says; they are simply seated next to each other "in an accidental, arbitrary, and completely exterior manner." These passengers "are not linked," but they are also "quite together" in this train, traveling in the same space at the same time. "They are between the disintegration of the 'crowd' and the aggregation of the group," Nancy writes, "both extremes remaining possible, virtual, and near at every moment." Being-with is nothing but this suspension between disintegration and aggregation: "a relation without relation, or rather, being exposed simultaneously to relationship and to absence of relationship." Exposed but not linked (or fused), the singularity is faced—at each moment, consciously or unconsciously, in "freedom" and "necessity"—with "the undecided decision" to respond to the other passengers as strangers or as neighbors, and so to move toward "solitude [or] collectivity," nonrelation or relation (*BIC* 7).

To the extent that the passengers on this metaphorical train are simply seated next to each other, side by side, suspended between disinterestedness and concern, they exist in and as their ecstatic (non)relation. These singularities are with-one-another, *Mitsein*-style—which means they share being and therefore states-of-mind (moods) that attest to their being-outside, in-the-world, together (exposed). And yet, they are also perfectly capable of maintaining a fundamental indifference toward one another, of continuing to file their nails or to read the paper (or *Being and Time*) without offering the slightest gesture of acknowledgment or concern. Indifference is the luxury of exposed existents who are not *faced* with the fact of their exposedness.

According to Nancy, who is with Georges Bataille and Maurice Blanchot on this one, "community," in the sense of social feeling, crystallizes not around a common essence or goal or project but around "the death of its members"—of those "whom we call, perhaps wrongly, it's 'members'"—that is, around "*the 'loss' (the impossibility) of their immanence*" (*IOC* 14). This loss may become the focus of epideictic effusions, of grand encomiums or eulogies, but the experience is not finally sublatable. Death marks the absolute limit of identification and (so) of understanding. A primordial rupture, the for-good withdrawal of the other—or simply exposure to its possibility—first of all gives the other *as* other, opening "me" to an outside and teaching me both my mortal truth (the inevitability of my birth and my death) and "the irredeemable excess" (the exposedness) that constitutes finite being. "Sharing," Nancy writes, "comes down to this: what community reveals to me, in presenting to me my birth and my death, is my existence outside myself"—my ekstasis, my exposedness (*IOC* 26). And yours. Finitude, "my" finitude, in other words, can communicate itself to me only through "your" mortality. Community is therefore "not the space of the *egos*—subjects and substances that are at bottom immortal" (*IOC* 15); gods, elves, fairies, and egos might form an association, consortium, or society, but they could not share community. Perhaps we could say instead that community is the space of shattered egos—or more carefully, it is where egos are shattered. That is ego's experience of finitude: being shattered.

"The community that is not a community of the gods also is neither a community of heroes nor of sovereigns," Blanchot writes. It produces no work and does not tend toward communitarian fusion. The only "purpose" it serves is to communicate to you your exposedness and so to shove you out of yourself, toward the other, to make you responsive to and responsible for the other (*Unavowable* 11). "If it sees its fellow-being die," Bataille once wrote, "a living being can subsist only *outside itself*."

> Each of us is then driven out of the confines of his person and loses himself as much as possible in the community of his fellow creatures. It is for this reason that it is necessary for communal life to maintain itself at a level *equal to death*. The lot of a great number of private lives is pettiness. But a community cannot

last except at the level of intensity of death—it decomposes as soon as it falls short of death's peculiar grandeur. (Nancy's translation, *IOC* 15)

Responsibility kicks in as *response* to finitude's deadly intensity; it kicks in when communal life holds itself "at a level *equal to death*" rather than sliding into tranquilized comforts and everyday absorptions, such as football or professional conferences or *Oprah*. The exposure to exposedness issues an obligation to respond, and no one has attended to this rhetorical imperative more directly or more concretely than Emmanuel Levinas—who would not in a million years have called it "rhetorical."

The Handoff. As Nancy was saying, the singularities seated side by side in being-with's train compartment are suspended between relation and nonrelation, held in "the simultaneous immanence of the retreat and the coming of the relation." Alluding, perhaps, to a major Levinasian motif, Nancy explains that this suspension—the exposedness of being-with—"is not yet even to be 'face to face.' It is anterior to entrapment by the stare that captures its prey or takes its hostage" (*BIC* 7). The capacity for indifference drops off in the shift toward the "face," where "I" am trapped, taken hostage. The relation with the face is a relation of nonindifference, Levinas tells us, that pivots neither on shared meaning nor on identification but on an obligation, an imperative that precedes understanding. Somehow, in the face to face, "I" am/is opened to an intensity "*equal to death*": it is the relation of a "host" to her guest or of a "hostage" to his captor, not simply being-with-the-other but being-*for*-the-other. The encounter with the face comes shrink-wrapped, in other words, with an obligation to respond, after which ignoring the other becomes a conscious *effort*. You might whip out your Blackberry or plug into your iPod or feign sleep or complete absorption in your magazine, iPad, or Nintendo DS, but the active refusal to be responsive is a response and so no longer simple indifference.

Levinas's singular descriptions of the face to face, of facing the face of the Other, will be the focus of chapter two. But let me note here that they depict a radically expropriating and nonreciprocal relation with which comprehension never manages to catch up. For him, the "face" connotes neither the front of the head in a literal sense nor the effect of routine figural operations. Face, in Levinas, has nothing to do with the color of the eyes or the shape of the lips or the size of the ears or how much the other resembles, say, the mother—according to him, as long as you are attuned to any of this, you are not encountering a face. Neither visible nor conceivable nor perceivable, face "is what cannot become content, which your thought would embrace; it is uncontainable, it leads you beyond" (*EI* 87).[10] What one encounters in the face to face *is* the other's finitude, the other's exposedness—that is to say, both his or her mortality (susceptibility to wounding, to ravaging illness, to "the cold and the heat of the seasons") and, simultaneously, his or her transcendence as sheer ungraspableness (*OTB* 91).

Face names the site of "my" encounter with the inassimilable alterity of the other, which provokes an interruption in identification and cognition: "The way in which the other presents himself, exceeding *the idea of the other in me*, we here name face" (*TI* 50). The face puts me into relation with what I can neither appropriate nor abdicate, overwhelming my powers of comprehension and so demolishing my delusions of transcendental symmetry (a.k.a. "intersubjectivity"). In the "face" of the other, "I" am/is under an intractable obligation, an ethico-rhetorical responsibility to respond. One possible response, of course, is to refuse to, or to respond with hostility and violence, to take the other out. It's also possible (even probable) that you will miss the face in an encounter with the other, approaching the other at and with an "angle," with the intent to harm or to persuade; this is why a very Platonic Levinas consistently locates rhetoric on the side of nonethical language. Not every communication with an other signals an encounter with the face. However, once encountered, the face (re)sounds a rhetorical imperative, and nonresponse is not an option.

To the extent that it signifies as a surplus of sociality (exposedness), the face "speaks," Levinas tells us. The relation with the face is already a language relation, a saying or an address, which is why in the encounter with the face "it is necessary to speak of something," Levinas writes, "of the rain and fine weather," of anything at all, "but to speak, to respond to him and already to answer for him" (*EI* 88). Levinas calls this language relation a "first discourse" or simply "conversation" (*entre-tien*). Ronell elaborates:

> Conversation is not that which fuses you to me; but the experience of Conversation induces, once again, the vertigo of expropriation. It is not only the case that I am not identical to myself when I begin to converse with you, but more severely perhaps: you are no longer the one I have interiorized or memorized. Breaking the secret contract that sealed you within me, you, in Conversation, are no longer you, or the you at least of whom I have preserved an image. . . . Conversing with you, I no longer see you, I am not even looking for you: I am oriented toward you generously. This is the non-violent transitivity of my inclination toward you. (*Dictations* xii–xxiii)

Conversation involves not a mutual appropriation but a double deterritorialization, a common but dissymmetrical *unworking* of "identity"—an exposition of exposedness. The relation with the face, then, is itself nonviolent yet expropriating: to encounter a face is to be both called into question and into service. As pure affective appeal, the face subjects one to the scandal of obligation in which ego, finding itself compelled to respond, is stripped of its sense of self-mastery and spontaneity. In his descriptions of the relation to the face, Levinas gives us to think a notion of generosity that is not freely given but compelled, the obligatory "generosity" of the host-age.

"Paradoxically enough," Levinas writes, "thinkers claim to derive communication out of self-coinciding." But the relation with the other "precedes any relationship of the ego with itself" as well as "the auto-affection of certainty to which one always tries to reduce communication." Even "inward dialogue," Levinas insists, is "beholden to the solidarity that sustains it" (*OTB* 119). The experience of or exposure to this fundamental solidarity, which gives "me" to be, takes place in the encounter with the face, in conversation. The face does not simply appear, so unlike intersubjective dialogue—which is a myth according to both Nancy and Levinas—conversation as such cannot be witnessed by a third party. It is the relation with "an addressor whose addressee I am, and about whom I know nothing," as Jean-François Lyotard puts it, "except that he or she situates me upon the addressee instance."

> The violence of the revelation is in the ego's expulsion from the addressor instance, from which it managed its work of enjoyment, power, and cognition. It is the scandal of an I displaced onto a you instance. The I turned you tries to repossess itself through the understanding of what dispossesses it. Another phrase is formed, in which the I returns in the addressor's situation, in order to legitimate or to reject—it doesn't matter which—the scandal of the other's phrase and of its own dispossession. This new phrase is always possible, like an inevitable temptation. But it cannot annul the event, it can only tame and master it, thereby disregarding the transcendence of the other. (*D* 110–11)

The scramble to "return" to the nominative position, Levinas tells us, is already a false nostalgia. Though ego operates on such hopes, I was never a subject in that sense; I am/is a subject to the precise extent that I respond(s). "By turning the I into its you [*toi*]," Lyotard continues, "the other makes him- or herself master, and turns the I into his or her hostage. The other is not master, however, because he or she dominates the I, but because he or she asks for the I"

(*D* 111). As weird as this may sound, Levinas insists that it is in the nonsubjective donation of the I that I is/am given at all: it's not so much that the subject responds to alterity, then, but that "the subject" *is* the response to alterity. It has no substance beyond this inessential solidarity, this receptivity and responsivity that are the conditions for symbolic exchange, for symbolicity as such.

When Nancy suggests that the singular being's neutral exposedness is anterior to "entrapment" by the face, he indicates that being-with-others is not *yet* being-for-others, that being-for could only derive from the originary and presubjective "fraternity" of being-with. Interestingly, however, in *Otherwise than Being* Levinas proposes something radically different: that if the face to face activates a kind of entrapment by which the I is captured and taken hostage, this can be the case only because the obligation is *preoriginary,* because the predicament of being-hostage is the condition for being at all and so simultaneously for being-with. Levinas describes this *preoriginary* predicament as "human fraternity itself" (*OTB* 116). (No sororities here; big surprise.) According to him, the existent (the "subject") emerges as such only in *response* to alterity and therefore exists for-the-other (nonindifference) before it ever gets the chance to exist for-itself (indifference). It is the underivable provocation to response that *institutes* the limit, the partition that separates what it also joins. Though he doesn't put it this way, Levinas situates a *rhetorical* imperative (an obligation to respond) prior to and as the condition for the gathering into presence associated with being-there, Da-sein. Forget ontology, epistemology—even ethics. What Levinas shows without seeing is that rhetoric is first philosophy.[11] Not (only) because the generative power of the trope is the ground for all thought, as Ernesto Grassi would have it, but because a nonsubjective persuasive appeal is what *calls* for tropological intervention each time.

Prior even to the contemporaneity of being-with, Levinas proposes, there is the "anachrony" of responsibility, a rhetorical imperative that serves as the condition for being and knowing. According to him, this response-ability is not only what brings an existent into being; it *is* the *clinamen,* the inclination toward the other. Being and knowing surely do follow, but if it were not for this irremissible inclination, this preoriginary obligation to respond, then in the face of the other I would nonchalantly file my nails. The face comes through each time as pure appeal, persuasion without a rhetorician, "command without tyranny" ("Freedom" 18). And there is no way to block it out, no way to "annul the event" of my expropriation, my depersonalization, in which I am turned inside out, ripped out of my "private" shelter *for*-the-other—"substituted" for the other, as Levinas says. (Blanchot describes it as a "mortal substitution" [*Un-avowable* 9].)

In the facing position, I am/is recalled, back to my responsibility, which in Levinas's hands is no longer restrained by intentional consciousness or the happy clarity of knowledge. The face teaches me an exorbitant responsibility without limits or final payoffs: "The debt increases in the measures that it is paid," Levinas writes (*OTB* 12). Yet, if it were not for this preoriginary obligation, the "unconditionality of being hostage," Levinas tells us, there would be no generosity in the world—no compassion, no pardon, no proximity, "even the little that there is" (*OTB* 117). The priority of the other is "presupposed in all human relationships," Levinas writes. And if that were not the case, "we would not even say, before an open door, 'After you, sir!'" (*EI* 89). What Levinas proposes is that there may be no way to get from being-with to being-for, from neutral exposedness to responsibility (from being to responding), unless a preoriginary "after you"—an underivable obligation to respond—(un)grounds them both. Rhetoric, I submit, is first philosophy.

Methodology

I hope you're still with me. After a few false starts I realize that there is really no way to assume a masterful scholarly pose here, as if I had a clear sense of how to proceed. It's not as if what I'm trying to present in these pages could be confirmed by a trip to the archive or some well-crafted empirical study, whether quantitative or qualitative. Let's just say that the question of method has proved quite agonizing. The task here—to expose a solidarity that precedes symbolicity—cannot be accomplished through representation (alone), through tireless exegesis, the constative work of describing and explicating; there is also, of course, no way to skip that work. The performative event of the saying takes place at (or as) the limit, the "unexposable *in*," but the saying by necessity gives a said that offers itself up once again to thematization and appropriation. Perhaps the most I can hope for here is that this text will testify to the saying's tortured rapport with the said, in which it barely hangs on. Heidegger claims that this sort of testimony is what poets are for, and I don't disagree; but I don't have the gift, and in any case I'm not sure that poetry alone would reach you, the ones for whom I write. Literature more broadly or even literary criticism would have been other ways to go, especially given fiction's remarkable powers of exposition (Ronell reminds us of "what Hegel drew from *Antigone* or Freud from *Oedipus Rex*" [*CW* 11]). A strictly philosophical or psychoanalytic frame might also have panned out. And if I were Avital Ronell, I might offer all of the above, and toss in some street theater, as well.[12] But given my specific limitations and capabilities, I will hold on to a specifically rhetorical perspective: I'll attempt to use rhetorical leverage to expose a preoriginary rhetoricity.

Still, the disciplinary boundaries wobble in the face of this "task." As Nancy notes, "the necessity of being-in-common is not that of a physical law, and whoever wants to expose it must also expose himself (that is what we call 'thought,' 'writing,' *and* their partition and sharing)" (*BIC* 9). There is no said without the saying, no meaning or sense without exposure, which indicates "the impossibility of communicating anything at all," as Nancy observes, "without touching the limit where all meaning [*sens*] spills out of itself, like a simple ink stain on a word, on the word 'meaning'" ("Exscription" 319). Sender-receiver theories of communication that focus narrowly on "speakers" and "messages" miss the fact that to address "you," in writing or speech (or, say, dance—any performance of the inscription), is already to touch the limit; and to be addressed, to "receive" an address, is first of all to be exposed to that exposedness. There is no communication except on this limit, this "site" of exposure where the address takes place and where the "masterful scholarly ethos" is toast. Hope lies in the fact that the appropriation of what is inscribed (the said) necessarily testifies to the inappropriable exposure that insists and resists. Writing and speaking are functions of this inessential solidarity, expositions not of who one is (identity) but of the fact that "we" are (relationality). "We do not seize control, we do not appropriate what is offered up [as the *in*]," Nancy writes (*BIC* 10). The exposure cannot be grasped in a concept or represented in significations. And yet, this "solidarity" is what is exposed in any address—in this address.

So far, I've been attempting to trope that which no figure can contain, to mediate a trace of the immediate, to attend to the unthematizable by necessarily and simultaneously thematizing it. Despite the built-in betrayal, this will have been the primary method of approach: a cautious figuring of the unfigurable, a reduction of the saying to the said. The secondary method, which is perhaps less familiar and which I have lifted from *Otherwise than Being*, involves a kind of reversal or rewinding—the reduction of the said to the saying. In Levinas's words, this approach attempts "to awaken in the said the saying which is absorbed in it" (*OTB* 43). It attempts, that is, to allow the saying to show itself within the said by performatively interrupting it. Levinas acknowledges that it is necessary that "the saying on the hither side be thematized, that is, manifest itself, that it enter into a position and a book" (43). But he goes on to argue that the "reduction" of the said to the saying is also necessary; indeed, he insists that it's the task of philosophy to not allow "what is beyond essence" to "congeal into essence" (44). One philosophical approach that had taken up the task of this reduction long before Levinas labeled it as such is, of course, deconstruction, which I would describe as a *rhetorical* philosophy. I would further argue, contra Levinas, that this reduction is first of all the task of rhetoric: philosophy picked it up when it took its rhetorical turn.

These two methods, these opposing reductions, will operate in tandem here, without much ado or metacommentary. And the goal, simultaneously modest and overreaching, will be twofold: to offer a theoretical contribution to rhetorical studies and to excavate the rhetorical basis for contemporary theories of relationality. To that end, this text offers itself up—tentatively, experimentally (let's see if this works)—*as* a rhetoric of the saying, a work devoted specifically to excavating, examining, and affirming the saying *as* rhetoric, as an extra-symbolic rhetorical appeal.

1
Identification

Identification is affirmed with earnestness precisely because there is division. Identification is compensatory to division. If men were not apart from one another, there would be no need for the rhetorician to proclaim their unity.

Kenneth Burke, *A Rhetoric of Motives*

Identification, in fact, is ambivalent from the very first; it can turn into an expression of tenderness as easily as into a wish for someone's removal. It behaves like a derivative of the first, *oral* phase of the organization of the libido, in which the object that we long for and prize is assimilated by eating and is in that way annihilated as such. The cannibal, as we know, has remained at this standpoint; he has a devouring affection for his enemies and only devours people of whom he is fond.

Sigmund Freud, *Group Psychology and the Analysis of the Ego*

According to Jack Selzer's delightful early history, *Kenneth Burke in Greenwich Village*, Burke's friends at the *Dial* probably introduced him to Sigmund Freud's work sometime in the early 1920s. The impact was profound and sustained: Burke loved Freud. In the 1939 essay "Freud—and the Analysis of Poetry," for instance, Burke writes: "the reading of Freud I find suggestive almost to the point of bewilderment. Accordingly, what I would most like to do would be simply to take representative excerpts from his work, copy them out, and write glosses upon them" (*Philosophy* 258). I'm not the first to observe that Burke spent much of his career, in fact, tweaking, applying, and extending Freud's ideas. Ellen Quandahl, David Blakesley, and others have demonstrated that Burke, in Freud's footsteps, set out to expose human motivations by analyzing language, and that he lifted several of his own key terms, such as "identification" and "motive," from *The Interpretation of Dreams*. As Roderick Hart and Suzanne Daughton bluntly put it, Burke "was Freudian to his core" (262).

And yet, anyone who has studied Freud's work on identification (or anyone who has seen the film *All About Eve*, for that matter) will already have detected the telltale signs of a simmering rivalry. Although Burke never denounced Freud and loved him to the end, his anxiety of influence did take a parricidal turn that expressed itself—in part and interestingly enough—in Burke's own theory of identification, which he himself described as "*post*-Freudian" ("Methodological Repression" 407–8).[1]

Burke based his theory of identification on Freud's, and the overlap is readily discernable.[2] According to the more or less "official" interpretation, Freud maintains a clean distinction between desire and the purely secondary motivation of identification: boy *wants* momma, daddy *has* momma, so boy wants to *be* daddy, identifies with him, takes him as the ideal model (*GP* 47). Burke agreed with Freud that humans are motivated by desire at least as much as by reason, but he ditched the Oedipal narrative, arguing that the most fundamental human desire is social rather than sexual, and that identification is a response to that desire. By all appearances then, the disagreement is in the details, since both Freud and Burke describe identification as a social act that partially unifies discrete individuals, a mode of "symbolic action" (as Burke would say) that resides squarely within the representational arena (or the dramatistic frame).

What gets deep-sixed in Burke's articulated revision, however, are Freud's less "official" reflections on an immediate, *affective* identification with the other (the "m/other"), who is not (yet) a discrete object or image or form. This "primary identification," as Freud sometimes calls it, precedes the very distinction between ego and model, and inasmuch as it is precisely *not* compensatory to division, it remains stubbornly on the motion side of Burke's action/motion loci. Burke had studied at least two of the works in which Freud explicitly addressed the problem of a nonrepresentational identification (*Group Psychology* and *The Ego and the Id*), so it may be telling that he never directly challenges it—or even mentions it. In any case, here we'll be digging up something of what Burke buried, since he covers over a more radically generalized rhetoricity, an affectability or persuadability that precedes and exceeds symbolic intervention.

Dramatizing Identification

In *A Rhetoric of Motives*, published in 1950, Burke follows Aristotle's lead in suggesting that rhetoric's "basic function" is persuasive, but he also argues that persuasion's very condition of possibility is identification; indeed, that any persuasive act is first of all an identifying act: "You persuade a man only insofar as you can talk his language by speech, gesture, tonality, order, image, attitude, idea, identifying your ways with his" (55). According to Burke, the father of modern rhetorical studies, the primary aim of rhetoric is not to win an argument but to make a connection, shifting the imagery of the persuasive encounter from a duel to a "courtship":

> A is not identical with his colleague, B. But insofar as their interests are joined, A is *identified* with B. Or he may *identify himself* with B even when their interests are not joined, if he assumes they are, or is persuaded to believe so.
>
> Here are the ambiguities of substance. In being identified with B, A is "substantially one" with a person other than himself. Yet at the same time he remains unique, an individual locus of motives. Thus he is both joined and separate, at once a distinct substance and consubstantial with another. (*RM* 20–21)

According to Burke, it is because neither A nor B is an absolute identity, because they share *no* essence in common, and because they are *not* identical or conjoined in any actual sense, that there can and must be rhetorical identification, a "mediatory ground" that establishes their consubstantiality without accomplishing their complete unity.[3] Identification, or what Burke also calls "consubstantiation," is both the mode by which individual existents establish a sense of identity and the mode by which they establish a relation to one another. As he puts it in *Attitudes Toward History*, identification "is hardly other than a name for the function of sociality" (267).

It can also go wrong, of course. Too much identification, too much unification, too much cooperation within any group, Burke warns, can be deadly for everyone else. He calls the "ultimate *disease* of cooperation: *war*" and notes that "you will understand war much better if you think of it, not simply as strife come to a head, but rather as a disease, or perversion of communion" (*RM* 22). Burke, writing the *Rhetoric* in the aftermath of a devastating war, pins his hopes for a survivable coexistence not so much on the act of identification, which is ontologically guaranteed, but on the human capacity to *resist* a little, to maintain a crucial distance through reasoned critique.[4] As Timothy Crusius puts it, for Burke "the problem, then, is not with identification *per se* (trust, faith) but with faulty or malign identifications, which must be exposed, critiqued, discarded, and replaced with sounder loyalties" (86). Burke's quiet rivalry with Freud drops anchor here, in Burke's insistance that identification is a symbolic act—whether conscious or unconscious—that therefore remains available for sober critique and reasoned adjustment.

According to Burke, there is no essential identity; what goes for your individual "substance" is not an essence but the incalculable totality of your complex and contradictory identifications, through which you variously (and vicariously) become able to say "I." Like the "official" Freudian version on which it's based, "rhetorical identification" depends on symbolic representation, on the production and intervention of meaningful figures, which Burke says are already persuasive: "wherever there is 'meaning,' there is 'persuasion'" (*RM* 172). Or, as Crusius observes, in Burke, "shared meaning is the very basis for identification" (86). There can be no identity without identification, and there can be no identification without figuration, without the suasive force of meaningful figures.

Now, we'll need to catch two nonharmonious Burkean drifts here: First of all, this indicates that what I habitually call "my" identity is the product of an identification with figures or symbols that reside outside my self, that the relation to symbolic structure precedes the relation to the self. Inasmuch as "my" identity is an effect of "my" inscription by this structure, I am always already other than myself, nonpresent to myself, inessential. Or, from another angle, "I" am *essentially* an actor, says a very Nietzschean Burke, "enact[ing] rôles" that are available to me as a "member of a group," which "is the only active mode of identification possible," since "all *individualistic* concepts of identity dissolve into the nothingness of mysticism and the absolute" (*Philosophy* 310–11). "Identity is not individual," Burke insists; it is constituted via the enactment of a series of dissociated and frequently contradictory roles defined by the groups with which one identifies (*Attitudes* 263). And my identification with other existents necessarily triangulates through the symbolic structures that grant my identity.

Paradoxically, however, and here's the second drift, to say that identification depends on shared *meaning*, on the intervention of already meaningful figures, is also to presume—as the condition for identification—a subject or ego who knows itself as and through its representations. It is to presume the prior activation of a human *tupos* itself, which covertly operates as the figure *of* meaning as well as the ground for any possible relation.[5] Indeed, for Burke, everything begins with an "individual" who is individuated by nature itself: the figures of self and other are not first of all a function of symbolic structure but of biology, says Burke. Each human organism is given as such in the material separation of one central nervous system from another, which results in the "*divisiveness* of the individual human organism from birth to death" (*RM* 130).[6] Prior to language acquisition, psychosexual development, and class consciousness, Burke proposes, there is biological estrangement, ontology's insurance premium for securing his entire rhetoric of relationality.[7] And any reference to some "Edenic" existence before this "fall" into divisiveness, Burke writes, belongs to mythology, to the "myth of a power prior to all parturition," in which "divided things were not yet proud in the private property of their divisiveness" (*RM* 140). For him, the division between self and other is the "state of nature" that is identification's motivating force: identification's job is to transcend this natural state of division, and rhetoric's job is identification.

In an exemplary instance of the way in which texts, as he says, can embody contradictory "*wishes*, each proclaimed in its own right, without regard to the others" (*Language* 68), Burke describes identity as an effect of the processes of identification *and* identification as the achievement of an already discernable (biological) "identity." The itinerary is complicated, and these descriptions contest and check each other throughout the *Rhetoric*. But whenever Burke feels forced to make a decision, to lay out the ultimate order of things, he comes down on the side of originary divisiveness, and there is no other choice.[8] From the moment he determines that identification is a function of (rather than a condition for) shared meaning—as soon as he situates identification *within* the arena of representation, in other words—he has already presumed a prior divisiveness and engaged the necessary contradiction.

According to Burke, "in parturition begins the centrality of the nervous system" (*RM* 146), and our very concepts of ownership and private property—indeed, of all our egoistic impulses—originate in this irreparable biological predicament: "What the body eats and drinks becomes its special private property; the body's pleasures and pains are exclusively its own pleasures and pains." But if you then "bring together a number of individual nervous systems, each with its own centrality," relational impulses intervene; there will be "vicarious sharing by empathy, by sympathy, the 'imaginative' identification with one another's states of mind." This Scramble of egoistic and relational motives is the rhetorical situation into which "man" is born, says Burke, an endless dialectical struggle between "the original biological goading that is located in the divisive centrality of the nervous system" and the inborn desire to transcend this state of nature through the mediatory ground of identification (*RM* 130).

Barbara Biesecker surmises, correctly I think, that "Burke's thinking of the social finds its resources in the newly determined space of the individual: in the predication of the human being *per se* is the possibility for the social" (47). And there is the problem. Who is this "individual," this human being *per se* who precedes predication and so predates the processes of identification? Who is *there*, there *already*, to experience alienation, to desire sociality? Burke's response: "*homo dialecticus*," whose inborn rationality includes the superpersonal "resources of classification, of abstraction, of comparison and contrast, of merger and division, of derivation, and the like [which] characterize the thinking of man *generically*" (*RM* 276, 285). Essentially enclosed and alienated, *homo dialecticus* already desires to transcend this state of nature—"[b]iologically, it is of the essence of man to desire" (*RM* 275)—and is ontologically equipped to do so via the inborn powers of his or her own imagination. So though Burke challenges psychoanalytic criticism for reducing the desire for social intercourse to a sexual desire, he is very much with the "official" Freud in his refusal to question the ontological priority of desire itself, which, despite it all, presumes a subject who *has* desires, be they conscious or unconscious.

In his response to Fredric Jameson, who suggests that the "centrality of the self" is an "optical illusion" (520), Burke rather impatiently explains again that he makes a clean distinction between the individual as a biological organism and the individual as a social/ideological construct, presumably contending that the former is *not* already a construct: "I locate the *individual* (as distinct from the kind of 'ideological' identity that is intended in a social term, such as 'individualism') in the human body, the 'original economic plant' distinct from all others owing to the divisive centrality of each body's particular nervous system" ("Methodological Repression" 404). Inasmuch as the individual is biologically individuated, Burke continues, it exists "as a separate organism possessing immediate sensations, not thus shared in their immediacy by other organisms." He grants that "the individual, as a 'person,' dissolves into quite a complexity of *identifications* in the sociopolitical realm," but he insists that this individual is first of all an irreparably *separate* organism (413).[9]

That somewhat puzzling proposition deserves our attention precisely because it seems so improbable coming from Burke—the thinker, *par excellence*, of the paradox of substance—and because he repeats it over and over like a refrain, as if it were deflecting a traumatic insight. Now, it would not be my first choice to venture into the arena of neuroscience here, but I feel compelled to try to speak Burke's language, to identify my ways with his. So: who can deny that sense organs and sensory neurons, which operate together not so much *at* but *as* threshold, already indicate an ex-centric structure, an inside-outside similar to a Klein jar or Möbius strip?[10] Mirror neurons, which were discovered in the last decade of Burke's life, offer further confirmation. Mirror neurons reside in the premotor area of the brain, which is the area that primes the next movements in a motor sequence. What's so interesting about them is that they act as both sensory and motor neurons, firing in association not only with the execution but also with the observation of an action. This means that the same mirror neurons fire in my brain whether I actually grab a pencil myself or I see you grab one, indicating no capacity to distinguish between my grasping hand and what is typically (and hastily) described as a visual representation of it: *your* grasping hand.

The same basic thing purportedly happens with nongoal-directed "biological movements": neurons in my motor areas start to "resonate" when *you* move.[11] And this is not learned activity, at least not in the beginning. Almost immediately after birth (as early as forty-two minutes after, according to recent studies) infants will imitate a number of facial gestures: when an infant witnesses an adult open her mouth or stick out her tongue, for example, the mere observation often triggers the related neurons in the motor cortex that physically mime that action—the infant's mouth opens and the tongue comes out.[12] Researchers insist that this early imitation is "non-reflexive, volitional, and intentional," demonstrating a nascent intersubjectivity (Meltzoff and Moore, "Infant Intersubjectivity" 56). This conclusion, however, relies on the presumption that the infant's responses are *its own*, that mimetic identification begins with an individual subject (agent) who imitates, with an original who (consciously or unconsciously) mimes a model. Here, forty-two minutes into it, nothing could be more uncertain. In any case, this identification surely does not depend on shared meaning: a mimetic rapport precedes understanding, affection precedes projection.

Despite the authors' distinctly humanist frame-ups, it's difficult not to read published reports on the activity of mirror neurons and resonance mechanisms as eloquent deconstructions of Burke's ultimate order of things, shattering the presumption of an originary biological disconnect between self and other. The "centrality" of each individual nervous system can hardly be characterized as "divisive" when it doesn't manage consistently to distinguish between self and other; indeed, at the level of the organism, a rather astonishing condition of indistinction announces itself. It's not only that "I" appear to be hardwired to mime "your" actions but, more disturbingly perhaps, that "I" may *be* "your" actions, that there may be no "me" until "I" perform "you." What is at issue here, maybe, is what Philippe Lacoue-Labarthe has termed a "constitutive mimesis," an originary mimetic rapport that exposes "the primitive, native lapse or default of identity," even at the level of the organism (116).

What's so confusing about all of this is that Burke himself suggests much the same thing in other terms. To say that the subject is *essentially* an actor, as Burke does, is already to imply its general absence of identity, as well as its "pure and disquieting plasticity," as Lacoue-Labarthe puts it, "which potentially authorizes the varying appropriation of all characters and all functions (all the roles), that kind of 'typical virtuosity' which doubtless requires a 'subjective' base—a 'wax'—but without any other property than an infinite malleability: instability 'itself'" (115). Nonetheless, Burke insists that the organism, the "wax," both is estranged and knows it's estranged, which allows him to interpret identification as an active response to a passive estrangement. This is why he can write in the *Rhetoric* that empathy and sympathy are "'imaginative' identifications" with another's state of mind (130), that they are affects that one "individual" *has* in regard to another, imaginative projections based on comparison or analogy—rather than that these affects are affections, that the "other" with whom "I" identify affects me with "my" affect precisely because "I" have no affect of my own—indeed, that there is no "my own" prior to identification.

By positing an estranged and desiring "individual" holding steady beneath the swirl of identifications, Burke is able to preempt any consideration of this individual's genesis in identification.[13] What this uncharacteristic lapse into metaphysical prejudices buys him, then, is a strategic pick against a rush of impossible questions: What if identification precedes not only any sense of identity but also, and *therefore*, any sense of divisiveness, as well? What if the identity of the organism *itself* is in the other? What if repetition is originary? In short, what if the real question, as Avital Ronell puts it in *The Telephone Book*, is not how to make a connection (that was the beginning) but "*how to make a disconnection*" (194)? This was Martin Heidegger's question, obviously, but it was Freud's too: a question of finitude. The first other, they both say, is a dead other, since death sets the absolute limit on identification. Emmanuel Levinas did not pose this question as such, but he did propose that the language relation, as "discourse" or "conversation" (*entre-tien*), was ethical inasmuch as it instituted a *distance* between the interlocutors, thereby opening the possibility for proximity. The distance, the interruption in identification, they all separately suggest, must be *achieved* somehow—which is not to say that it would amount to an achievement of the will.

These impossible questions, blocked by the barricade of biological estrangement, imply that the entire logic of identification has to be rethought: it can no longer be understood as an identification *of* one *with* another, at least not at first, since it would necessarily precede the very distinction between self and other. Identification could not operate among self-enclosed organisms; it would have to belong to the realm of affectable beings, infinitely open to the other's affection, inspiration, alteration; it would have to belong to the realm of a radically generalized rhetoricity, then, an affectability or persuadability that is at work prior to and in excess of any shared meaning. As Lacoue-Labarthe and Jean-Luc Nancy observe in a very early piece on identification in Freud, "to be affectable is to be always already-affected," to be nothing other than affected, nothing other than this endless repetition of each time originary alterations ("The Unconscious" 199).

To get a sense of what Burke is avoiding here, we'll need to go back to his most important source—to Freud—who never stopped wrestling with precisely what Burke's "post-Freudian" notion of identification silently sheers off. It's true that even when Freud describes an Oedipal *prehistory*, he tends to maintain the distinction between identificatory and libidinal bonds and to depend on his cast of usual suspects—the mother, the father, and an ego who takes the father as a model and the mother as an object. However, Freud also had the guts—here and there, against the grain—to explore a prehistory *to* that prehistory in which identification is "anterior and even interior to any libidinal bond" (Borch-Jacobsen, *ET* 8).

Primary Identification

Freud begins the seventh chapter of *Group Psychology* (1921) with a revelation that, save the reference to psychoanalysis, Burke could easily have written: "Identification is known to psycho-analysis as the earliest expression of an emotional tie with another person" (105). However, Freud goes on to indicate that this very first "emotional tie" is formative of the ego—so we're really talking about the "passionate attachment," as Judith Butler puts it in *Psychic Life*, of something or someone who doesn't yet exist, a relation (without relation) to the other that is older than and productive of the relation to the self. This identification, Freud continues, "behaves like a derivative of the first, *oral* phase of the organization of the libido, in which the object that we long for and prize is assimilated by eating and is in that way annihilated as such" (105). According to him, you are *who* you eat: the genesis of the ego involves a devouring affection, a fusional sort of cannibalism that you are not yet around to remember (or even to repress). A few years later in *The Ego and the Id* (1923), Freud writes:

> [T]he effects of the first identifications made in earliest childhood will be general and lasting. This leads us back to the origin of the ego-ideal, for behind it there lies hidden an individual's first and most important identification, his identification with the father in his own personal prehistory. This is apparently not in the first instance the consequence or outcome of an object-cathexis; it is a direct and immediate identification and takes place earlier than any object-cathexis. (31)

Though Freud stubbornly describes this "first and most important identification" as an "identification with the father"—or even, according to his footnoted second choice, with "the parents"—the qualifiers "directly and immediately" imply that he is trying to suggest something else: that this formative identification would precede any representational scission between identity and alterity and so would be prior to the intervention of a specular object or ideal model. In a sociality or collectivity prior to all individual history, ego is formed "directly and immediately" through a *blind* identification in which a not-yet-I swallows the not-yet-other alive.[14]

Seventeen years later, in "An Outline of Psycho-Analysis" (1940), Freud drops all reference to ego-model pairs and explicitly details a pre-egoic identification: "to begin with, the child does not distinguish between the breast and its own body," but "when the breast has to be separated from the body and shifted to the *outside* because the child so often finds it absent, it carries with it as an *object* a part of the original narcissistic libidinal cathexis" (188).[15] There is first an objectless identification with the nurturing breast, Freud is suggesting—the breast is part of "me"—and it's only afterwards, after it has gone MIA too many times, that this breast is "shifted to the outside," becoming an object of desire. Roughly a year later in "Findings, Ideas, Problems" (1941), Freud further muses: "'Having' and 'being' in children. Children like expressing an object-relation by an identification: 'I am the object.' 'Having' is the later of the two; after the loss of the object it relapses into 'being.' Example: the breast. 'The breast is a part of me, I am the breast.' Only later: 'I have it,' that is, 'I am not it'" (*SE* 23:299).

The intrinsically antisocial ("hateful") dimension of identification exposes itself in the total annihilation of otherness expressed in the present tense form of the verb "to be": If I *am* the breast, then I identify not with but *as* (or in) the breast, and I *see* nothing—no object, no imago, no mirror. I *am* what I mime. This is a mimetic event, to be sure, but in this case there is no specular distance between the "I" and its "model." A kind of "Narcissus without a mirror," Mikkel Borch-Jacobsen writes, this I "instantly drown[s] himself in the water of his reflection" without ever managing "to think himself, to want or desire himself" (*ET* 151–52). "To identify oneself with the object," Borch-Jacobsen writes elsewhere, "is to put oneself in its place or to place it within oneself, to kill it and live off its death. If I *am* the breast, then that breast is *nothing*—outside of myself, who have always already swallowed it up (and consequently *I* shall never come back to that place where *it* was I before I was)" (*FS* 181).

Burke describes identification as another name for the function of sociality, but what Freud gives us to think is that sociality, the birth of the relation as such, would require a prior disidentification: the breast is finally "shifted to the outside because the child so often finds it absent." Both self and other would be established in this crucial "shift," which could be described as a separation of "me" from "myself," except that there would be no "me" at all prior to this separation. The almost unthinkable claim being posited here is that both individuation and the relation to alterity are born in this experience of disidentification: a dissociation that takes place at the very moment of association, an untying tie in which identity appears in (or as) the movement of its disappearance.

And/but apparently this "birth" is itself a repetition. Already in *Inhibitions, Symptoms and Anxiety*, Freud had proposed that the birth event is the first (and paradigmatic) instance of anxiety, which stems not from the fetus's conscious perception of danger (because how could it know?) but from an awareness "of some vast disturbance in the economy of its narcissistic libido" (135). This "disturbance" is birth itself, the separation of "me" from "myself" in the very advent of becoming a self. In contradistinction to Burke's clean snip of the umbilicus, Lacoue-Labarthe and Nancy observe that "what is at stake here is the incision of an outside in an inside, a withdrawal of identity in the advent of identity. Or again, it is a dependence in the advent of autonomy: the dependence of birth, that of prematuration, and finally that which lasts an entire life" (200).

Perhaps Burke's "individual" finally comes into play here, as a product of the experience of disidentification and individuation, and perhaps that sets the stage for the secondary or "post-Oedipal" identification that both Freud and Burke define as "social"—the identification *of* one *with* another. There is, of course, no denying that specular and symbolic identifications take place, everywhere and all the time, but as Borch-Jacobsen observes, they "cannot really be produced elsewhere than on the (abyssal, non-'subjectal') ground of a preliminary *affection*, by the 'other' that 'I' *am* 'myself,'" prior to any perception or representation (*Lacan* 66). And nothing indicates that the originary narcissistic tendency upon which "social" identifications are produced can be permanently displaced or overcome. If identification precedes and is the condition for identity, then how could there be any biological, ontological, or symbolic prophylactic against devouring affection, any way retroactively to switch off the swallowing machine? Though he ultimately protects his Oedipal narrative, Freud does attempt several times to tackle this problem in his career-long struggles with what he calls "the riddle of suggestive influence" (*GP* 117).[16] And what gets exposed, each time, is the repetitive nature of "primary identification," which confounds all attempts at chronological description.

The Hypnosuggestive Technique

Between 1886 and 1896, Freud employed the therapeutic technique of hypnosis, which typically counts on a series of verbal suggestions through which the hypnotist talks the patient into a state of "mental compliance," literally persuading the patient to become persuadable, affectable, suggestible vis-à-vis the hypnotist ("Psychical Treatment" 293–95). When patients fall into a hypnotic state, Freud explains, they demonstrate an extreme "docility" in their relation to the hypnotist, becoming "obedient and credulous—in the case of deep hypnosis, to an almost unlimited extent" (294–95). "Suggestion" is the technical name for "the words spoken by the hypnotist which have the[se] magical results," Freud writes, and he confirms all of Plato's suspicions about rhetoric when he says that in the suasive force of suggestion, "words have once more regained their magic" (296). Why magic? Because suggestion names the power of an "influence without logical foundation" (*GP* 88–90).

In his preface to the German edition of Bernheim's *Suggestive Therapeutics*, Freud writes: "What distinguishes suggestion from other kinds of psychical influence, such as a command or the giving of a piece of information or instruction, is that in the case of suggestion, an idea is aroused in another person's brain which is not examined in regard to its origin but is accepted just as though it had arisen spontaneously in that brain" (82). Suggestion, as Borch-Jacobsen observes, "possesses the remarkable property of annulling (at least for the hypnotized person) the distance between locutor and listener, emitter and receiver."[17] While the other sorts of "psychical influence" that Freud mentions consist in communication with the other, suggestion consists in the constitution of that other—*again*. It involves "the birth of the subject," Borch-Jacobsen writes, "perhaps not a repetition of the birth event—but birth as repetition, or as primal identification: in it the subject comes into being (always anew: this birth is constantly repeated) as an echo or duplicate of the other, in a sort of lag with respect to its own origin and its own identity" (*FS* 231).[18]

In "Psychical (or mental) Treatment," published in 1905, Freud noted that suggestion's capacity to "cure" hysteria and certain other ailments points to the astonishing "physical influence of an idea," to the "magical" power of language to "remove the symptoms of illness" (296, 292). By then Freud had already ditched hypnosuggestion as a therapeutic technique, but not because it didn't work; sixteen years later in *Group Psychology* he was still convinced that suggestibility is "an irreducible, primitive phenomenon, a fundamental fact of the mental life of man" (89). On the contrary, Freud felt compelled to give up the use of suggestion in his practice because it worked too well, so well that it offended his humanist sensibilities, or, as Burke puts it, his "individualistic libertarianism" (*Language* 79): a patient, Freud tells us, should not be subjected to the suggestions of analysts, at least not without recourse to countersuggestion. But Freud also felt compelled to give up the practice of suggestion because its undeniable success couldn't be adequately explained; what Freud couldn't tolerate, he tells us in *Group Psychology*, was that "suggestion, which explained everything, was itself to be exempt from explanation" (87). "The hypnosuggestive technique was expressly rejected by Freud," Borch-Jacobsen observes, "for a very simple reason, which is, at bottom, reason itself. . . . [F]or how is one to say the truth about this false power, this *pseudologos* that makes one believe in no-matter-what?" (*ET* 68). Analysts who use hypnosuggestion are like the rhetoricians in Plato's *Phaedrus*: they don't *know* what they're doing, "they can't produce the truth of their own psychagogic discourse" (*ET* 68). Freud founds the "science" of psychoanalysis by trading in the analyst's suggestions for the patient's "free-associations"—that is, by trading in persuasion for interpretation, performative for constative language, or again, by trading in rhetoric as persuasion for rhetoric as trope—and from then on the analyst was for the most part to keep his or her mouth shut.

Nonetheless, and to Freud's great consternation, the problem of suggestibility shows up again spontaneously in analysis in the form of the transference. No matter how tightly the analyst zips it, Freud discovers, the patient still submits to his or her influence, demonstrating "the same dynamic factor which the hypnotists have named 'suggestibility,' which is the agent of hypnotic rapport" (*An Autobiographical Study* 42). Indeed, Freud finally has to admit, with Gustav Le Bon, that the paradigmatic relation to others is hypnosis, that the social tie is comprised not of thinking subjects but of *hypnotized things*: "Hypnosis is not a good object for comparison with a group formation because it is truer to say that it is identical with it" (*GP* 114–15). Group formation involves a collective hypnosis, and the hypnotist, says Freud, could be a chief, father, or *führer*, a party or an ideology or some other "leading idea," such as that of "country" or "national glory." However, according to him—and here's the recuperative gesture—the identifications among group members result from a prior love for the hypnotist, the unifying figure. There is no herd instinct, he still argues, no natural sociability; there is instead a *horde* instinct. Love for the same leader holds the group together, and when that leader goes down, Freud insists, panic sets in, prompting the group to dissolve into its constitutive parts: individual Narcissi estranged and opposed to one another.

Paradoxically, however, the defining feature of the phenomenon of "panic fear" is contagion, which indicates not estrangement but exposedness. As Borch-Jacobsen observes, "panic fear" announces "an uncontrollable breaching of the ego by (the affects of) others; or, if you will, a mimetic, contagious, suggested narcissism" (*ET* 9; also *FS* 166–67). The infectious nature of panic indicates "a gaping, more or less bewildered opening toward others," as he puts it, in which "each imitates the 'every man for himself' of the others" (*ET* 9). What Freud shows but can't quite embrace is that "the sympathetic (suggestive, imitative) bond" of identification is precisely what remains when the leader/hypnotist is subtracted from the equation (*FS* 167). "What is the transference," Borch-Jacobsen asks, "if not hypnosis without a hypnotist, persuasion without a rhetorician, since it is produced in the absence of any direct suggestion?" The phenomenon of positive "transference reveals that the influence of the hypnotist" is grounded not in some specific hypnotic technique but in "an a priori affectability (a 'spontaneous receptivity') in the patient—that is to say, [in] the 'rhetoricity' of the affect as such, a rhetoricity anterior to any verbal persuasion and also to any metaphoric expression of passions" (*ET* 71).[19] And we won't even mention the equally impressive phenomenon of countertransference.

The "Suggect" of Desire

Both Freud and Burke ground their theories of identification in the subject of desire. "What would be inexplicable, unacceptable," however, as Borch-Jacobsen puts it, "would be the absence of anyone to want or desire anything at all—except the strange and disquieting suggest of hypnosis, always already in submission, subjected to the will of another" (*FS* 149). And Burke just can't go there, not without throwing into question his entire ontology of the social. He encounters but then artfully dodges the problem when he mentions, seemingly in passing, the "rhetoric of hysteria." Since even a hysterical fit is addressed to an audience, Burke observes, it must be situated squarely within the dramatistic frame: "even a catatonic lapse into sheer automatism, beyond the reach of all normally linguistic communication, is in its origins communicative, addressed, though it be a paralogical appeal that ends all appeals" (*RM* 39). This observation is followed by a new heading on a new page: "Rhetoric and Primitive Magic." So by all appearances, Burke has finished with the topic of hysterical rhetoric, finished without so much as touching on the question of "suggestibility," which is both the chief feature of hysteria and what could quite possibly be the "ultimate" rhetorical question. What suggestibility suggests is a human capacity to be "directly and immediately" induced to action or attitude by another, sans all logical foundation and cognitive discretion; it involves a nonrepresentable and each time originary identification that takes place behind the back and beyond the reach of critical faculties.

So, we witness Burke bring up but then very quickly drop the "rhetoric of hysteria." And when he argues, two pages later under the new heading "Rhetoric and Primitive Magic," that the "art" of rhetoric is "not 'magical'" (41), he appears to be making an unrelated and fairly commonsensical observation:

> The approach to rhetoric in terms of "word magic" gets the whole subject turned backwards. Originally, the magical use of symbolism to affect natural processes by rituals and incantations was a mistaken transference of a proper linguistic function to an area for which it was not fit. The realistic use of addressed language to *induce action in people* became the magical use of addressed language to *induce motion in things* (things by nature alien to purely linguistic orders of motivation). (*RM* 42)

This important reclaiming of the properly rhetorical use of language also instantly forecloses any thinking of the problem of suggestion, which is something like the ability of addressed language to induce *motion* in *people,* even when the addressor says nothing, that is, even when the magic words, as Cheryl Glenn might say, go "unspoken." But this impossible possibility, which becomes necessary as soon as identification is understood as the condition for identity, is precisely what the principle of ontobiological divisiveness stiffens against. Unlike political persuasion, suggestion is an improper rhetoric, a bastard form that induces action (or attitude) without properly persuading, a directly suasive "discourse" that defies the presumed distance between self and other, evading cognitive discretion and so all possibility for deliberation.

A few years later in *Language as Symbolic Action* (1966), Burke explicitly articulates the problem of suggestibility in terms of ideology. Citing psychogenic illnesses as an example of symbol misuse, he argues that when symbolic action is "improperly criticized," "the realm of symbolicity may affect the sheerly biologic motions of animality" (6). You may actually gag or spew, for instance, if you try to eat foods that are "perfectly wholesome" and "prized" in other cultures but considered disgusting in your own. And then this: "Instances of 'hexing' are of the same sort (as when a tribesman, on entering his tent, finds there the sign that for some reason those in authority have decreed his death by magic, and he promptly begins to waste away and die under the burden of this sheer thought)" (7). Here, Burke affirms the astonishing "physical influence of an idea," that is, language's capacity (as ideology) to induce *motion* in *people,* but he nonetheless retains an almost absolute faith in the power of reason. Persuadability remains a function of shared meaning; symbolic structure still mediates between listener and locutor, which leaves a space for cognition and so for a more *proper* critique.

Freud's work demonstrated, however, that suggestive influence is less rational, less manageable, less consciously *correctable* than Burke allows. What Freud rediscovers, mostly despite himself, is basically a new version of "the 'pathic' part of ancient rhetoric"—except that this version involves not an emotional appeal but an immediate affection, a kind of "mimetico-affective contagion," as Borch-Jacobsen puts it, that indicates, once again, the absence of any proper divisiveness, of any *subjectum,* and finally of any subject—including any subject *of* representation (*ET* 67). What suggestibility suggests, in other words, is that identification is not simply rhetoric's most fundamental aim; it's also and therefore rhetorical theory's most fundamental *problem.* This problem, which is not simply solvable, effectively undercuts any theory of relationality grounded in representation, and therefore any hope of securing a crucial distance between self and other through reasoned critique or other forms of symbolic action.

The Voice of Conscience

Perhaps Burke's theory of ontobiological divisiveness, along with its attendant faith in critique, was installed as a defense against the threat that Freud's scattered insights posed, the threat of an originary repetition, of an abyssal mimesis propelled along by an irrepressible narcissistic tendency from which symbolic structure could provide no real transcendence. However, the laceration one suffers when the breast goes MIA or when one encounters the dead other (Freud's *der Tote*) or when one engages in conversation (Levinas's *entre-tien*) with an other, for example, is not the effect of a critical intervention; it emerges instead from a *failure* of identification, an interruption in narcissistic appropriation. According to a certain Freud, devouring affection is interrupted (temporarily) not by the Law or by the will or by the unstoppable powers of the critical faculty but by a surplus of alterity that remains indigestible, inassimilable, unabsorbable. Burke insisted in *Language as Symbolic Action* that "there are no negatives in nature and that this ingenious addition to the universe is solely the product of human symbol systems" (9). However, what Freud exposes is a pre- or extra-symbolic "experience" of the negative, a "thou shalt not" that issues not from human symbol systems or the Law (of the father) but from an originary dissociation that operates as the condition for both. The other *as* other shows up in this interruption in identification, which installs a bewildering and (temporarily) ineffaceable distance. What Freud calls the "voice of conscience" owes itself to this failure of identification, to this "self"-shattering dissociation, in which "I" experience "my" vulnerability, "my" destitution, "my" debilitating dependence—my finitude and yours—in the very moment that "I" experience my "self."

In "Thoughts for the Times on War and Death," Freud writes:

> What came into existence beside the dead body of the loved one was not only the doctrine of the soul, the belief in immortality and a powerful source of man's sense of guilt, but also the earliest ethical commandments. The first and most important prohibition made by the awakening conscience was "Thou shalt not kill." It was acquired in relation to dead people who were loved, as a reaction against the satisfaction of the hatred hidden behind the grief for them. (295)

The voice of conscience and the experience of guilt emerge in the anxious apprehension of death "beside the dead body of the loved one." Contrary to the myth elaborated in *Totem and Taboo*, Freud here indicates that this dead one need not be a murdered "father" but anyone with whom one is identified.[20] When "primeval man" is confronted with a dead loved one, any dead loved one, Freud continues, "in his pain, he [is] forced to learn that one can die, too, oneself, and his whole being revolt[s] against the admission; for each of these loved ones was, after all, a part of his own beloved self" ("Thoughts" 293). You necessarily gain a particular sense of certitude in an encounter with *der Tote*, but it can only be an unsettling one: "the certainty of a *cogito* whose formula is not 'I am' but 'he is/you are dead,'" as Nancy and Lacoue-Labarthe put it ("*La panique*" 27). If I may tweak their drift just a bit: "he is," and so, given your devouring affection, "*you* are," you are *too*. How to throw up the dead one? Facing "the dead body of the loved one" means facing what is absolutely inappropriable: your own death, your own dying (*le mourir*), your finitude—which is to say your non-selfsufficiency, your exposedness, your "infinite lack of an infinite identity," as Nancy has put it (*Inoperative* xxxviii).

According to Freud, the *relation* to alterity (already ethical) is born here, in the interruption of narcissistic appropriation, in a disidentification that serves as the condition for symbolic intervention.[21] What's at stake in Burke's truncated rearticulation of Freud's theory of identification, then, is "social feeling" itself. It is not in identification but in its failure, in the withdrawal of identity, that I am exposed to my predicament of exposedness and become capable of demonstrating concern for another finite existent. In Freud the social tie, Lacoue-Labarthe and Nancy write, amounts to this dissociating association, an untying tie that "would therefore be formed of this identification with the withdrawal" ("The Unconscious" 203). As nonintuitive as this may sound, what Freud exposes is that *dissociation* is productive of the exteriority that sociality implies, that it is through disidentification, dislocation, depropriation that social feeling emerges and (so) something like society becomes possible. It's only in the failure of identification, each time, that "I" am opened to the other *as* other and get the chance to experience something like responsibility for the other that exceeds (and conflicts with) "my" narcissistic passions.

But this failure cannot be *produced* through reason or critique. Indeed, what Burke censored in Freud—consciously or unconsciously—is the possibility that no flex of reason, no amount of proper critique, can secure the interpersonal distance on which Burke had pinned his hopes. According to Freud, an affectability or persuadability operates irrepressibly and below the radar of the critical faculties. None of this suggests, of course, that critiquable (symbolic) identifications do not take place (everywhere and all the time), nor does it suggest that symbolic identifications are insignificant or that critiquing them is unnecessary. It is surely one task of rhetorical studies to soberly analyze and to provoke resistance to certain dangerous (or simply distasteful) alliances when they disclose themselves to consciousness. However, there may be nothing more dangerous than too much faith in reasoned critique. It seems to me that Freud presents rhetorical studies with another, equally important task: to think the limits of reason by tracking the implications—for society, for politics, for ethics—of a radically generalized rhetoricity that precedes and exceeds symbolic intervention. It seems necessary today, at the very least, to begin exploring the sorts of rhetorical analyses that become possible only when identification is no longer presumed to be compensatory to division.[22]

2

Figuration

But it is life that is still not arrested
in the absolute immobility of a death mask.

Emmanuel Levinas, *Otherwise than Being*

Emmanuel Levinas—after Freud but
with a very different twist—also depicts the interruption in identification as an
encounter with the other *as* other, with a surplus of alterity that I can neither
appropriate nor abdicate, and that therefore calls my self-sufficiency and spontaneity into question. Levinas describes this encounter as the opening of ethics:
"We name this calling into question of my spontaneity by the presence of the
other, ethics" (*TI* 43). Pace Burke, he proposes that this is an *extra*-symbolic
"experience" of the negative, which operates not as a "simple rule of conduct"
but as "the principle of discourse itself," the very condition for the language
relation. And pace Freud, he suggests that this originary "No" first expresses
itself not in an encounter with *der Tote* but in an encounter with what he calls
"the face of the Other" (*le visage d'Autrui*): "To see a face is already to hear:
'You shall not kill'" (*DF* 8–9). This "saying" of the face is both an invitation to
speak, Levinas tells us, and an interdiction against murder. Explicating what
"face" signifies for Levinas is no simple task, especially since he insists that what
he calls face does not, contra Paul de Man, operate as a mere figure of speech
or of thought.[1] In what follows, we will unpack this paraconcept carefully, me-
thodically. What is clear up front, however, is that the relation to the other,
the ethical relation, according to Levinas, is opened in an interdiction against
murder by figuration that issues from "the face of the Other." That is, Levinas
proposes that the *relation* with the other is not a function of symbolic exchange
but of an extra-symbolic "No" that is aimed directly at rhetoric's intralinguistic
function: figuration.

Figuration is typically described as an exercise in stylistic ornament, an artful deviation from the ordinary signification or arrangement of words, and it is traditionally viewed as a constative act, a reiteration of established meaning through productive or striking substitutions. This approach retains the comforting fiction of a knowing and speaking subject who understands the world and communicates that understanding with eloquence and grace. Nietzsche, of course, famously described figuration as an instituting gesture, an initial positing of what we then call truth. Heidegger, too, describes figuration as a performative function of language; when he wants to reflect on this function in *On the Way to Language,* he turns to a line in Stefan George's poem "The Word": "Where word breaks off no thing may be." In his often cited paraphrase, "No thing is where the word is lacking," Heidegger understands "thing" in the broadest possible sense as "anything that in any way *is,*" including a god. "Only where the word for the thing has been found," Heidegger writes, "is the thing a thing. Only thus *is* it. . . . The word alone gives being to the thing" (60–62).[2] Such diverse thinkers as Levinas and de Man also describe figuration as a performative gesture that *gives* form to formless indeterminacy, as de Man puts it, making "the unknown visible and accessible to the mind and the senses" (*RR* 80). Or, as Levinas suggests, rhetoric as figuration is what *gives* "objects" to be seen and thought: thought does not begin "with the reception of a datum by perception" but with the "language that has formed it" ("Everyday" 135–36). Approached from this angle, figuration gives world by giving meaning; it is the very condition for knowing, and without it, there would be no-thing, nothing to know and nothing to understand—not even a "you" or an "I."

In *First Philosophy of Spirit,* a very early text by Hegel, we read that what's at stake in this engendering of objects for consciousness, however, is existence as such: "Adam's first act, which made him master of the animals, was to give them names, that is, he annihilated them in their existence (as existing creatures)" (Blanchot's translation, *WF* 323). The first function of language, says Hegel, is denomination, and the first function of denomination is annihilation: the name wipes out the existent to bring an idea to life inside language. In this sense, Simon Critchley suggests, Adam was our first serial killer (*Very Little* 53). All signification is born atop an "immense hecatomb," as Maurice Blanchot puts it, in which singular existents are negated (Lacan, Blanchot, and Levinas all say "murdered") for the sake of exchangeable and masterable figures/concepts, granting the death of the real in exchange for the life of the spirit, in Hegel's parlance.[3] One can only really grasp what comes into consciousness DOA, and the work of language—naming, signifying, asserting, describing, the whole of its dialectical activity—is, according to Blanchot, "the speech of death," through which "meaning comes toward us, and we toward it" (*IC* 35).

In very different ways and to very different ends, de Man and Levinas draw on Hegel, Heidegger, and Blanchot to suggest that the successful figuring of the human face is the condition for "speaking consciousness." According to them, in other words, the supposed referent (the speaking subject) is an *effect* of the figure rather than the other way around, and their insistence that face *is* figure defaces any notion of a preexisting referent to which it might refer. Both agree, also, that face-as-figure is itself *dis*figured each time it faces and speaks: the performative "event" of the saying, each time, irrepressibly shatters the face enfaced in the said (constative realm), exposing a fissure in the tropological field, a trace of alterity that resists all modes of knowing. Levinas, however, takes the insight one provocative step further, proposing that it is this defaced face, this interruption in figuration that opens the ethical relation, issuing both an invitation to speak and an interdiction against murder. To speak or to kill? These are your options in *le visage d'Autrui*: conversation or (re)figuration.

Giving Face

In *Immortality*, Milan Kundera dramatizes knowing's troubling dependence on figuration:

> She opened her magazine again and said, "If you put the pictures of two different faces side by side, your eye is struck by everything that makes one different from the other. But if you have two hundred and twenty-three faces side by side, you suddenly realize that it's all just one face in many variations and that no such thing as an individual ever existed."
>
> "Agnes," said Paul, and his voice had suddenly become serious. "Your face does not resemble any other. . . . Don't smile. I really mean it. If you love somebody you love his face and then it becomes totally different from everyone else's."
>
> "Yes, you know me for my face, you know me as a face and you never knew me any other way. Therefore it could never occur to you that my face is not my self."
>
> Paul answered with the patient concern of an old doctor, "Why do you think your face is not you? Who is behind your face?"

"Just imagine living in a world without mirrors. You'd dream about your
face and imagine it as an outer reflection of what is inside you. And then, when
you reached forty, someone put a mirror before you for the first time in your
life. Imagine your fright! You'd see the face of a stranger. And you'd know quite
clearly what you are unable to grasp: your face is not you."

"Agnes," said Paul, and he rose from his armchair. He stood close to her. In
his eyes she saw love, and in his features, his mother.

. . .

"It must have happened some time toward the end of my childhood: I kept
looking in the mirror for such a long time that I finally believed that what I was
seeing was my self. My recollection of this period is very vague, but I know that
the discovery of the self must have been intoxicating. Yet there comes a time
when you stand in front of the mirror and ask yourself: this is my self? And
why? Why did I want to identify with *this*? What do I care about this face? And
at that moment everything starts to crumble. Everything starts to crumble."
(35–36)

Agnes allegorizes the supposedly specular moment that grounds all understanding, and specifically self-understanding, when she says she looked into
the mirror and recognized her self. This event of self-identification takes place
at the end of her childhood, suggesting that it is the effect of both visual and
verbal processes of figuration. What Agnes is struggling with now, however,
amounts to a traumatic experience of disidentification: "her" face doesn't express the extreme particularity that she experiences herself to be but instead
a generality that swallows what she presumes is her individuality ("it's all just
one face in many variations"). Functioning as figure/*schēma*, her face presents
her as a knowable entity only by *mis*representing "what is inside" her, as if she
had been fitted with the "face of a stranger" with which even she had come to
identify.

Agnes detects a distance between the representation (image) and the thing it
is supposed to represent (self), and she wrestles with the implications of sporting
a nonrepresentational face. But what she can't quite embrace is the possibility of
an *irreducible* figurality; that is, she now understands at some level that knowing
depends on figuration, but she doesn't quite snap to the conclusion that rhetoric (as figuration and so thematization) *constitutes* the hermeneutic dimension
and therefore that all intelligibility, including self-intelligibility, is a tropological
product. Maintaining a clean distinction between the ontological status of her
self (what's inside her) and the figural status of her reflected image, Agnes grasps

a slightly truncated version of the Lacanian mirror stage: she realizes that what she recognized in the mirror as her self was in fact a misrecognition and a *captation*. And Paul, she suggests, has made the same mistake—he knows and loves her *as* her face, but if her face is not her self, then what he knows and loves is not her, and therefore Agnes presumes, among other things, that their relationship is a sham. In the instant that the understanding grounding her identity and so their love is understood to be a misunderstanding "everything starts to crumble."

If we were to read Kundera across de Man, we might say that what Paul is able to *know* amounts to the substantializing effect of two intertwined figures of thought, apostrophe and prosopopoeia, which collude to *give* a face and (so) a voice to a name, Agnes. Apostrophe, in de Man's work, names an address to "an absent, deceased, or voiceless entity" as if it were present, conscious, and able to reply, thus *bestowing* it with the power of speech (*RR* 75). And prosopopoeia names the representation of this entity's speech: "Voice assumes mouth, eye, and finally face, a chain that is manifest in the etymology of the trope's name, *prosopon poien*, to confer a mask or a face (*prosopon*)" (76). The face is the "locus of speech," de Man observes, "the necessary condition for the existence of articulated language" (89). In defining prosopopoeia (the giving of face) as the trope of apostrophe (the giving of voice), de Man implies that "voice," the conception and/or experience of a speaking consciousness, is a fiction engendered by the figure of the face; the "speaking consciousness," then—the self-present, self-conscious subject who speaks—is *the figure of a figure.*

Agnes proposes that in a world without mirrors you would "dream about your face" and be horrified to learn that it is not "an outer reflection of what's inside you," that all your friends and loves and enemies are in a relation with "the face of a stranger." But de Man would not suggest that "your face is not you," as if there exists some other, essential you to which your face does not do justice. Rather, he'd suggest that there is no intelligible or essential "you" at all until you are given (as) face, until you are inscribed, troped as an enunciating subject. This originary troping, this immemorial site of self-inscription is the (disastrous) scene of your birth—and/but also of your death: You are born into presence precisely inasmuch as you dissolve into your inscription, inasmuch as you are reduced to the status of a figure. You are therefore born dead. Or missing. DOA or MIA, you only ever *appear* as an apparition, a ghostly figure, the presence of an absence. Or the absence of a presence. Your face is what there is to *know* about you, and all there is to know; and yet, your very presence *as* a so-called speaking subject indicates that the you to which the face is supposed to refer has always already been snuffed out; wherever there is voice, there are ghosts.[4] "Dying means: you are dead already, in an immemorial past, of a death which was not yours," Blanchot writes, "which you have thus neither known nor lived, but under the threat of which you believe you are called upon to live" (*WD* 65).

Cynthia Chase points out that the Oxford English Dictionary translates *prosopon* as "face, person" and *poiein* as "make," and she notes that de Man's decision to translate "*prosopon* as 'face' or 'mask,' not as 'person,' is to imply that the face is the condition—not the equivalent—of the existence of a person" (83). According to him, even "humans" must be *person*ified (figured, enfaced), in other words, to achieve the status of a person, of a human agent, leading de Man to insist on a distinction between anthropomorphism and proso-popoeia.[5] Anthropomorphism is a humanist gesture that takes the essence of the "human" for granted: presuming human beings are essentially conscious and present entities endowed with the power of speech, it then projects this "human essence" onto some supposedly different sort of essence. De Man writes that anthropomorphism

> is not just a trope but an identification on the level of substance. It takes one entity for another and thus implies the constitution of specific entities prior to their confusion, the *taking* of something for something else that can then be assumed to be *given*. Anthropomorphism freezes the infinite chain of tropo-logical transformations and propositions into one single assertion or essence which, as such, excludes all others. It is no longer a proposition but a proper name. (*RR* 241)

Anthropomorphism's substantializing tendency freezes the endless troping of language into a seemingly immutable figure (*forma*), which it presents as natu-ral, essential. In "taking the natural as human," Chase comments, it "takes the human as given" (83), effacing the distance between "man" and "nature"—or, in Heideggerian terminology, between "world" (*techné*) and "earth" (*physis*).[6] De Man continues: "Anthropomorphism seems to be the illusionary resuscita-tion of the natural breath of language frozen into stone by the semantic power of the trope. It is a figural affirmation that claims to overcome the deadly nega-tive power invested in the figure" (*RR* 247), that claims to have landed on sub-stance—the bottom turtle, which is "man"—rather than on another trope.

Chase notes that for de Man prosopopoeia, on the other hand, proceeds without substantializing its gesture, taking the human to be "dependent upon the giving of a figure, that of 'face'" (84), rather than the other way around. Anthropomorphism is possible only because it mistakes a tropological effect for an essence, only because it confuses the face posited by a rhetorical process for a natural phenomenon, for a face given in nature. "De Man not merely reads *prosopopoeia* as the giving of face," Chase emphasizes, "he reads *face* as that which is given by prosopopoeia. Face is not the natural given of the human person. It is given in a mode of discourse, given by an act of language. What is given by this act is figure. Figure is no less than our very face" (84). Indeed, in French one definition of *figure* is "face." De Man's use of prosopopoeia therefore denies access to any "independently existing phenomenon," to "the face we think we always have," Chase observes. "Prosopopoeia, or the giving of face, is *de*-facement, then, insofar as if face is given by an act of language it is 'only' a figure" (85). The notion of a substantial self, which the posited face posits, is shattered in the face's emergence as a mere figure of speech (or of thought); therefore, prosopopoeia *defaces* and *effaces* precisely to the extent that it *enfaces*. What it defaces is essential selfhood, the very idea of a preexisting and substantial self that the face would (mis)represent. De Man is explicit about this: face must be *put in place* by language. "*Prosopon-poiein*," he writes, "means to *give* a face and therefore implies that the original face can be missing or nonexistent. The trope which coins a name for a still unnamed entity, which gives face to the faceless is, of course, catachresis" (*Resistance* 44). So prosopopoeia operates via catachresis, which is typically understood to be a misuse or abuse of figure, to put a face in the place of an originally *missing* essence. A certain catachrestic enfacement that gives form to a formless indeterminacy is the condition of possibility for perceiving any existent *as* a speaking consciousness.

Despite their significant differences, however, Chase reminds us that both prosopopoeia and anthropomorphism are ultimately unsuccessful strategies that attempt to slap a mask of consciousness or cognition over language's random positing power. "Both strategies arise," Chase writes, "from the necessity to establish the phenomenality of the poetic voice, which is the principle of intelligibility . . . of language in general" (107). Language's power to mean—"the semantic power of the trope"—involves the positing of a face: the poetic voice that brings "world" into being relies on what de Man calls the "face-making, totalizing power" of language to offer it a sur*face*, a channel, a mouth through which to speak. This power is clearly generative: it brings "I" into being, granting word and world by giving face and voice. But as de Man suggests in his reading of Wordsworth's *Prelude*, "the face, which is the power to surface from

the sea of infinite distinctions in which we risk to drown, can find no surface";
the face-making power of language is "the relentless undoer of its own claims"
(*RR* 91, 92). Language's random positing power, which makes meaning possible and continuously interrupts it, never stops and is not stoppable. "De Man
arranged for a new alignment of the constative and performative edges of language," Avital Ronell writes in *Stupidity*, "where the constative (discovering,
unveiling, pointing out, saying what is) is always shown to be unsettled by the
performative intrusion (producing, instituting, transforming)" (97). Rhetoric,
as the figural structure of language, demonstrates an implacable determination to deterritorialize its own cognitive territories, to disfigure its own figures,
deface its own face(s). "The repetitive erasures by which language performs
the erasure of its own positions," de Man writes, "can be called disfiguration"
(*RR* 119), and the face/figure of the speaking subject is defaced/disfigured
as soon as it—that is, *language*—begins to speak. So this generative power
that gives face and voice is simultaneously and doubly mortifying. It is also,
paradoxically, silencing: inasmuch as "I" come(s) into being as a figure, each
time, "I" am/is a plastic image, "frozen into stone by the semantic power of the
trope"—frozen and so intelligible but also, as de Man says, "mute as pictures
are mute" (*RR* 80).[7]

Face Off: On Being Mute

In an essay called "Language," Heidegger emphasizes that language is not simply "a human faculty" (*OTWL* 107), as humanism wants/hopes, but that language *itself* speaks—if "language *speaks*," he observes, "this means at the same
time and before all else: *language* speaks" ("Language" 198). This speaking of
language, which exceeds all human appropriation, all conscious articulation,
Heidegger writes, "takes place as that which grants an abode for the being of
mortals." Mortal beings dwell inside language, which is also what brings them
into being: to say that "language speaks" is to acknowledge that "it is language
that first brings man about, brings him into existence" ("Language" 192). When
we mortals speak, then, we speak according to a prior granting that involves a
prior listening. In his reading of the *Prelude*, de Man tropes it slightly differently,
shifting from an ear to an eye: "one can speak only because one can *look* upon
a mode of speech which is not quite our own" (*RR* 90, my emphasis). But back
to Heidegger, who stays with the ear:

Speaking is of itself a listening. Speaking is listening to the language which we speak. Thus, it is a listening not while but before we are speaking. This listening to language also comes before all other kinds of listening that we know, in a most inconspicuous manner. We do not merely speak *the* language—we speak *by way of* it. We can do so solely because we always have already listened to the language. What do we hear? We hear language speaking. (*OTWL* 124)

According to him, an originary relation to language, a relation to language that precedes and is productive of "self," is what makes both speaking and all other (determinate) relations possible. Relationality opens with language, which is why Heidegger calls language "the relation of all relations" (*OTWL* 107). De Man's reading of Wordsworth exposes something similar: "Man can address and face other men, within life and beyond the grave, because he has a face, but he has a face only because he partakes of a mode of discourse that is neither entirely natural nor entirely human" (*RR* 90). This originary relation with language is the condition of possibility for all "human" relations and all "human" speech. It is also their condition of impossibility.

De Man insists that the speaking consciousness is in fact mute because it is language that speaks—language speaks this "consciousness" into being as a figure, effecting an (immemorial) appropriation that gets reenacted each time language speaks through and in place of the "I." De Man explores this ventriloquizing scene explicitly in his essays on Hegel, who, in the *Phenomenology of Spirit*, snaps to an impasse between meaning (*Meinung*) and saying (*sagen*). Here's Hegel:

It is as a universal too that we *utter* what the sensuous [content] is. What we say is: "This," i.e. the *universal* This; or, "it is," i.e. *Being in General*. Of course, we do not *envisage* the universal This or Being in general, but we *utter* the universal; in other words, we do not strictly say what in sense-certainty we *mean* to say. But language, as we see, is the more truthful; in it we ourselves directly refute what we *mean* to say, and since the universal is the true [content] of sense-certainty and language expresses this true [content] alone, it is just not possible for us ever to say, or express in words, a sensuous being that we mean. (60)

Hegel situates *real* truth in the universal rather than in sense-certainty, sizing up the true content of the particularity one sensuously experiences *as* the universal. One cannot ever *say* what one *means* because language's meaning-making power operates figuratively. Though one means to say the particular experience of what one immediately grasps in "sense-certainty"—or perhaps, to add another dimension to Hegel, one means to say the radically singular interruption of experience in enigma or trauma—one is only ever able to *say* the universal, the general, the figural. When I say "now," the uniqueness of this singular instant or interval or lapse that I *mean* to say has already disappeared into the word, into the general form/figure of a kind of eternal presence, which is precisely what I do *not* mean. Agnes: "But if you have two hundred and twenty-three faces side by side, you suddenly realize that it's all just one face in many variations and that no such thing as an individual ever existed."

By extension, when I say "I," Hegel notes elsewhere, I mean *this* I and no other, but what "I" say is the universal and so "is precisely anyone" (qtd. in de Man, *Aesthetic* 98). De Man observes that this contradiction between meaning and saying indicates that "the position of the I, which is the condition for thought, implies its eradication . . . the undoing, the erasure of any relationship, logical or otherwise, that could be conceived between what the I is and what it says it is" (*Aesthetic* 98–99).[8] In the saying/positing of "I," Chase explains, I am/is undone, erased as a conscious, preexisting entity "or a subject with predicates"—and this erasure, she points out, also obliterates the very possibility of "relating subject to predicate" (92). If the so-called speaking subject cannot "say an 'I' that stands in any relation to it," she observes, "it becomes a subject incapable of functioning as a subject" (93), marking the impossibility of linking speech to the intentions of a speaking consciousness. Language grants the figure of the self-subject but then sets it to autodestruct, ensuring that it'll be taken out by its very "own" speech. Inasmuch as language speaks through "us," de Man observes, "we speak only as a ventriloquist's dummy. . . . The self is deprived of any locutionary power; to all intents and purposes, it may as well be mute" (*Aesthetic* 112).

But it is not only that each time "I" opens its mouth, language speaks in its place; it is also that each time language speaks, it immediately "echos," as Claire Nouvet puts it, diffracting or laterally sliding into an endless proliferation of "alternative meanings that no consciousness can pretend to comprehend" (108). Each time it speaks, "'I' disappears in a play of signifiers" over which it has no control, undergoing a reenactment of its own immemorial appropriation by language:

> As soon as "I" speaks, "I" loses a consciousness which it never had, and becomes the figure that we posit *in place of* a consciousness which is, from the

moment we speak, lost. In this sense, the speaking "I" marks the absence, the original disappearance of the subject. It is a figure of the subject put in place of a missing subject. It "stands" for a disappearance. (Nouvet 108)

Apostrophe and prosopopoeia are the figural operations that *give* the figure of the "I," the speaking consciousness, turning an echo into a "somebody" and (so) granting the poetic voice a sur*face* through which to speak. But as soon as this "I" speaks it disfigures, as soon as "I" opens its mouth, it is already gone, already obliterated as a conscious subject. As soon "I" tries to speak, in other words, the Other, the echoing of language, speaks instead, blowing the "I" away. "The Other which estranges 'I' from what is abusively called its 'own' speech," writes Nouvet, "therefore marks an original loss of speech, since when 'I' believes it speaks, the echoing Other which speaks in its place in fact reduces it to muteness" (108).

Significantly, for Nouvet the Other (capital "O") is the echoing of language and not a "human" other. The Other, she writes, "is to be considered less a being than an operation: it is 'other' to the extent that it 'alters.'" The Other is a "process of alteration" that sets "language in motion," initiating "its endless drift, its endless lateral sliding," which from the very beginning, diffracts any utterance into "a potentiality of alternative meanings." So even when, as in Ovid's Narcissus myth, one calls out for an other, another *person*—"Is there anyone around?"—the Other alters the question/call "as soon as it is uttered," *answering* the question by sending it back in all its otherness, as an echoing of alternative meanings that one cannot control and could never comprehend. This means, Nouvet observes, "that 'I' does not know what it is calling for when it calls out for the proximity of the other; the Other speaks as soon as 'I' calls out for the other, and in its place" (109–10). Forever denied the nominative position to which it aspires, the "I," when it calls out for an other, is already "withdrawn from the call, dispossessed of what it believed to be its own speech by the unrecognized Other which echoes in its place. In the very gesture of calling, 'I' is therefore deprived of the power to call, condemned to an apparently insurmountable muteness" (110). The Other that inhabits the call to the other from the start responds by "violently altering" it and "rendering uncertain the very presence of the caller; it is no longer certain that there is someone here as soon as 'I' asks: 'Is there anyone around?'" (Nouvet 110).[9]

The very notion of intersubjective dialogue is the effect of a "merciful subjective error," as Nouvet puts it (111), which shields me from my radical inability to address another and to respond to another's address as the subject of my "own" speech. The figure/fiction of the intersubjective buttresses the hope that one is a knowing and speaking subject in control of one's "own" language—this hope, however, is constantly dashed. "It is upon losing what we have to say that we speak," Blanchot writes, "upon an imminent and immemorial disaster. We speak suggesting that something not being said is speaking: the loss of what we were to say" (*WD* 21). The figure of speaking consciousness is shattered each time "I" opens its mouth: each time "I" speak/s, the Other that echoes in its place kills off all hope for a speaking consciousness—which nonetheless doesn't excuse "me" from "my" responsibility to respond, to respond without the power to do so, *parler sans pouvoir*, as Blanchot says. We are getting there.

"My" death has already taken place: the scene of "my" birth as a conscious and intelligible self is also a murder scene. "I" was born by having been knocked off; the speaking "I," which is always already not one, is the "subject" of a lethal inscription that brings it into being precisely by doing it in. The essential self comes into being only as it is falling into its "own" image, which is, Nouvet reminds us, "like all mirror images, an inverted image, an image which indeed occasions the inversion, the reversal, the 'falling,' of the very notion of a substantial, ontological self" (127). This is an immemorial death that cannot be remembered by a self as if it were simply a past event that happened to it; because this "event" is precisely what generates the figure of the essential self in the first place, there is no one around to experience it. And yet, each time "I" speaks, it is doomed to reenact this inaugural trauma, the dissolution of its purported antecedent into its image, setting its own murder scene to perpetual replay. "In the disaster," Blanchot writes "I disappear without dying (or I die without disappearing)" (*WD* 119).

Agnes's mistake was to preserve a clean distinction between the self and "its" image, to presume the ontological status of a self that turns out to be the figure of a figure. If the essential or ontological self can be confused with a mirror image in the first place, that's "because it is 'itself' an imago," Nouvet observes, an idealized and mute mental image that represents no original (125). Agnes was actually closer to this disastrous truth when she looked into the mirror and believed what she was seeing *was* her self, that she *was* what the mirror reflected. When she states her apparently demystified position, "your face is not you," she suggests that the image the mirror is able to reflect is not representative of her unique, essential self. Realizing that she has been duped by the figural status of the face, she nonetheless does not snap to the figural status of the *self* as a speaking consciousness.

According to Nouvet's innovative reading, Narcissus, on the other hand, does come to recognize his "own" figural status. When he looks into the pool and speaks to "his" imago, whose "sweet lips" move in mute response, Narcissus suddenly exclaims, "*Iste ego sum,*" which is translated as "Oh, I am he!" "I am that one," or "The ego is that one." The standard interpretation is that Narcissus has just realized that he has fallen in love with his own reflection, with a *mere* image. But Nouvet suggests that he also, perhaps unwittingly, defines "the ego as the other, as an 'other' which is not, however, another subject, a subjective otherness, but a mute and unresponsive imago that the water reflects" (124). When Narcissus says "I am that one," he equates the supposedly substantial, speaking self with a mute and lifeless imago, an "originary simulacrum, a mere figure," a "nonself, an image deprived of subjectivity" (125). And Nouvet points out that it is precisely when he recognizes that the self is a simulacrum that he begins to die, allegorizing the immemorial trauma: "To recognize the self as an originary simulacrum is to recognize that the constitution of the self coincides with its decomposition, that the self 'appears' as originally missing, a simulacrum referring to no 'original.' It is in that sense that the self 'dies' in the very process of constituting itself" (125).

But the death of the essential self, which in any case has always already occurred, opens the possibility for an entirely other sense of the "self" that is not defined by form or consciousness, a "self on the hither side of my identity," as Levinas puts it, "prior to all self consciousness" and "older than the plot of egoism" (*OTB* 92). In Blanchot's unusual reading of the Narcissus myth, which in part inspires Nouvet's reading, it is this inessential "self" that Narcissus "sees" in the pool. The significant advantage Narcissus has over Agnes is that he catches sight of his face on the surface of the *water,* which allows both for the clarity of an image to appear and/but also prevents the "stable fixity of sheer visibility (which [can] be appropriated)." Narcissus, in other words, doesn't "see" the "distinct and definite image" that a mirror can reflect; rather he "sees" what escapes sight: "the invisible in the visible—in the picture the undepicted, the unstable unknown of a representation without presence, which reflects no model" (*WD* 134).[10]

Both on and as a watery surface, the figure of the face itself disfigures, revealing a kind of "presence" diverted from any present, an enigmatic surplus that overflows its "own" form and so exceeds vision's appropriative gaze. Representing nothing, what this disfiguring "figure" of the face expresses escapes all comprehension, all knowledge, and so all power. What it exposes is not a substantial or essential self but, as Levinas puts it, "the gleam of exteriority" that precedes and exceeds form/figure (*TI* 24). When Narcissus points to this manifestation of a face over and beyond form and exclaims "I am that one!" he affirms that the "self" is an irremediable exposedness unprotected by the borders of a figure—he affirms that the "self," in other words, is delimited neither by consciousness nor by the outline of a phenomenological *entity*.[11] Whereas the young Agnes looks into a mirror and believes what she's seeing is her essential self, Narcissus looks into the pool and "sees" the self as that which no essence or entity could possibly contain. If Agnes's experience allegorizes the figural grounding for all (self) knowledge, Narcissus's experience allegorizes the utter collapse of that ground in what Levinas calls the "epiphany of the face" (*TI* 66).

The Epiphany of the Face

According to de Man, what we take to be the phenomenon of the face is already a figure; that is, the phenomenality of the face is an effect of its figurality. And inasmuch as that supposed phenomenality amounts to the thematizing figure that also manifests it, it is frozen, plastic, mute—dead. Levinas would not disagree. But "the epiphany of the face is alive," he writes: "Its life consists in *undoing* the form in which every entity, when it enters into immanence, that is, when it exposes itself as a theme, is already dissimulated" ("Trace" 351; my emphasis). In Levinas's work "the face"—which is never my own but always the Other's (*le visage d'Autrui*)—names neither a natural phenomenon nor the figure that is given in prosopopoeia: it names instead the dissolution of that figure. Levinas doesn't put it this way, but it seems fair to say that "face" here operates as a (para)figure for disfiguration, for the eruption of an enigma *in* the phenomenon, which names an interruption in narcissistic appropriation (identification) and therefore the opening of ethics.

Disfiguration involves the spontaneous unworking of the work of the figure, which touches off an interruption in the movement of comprehension; it describes a depropriative instant in which a figure is suddenly divested of the meaning it is charged with transporting, leaving a shattered sur-face that reveals the tropological structure grounding all knowledge, including self-knowledge. Levinas proposes that when this interruption in cognition erupts in the interhuman relation, one is exposed to the unfigurable otherness in the other (*Autrui*).[12] In *le visage d'Autrui* the supposed intersubjectivity (transcendental symmetry) of the ego and the other is interrupted by a relationality prior to all mediation. Levinas characterizes this relation as one of nonindifference, and yet he insists that it is a function neither of shared meaning nor of identification since understanding is precisely what is disrupted in the face of the Other; rather, this relation consists in pure appeal, saying without a said, persuasion without a rhetorician:

> The way in which the other presents himself, exceeding *the idea of the other in me*, we here name face. This *mode* does not consist in figuring as a theme under my gaze, in spreading itself forth as a set of qualities forming an image. The face of the Other at each moment destroys and overflows the plastic image it leaves me, the idea existing to my own measure and to the measure of its *ideatum*— the adequate idea. It does not manifest itself by these qualities, but *kath 'auto*. It *expresses itself*. (*TI* 50–51)

"Face" names a kind of reversal of the gesture of prosopopoeia, then, in which the face-as-figure slips or is broken through, exposing not a "true essence" behind the mask but an infinite alterity irreducible to form, to concept, and therefore to essence. It "expresses itself" not through the qualities of a form but by shedding that form; it ex-presses itself *kath 'auto*, Levinas says, according to itself alone. What the face expresses, in other words, is *that it is*, in all its naked existence, unprotected and so unlimited and unmediated by form or context or idea. Exposition of exposedness. "The first content of expression is the expression itself," Levinas writes (*TI* 51). Face "expresses itself" not as meaningful figure but as an interruption that no figure (and therefore no understanding) can hold. And according to Levinas, "the whole body—a hand or a curve of the shoulder—can express as the face" (*TI* 262), as can the "skin" itself, and occasionally, the "saying" of a text.[13]

What *undoes* its "own" form is not, as Agnes would have it, a substantive essence that the form misrepresents but an exposed existence that no figure can finally absorb or contain—and therefore that "I" could not encounter except in the (non)event of that form's undoing. According to Levinas, the face figures the abrupt divestment of any tropological complexion whatsoever, and so of any semiotic meaning. In the face to face, you are exposed to the exposedness of the other, and so to your relation to radical alterity, to the wholly other, to the Other who (nonetheless) alters: *Autrui*. That is, Levinas's Other (capital "O") names neither Nouvet's play of the signifier nor a "category of the genre *autre*," as Derrida says ("Violence" 105), but the unfigurable otherness in the other existent—which Levinas tells us effects an "alteration without alienation" (*OTB* 141). If *le visage d'autre* is the effect of figuration, *le visage d'Autrui* effects a disfiguration.[14]

Levinas designates this otherness in the other with the term "illeity," which indicates a dimension of irreversibility, of nonreciprocity, a nonbridgeable distance that prevents "conjunction" between the "I" and the "you." In Levinas's work, "the face of the Other" signifies something like the presentation, in the other existent, of this irreversible otherness. Complicating Martin Buber's symmetrical and (so) reciprocal "I-thou" relation, Levinas proposes that "*[i]lleity* lies outside the 'thou' and the thematization of objects. A neologism formed with the *il* (he) or the *ille*, it indicates a way of concerning me without entering into conjunction with me." Illeity names a third-person-ness, a he-ness that comes through *in* the face to face, preventing simple identification and reciprocity between the "I" and the "you" (or "thou") (*OTB* 12–13).[15] Illeity means not only that my responsibility for the Other is a one-way street but also that *Autrui* will never be reducible to me or to an object of identification.

Blanchot proposes that in Levinas *Autrui* is the name for "what in the other exceeds me absolutely" (*IC* 61). *Autrui*, the other (existent) who presents him/ herself as a "face" and so exposes me to illeity, is "without a country," Levinas writes, "not an inhabitant, exposed to the cold and the heat of the seasons" (*OTB* 91).[16] Having no proper form, *Autrui* cannot be properly recognized or thematized, cannot enter into any sort of reciprocal pact. *Autrui* cannot enter into the world of representation at all—intersubjective deliberations are closed to *Autrui*, who (who?) nonetheless haunts them from the "Outside," as Blanchot might say. *Autrui* remains exterior to the work of the concept, inaccessible to cognition, and when I encounter *le visage d'Autrui*, it trips me up, stupefies me, interrupts my capacity to understand, to make sense, "turning my highest power into im-possibility," as Blanchot puts it (*IC* 54). Levinas describes the encounter with *Autrui* as a "traumatism of astonishment" (*TI* 71), a brush with inassimilable exteriority that reveals an irreparable structure of exposure—but without offering anything one could call *knowledge* and without closing the impassible distance between "us."[17]

And yet, *Autrui* is at the same time unbearably close to me, maintaining a proximity closer and older than any merely present presence, than any essence or entity, *affecting* me beyond the intervention of a mediating force, without the aid of figures and concepts: *Autrui* is an immediate "presence." The immediate precedes and exceeds "all direct relation, all mystical fusion, and all sensible contact," Blanchot writes. One does not grasp or comprehend the immediate; comprehension requires the distancing and imaging of a mediating force, which makes presence *present*, visible and accessible to cognition. But "immediate presence," Blanchot observes, "is presence of what could not be present, presence of the non-accessible, presence excluding or exceeding any present." The relation with *Autrui* is therefore in a strong sense "im-possible." The relation with *Autrui* is impossibility itself, impossibility being "a relation escaping power" (*IC* 38), a relation beyond comprehension's possibilities, a relation without relation, then, that affects "me," that is in fact constitutive of "me." And when "I" encounter(s) *Autrui*, it overwhelms "me," undoing "the core of what is identity in me," says Levinas (*OTB* 89).

In Levinas's texts, *le visage d'Autrui* figures "the rupture of the immanent order, of the order that I can embrace, of the order which I can hold in my thought, of the order which can become mine" (*IR* 48). It figures an interruption in identification and cognition that opens a dissociating association. The encounter with *Autrui* is a depropriating experience (or nonexperience[18]) with an immediate presence that exceeds all form, with what is in-visible and radically nonfigurable. "I" experience *Autrui* only as the disturbance of disfiguration, as an interruption in the work of the figure in which all "metaphor gives way to metamorphosis," as Steven Shaviro so beautifully puts it (154). That is, the encounter, the *experience* of my rapport with *Autrui* (a rapport that turns out to be older than "I" am) opens as this interruption, as this eruption of exteriority that pierces the smooth ordering both of my "world" and of my sense of interiority, making an entry while resisting my power absolutely. Levinas zeroes in on the instant of the divestment, on the interruption that exposes the trace of a nonfigurable surplus, the flickering of an imminent but never quite present presence, already gone, which he reads as the trace of an immemorial "*past* that was never a *now*" ("Phenomenon" 73). *Autrui*, he writes, is "the free one. Over him I have no power. He escapes my grasp by an essential dimension, even if I have him at my disposal. He is not wholly in my site" (*TI* 39).[19]

In Levinas, "the face of the Other" signifies a trace of that which is irreducible to the tropological field, to all form and concept, to the entire territory of the said; it exposes the trace of a relation that is even older than your reduction to the status of a figure and which overwhelms your powers of comprehension, producing in you "the idea of the Infinite." An experience of what Kant calls the mathematical sublime (but without the recuperative move), the encounter with *le visage d'Autrui* is a collision with a vastness that overwhelms the powers of comprehension.[20] Inasmuch as the idea of the infinite lights up *as* "the face of the Other," Levinas suggests that the face is the site of a rupture in the tropological field, in world as such, the entire arena of representation and thematizing consciousness. Still, and despite Levinas's many protestations, what he calls ethical language—the saying of the face, its expression—is itself rhetorical. Michael Hyde describes it as a "primordial epideictic discourse," a "rhetorical interruption" (*Call* 111). It operates as an affective appeal, an address that effects not the figuring of meaning but meaning's interruption, its disfiguration: the ethical relation takes place as a sublime trauma in which comprehension is eclipsed.

Phenomenon and Enigma

Levinas's analyses begin with the everyday experience of "world," with the "cultural whole" in which the figuration and manifestation of the other are produced, acknowledging that "the other is given in the concept of the totality to which he is immanent," and that s/he is "illuminated within this [cultural] whole, like a text by its context" ("Trace" 351). But Levinas works backwards from there "to a situation where the totality breaks up, a situation that conditions the totality itself." This situation is "the gleam of exteriority or of transcendence in the face of the Other" (*TI* 24), which *precedes and exceeds* manifestation, and therefore knowing. The figured other signifies as a phenomenon within the cultural whole and/but also expresses as a face outside any context, outside the tropological field, disturbing and breaking up the totality:

> [The other's] cultural signification is revealed and reveals as it were *horizontally*, on the basis of the historical world to which it belongs. According to the phenomenological expression, it reveals the horizons of this world. But this mundane signification is found to be disturbed and shaken by another presence, abstract, not integrated into the world. His presence consists in coming unto us, making an entry. This can be stated in this way: the phenomenon which is the apparition of the other is also a *face*. ("Trace" 351)

The figured/enfaced other shows up as an immanent phenomenon who can be understood, grasped, identified (with) via his/her context within the world; but at the same time, the other signifies otherwise, as another kind of presence, not immanent but both imminent and immemorial, as a disturbance, an interruption in the totalizing context: "The other who manifests himself in the face as it were breaks through his own plastic essence, like someone who opens a window on which his figure is outlined. His presence consists in divesting himself of the form which, however, manifests him. His manifestation is a surplus over the inevitable paralysis of manifestation" ("Trace" 351–52).

As a face, that is, the other presents him or herself as a phenomenon from which s/he is always already busting loose, as a phenomenon that cannot contain its "contents." Escaping all representation, the face "is the very collapse of phenomenality," Levinas writes: "Not because it is too brutal to appear, but because in a sense it is too weak, non-phenomenon because less than a phenomenon. The disclosing of a face is nudity, non-form, abandon of self, ageing, dying, more naked than nudity. It is poverty, skin with wrinkles" (OTB 88). Whereas the face given in prosopopoeia grants the condition of possibility for an intelligible "I" and "you" to manifest, Levinas's "face," an enigmatic para-figure for disfiguration, disrupts the mundane presence of that manifestation, signaling a surplus over the presence of any thematizing form, an uncontainable overflow that remains impervious to figuration's essentializing enclosures. This surplus manifests itself only as interruption, as a disturbance: an enigma erupting in the phenomenon, a *trace* of the infinite expressing itself in the finite. The face names "a trace of infinity which *passes* without being able to enter" (OTB 93).

So whereas the speaking consciousness that prosopopoeia engenders is mute as a picture, Levinas's face speaks: "The life of expression consists in undoing the form in which the existent, exposed as a theme, is thereby dissimulated. The face speaks. The manifestation of the face is *already* discourse" (TI 66; my emphasis). The saying or expression of the face, then, is a "first discourse," which designates a "way of coming from behind one's appearance, behind one's form—an opening in the openness" ("Trace" 352).[21] This saying has nothing to do with the communication of a message or an idea or bit of information; nor are we talking here about facial expressions that communicate a subject's mental or emotional states: "The primordial essence of expression and discourse does not reside in the information they would supply concerning an interior and hidden world" (TI 200). The discourse of the face expresses only itself according to itself (*kath 'auto*), shedding form and figure, exposing an irreparable exposedness, the impervious breach of exteriority. What is significant in the discourse of the face is that this radical alterity interrupts me by addressing me, appealing to me, turning me into its addressee. The face is signification, signification itself, according to Levinas, and/but it signifies in an immediate way, prior to the exchange of signs and sans the "as" structure (this *as* that) that underwrites any hermeneutical understanding within the context of a world. The face signifies "beyond every attribute" that would qualify it and reduce it to the realm of the knowable or the useable; it signifies "before we have projected light upon it," Levinas writes (*TI* 74):

> On the hither side of the ambiguity of being and entities, prior to the said, saying uncovers the one that speaks, not as an object disclosed by theory, but in the sense that one discloses oneself by neglecting one's defenses, leaving a shelter, exposing oneself to outrage, to insults and wounding. But saying is a denuding of denuding, a giving a sign of its very signifyingness, an expression of exposure, a hyperbolic passivity that disturbs the still waters, in which, without saying, passivity would be crawling with secret designs. (*OTB* 49)

Affecting me prior to and in excess of any meaning I might ascribe to it, the face of the Other "strikes me before striking me, as though I had heard before he spoke" (*OTB* 88).

As a phenomenon, as a product of the said, the face offers itself to my vision, making itself available to my grasp, to my powers of comprehension. But "in its epiphany, in expression, the sensible, still graspable, turns into total resistance to the grasp" (*TI* 197)—this is a resistance, however, that is without violence, without force. It is by *withdrawing* from the possibility of comprehension that the face of the Other shatters the "plastic image it leaves me," overflowing the "avidity of the gaze," and so interrupting my power, defying my very "ability for power" (*TI* 198). The expression of the face signifies extreme proximity, "an immediacy older than the abstracts of nature" through which "I" effect a distance; it signifies a "contact with the other," affection by the other that precedes apprehension. This contact, this affection, then, is not reducible to appropriation, but neither does it designate the fusional experience of ecstatic participation: "To be in contact is neither to invest the other and annul his alterity, nor to suppress myself in the other. In contact itself, the touching and the touched separate, as though the touched moved off, was always already other, did not have anything in common with me" (*OTB* 86). This dissociating association takes place as the immediate language relation with the Other, Levinas says, an address that requires a response.

The saying of the face comes through as a rhetorical imperative, an obligation to respond that holds the "I" and the other in an extreme proximity, in a nearness so excruciatingly close that s/he touches me, affects me, overwhelming my powers of comprehension but without absorbing me. In the face of the

Other, my power ceases: I lose my capacity to grasp, to comprehend, to know. On the other hand, "when the other appears to me as an entity in the plastic form of being an image," mediating forces are imposed on "our" proximity that grant me some semblance of control over myself and my world. When the other appears as conceptual image, as the said's delimited entity, and not as a face, s/he doesn't seem to disturb my power, and I seem "capable of accounting for everything by my own identity." But what this illusion of self-sufficiency indicates, Levinas tells us, is that the Other "is no longer near," that "the contact is broken." According to him, "immediacy is the collapse of representation into a face" (*OTB* 89, 91), and this face manifests itself as an interruption of my spontaneity, of my "joyous possession of the world" (*TI* 76). It is, again, precisely this interruption that Levinas calls ethics: "The strangeness of the Other, his irreducibility to the I, to my thoughts and my possessions, is precisely accomplished as a calling into question of my spontaneity, as ethics" (*TI* 43).

To Speak or to Kill

This interruption that calls me and my appropriation of "world" into question also introduces me to a relation that already obligates me. The face of the Other first of all *speaks* to me, Levinas insists, breaking through its plastic form, interrupting my power and possibility and offering an exposition of exposedness, the revelation of my "original relation with exterior being" (*TI* 66). The encounter with *Autrui* occurs solely in the language relation, in the saying of the face, which is before all else an invocation, a greeting, an appeal to which I cannot not respond: "I cannot evade by silence the discourse which the epiphany of the face opens" (*TI* 200–201). He obviously doesn't put it this way, but what else is Levinas describing here than a rhetorical imperative that comes in from out of nowhere, an obligation to respond that precedes comprehension, announcing itself not through the production of constative meaning but through its performative interruption? What else is he describing but an exemplary instance of persuasion without a rhetorician? This obligation, as unlocatable as it is undeniable, is the condition for symbolic exchange, he proposes, an "invitation" to speak. It is also a startling command, "an imperative given to your responsibility" (*IR* 48): "to see a face," as he bluntly puts it in *Difficult Freedom*, "is already to hear 'You shall not kill'" (8). The invitation is indissociable from the interdiction because to refuse the invitation is already to be guilty of "murder." To encounter a face is straightaway to *be faced* with the ethical dilemma: to speak or to kill? Blanchot observes that "should the self ever come under this command—speech or death—it will be because it is in the *presence* of *autrui*" (*IC* 61).

To Speak; Or If I Could, Baby, I'd Give You My World

To encounter a face is already to be addressed, greeted, and this greeting issues an obligation to respond. Before the face, "I" do not just stand there "contemplating it," Levinas notes: "I respond to it" (*EI* 88). I could take a train trip or go people watching at the local mall, for example, without ever encountering a face; once I do, however, the entertainment is over, trumped by an irremissible obligation. The first mention of the face in *Totality and Infinity* defines the relation with it as "conversation" (*entre-tien*)[22]:

> For the presence before the face, my orientation toward the Other, can lose the avidity proper to the gaze only by turning into generosity, incapable of approaching the other with empty hands. This relationship established over the things henceforth possibly common, that is, susceptible of being said, is the relationship of conversation. . . . To approach the Other in conversation is to welcome his expression, in which at each instant he overflows the idea a thought would carry away from it. It is therefore to receive from the Other beyond the capacity of the I, which means exactly: to have the idea of Infinity. (*TI* 50–51)

Conversation: "to be in relation with a substance overflowing its own idea in me, overflowing what Descartes calls its 'objective existence'" (*TI* 76). This "relationship of conversation," Levinas insists, here and everywhere, is *over* anything that might *henceforth* be said and so consciously/cognitively shared. In a significant rejoinder to Hegel, Levinas proposes that the radical singularity that the face expresses is unsayable not because its real truth lies in the universal but because it is the *condition* for and so remains *irreducible* to universality, preceding and exceeding any empirical articulation as well as the rhetorical/grammatical position of the "I." Anything that can be said is, for Levinas, the function of an always prior saying that remains inarticulable as such, irreducible to "the thematization and exposition of a said" ("Everyday" 141–42).[23]

Language, Levinas insists, should not be understood primarily as "the communication of an idea or as information," but also and "perhaps above all—as the fact of encountering the other as other" (*IR* 47). The language relation involves encountering the other as a being "who stands beyond every attribute, which would precisely have as its effect to qualify him, that is, to reduce him to what is common to him and other beings—a being, consequently, completely naked" (*TI* 74). A being exposed. Anterior to the communication of any generalized message that might henceforth be consciously shared, Levinas tells us, there is the speech before speech, the saying that is the condition for every said, the encounter with naked and so defenseless and absolutely ungraspable singularity, which comes through as an interpellation (interruption), a call from the Other to which "I" can only respond, and which is already presupposed in any exchange of messages, any interpretation, any "decoding of signs" (*OTB* 92).[24]

The nakedness of the face, Levinas insists, "extends into the nakedness of the body that is cold and that is ashamed of its nakedness. Existence *kath 'auto* is, in the world, a destitution. There is here a relation between me and the other beyond rhetoric" (*TI* 75). Well, there is here, we might say, a *relation* between the other and me that precedes and exceeds figuration and representation, a relation between the other and me that attests to a *rhetorical imperative* (a responsibility to respond) that would be the condition for all thematization, all generalization:

> The gaze that supplicates and demands, that can supplicate only because it demands, deprived of everything because entitled to everything, and which one recognizes in giving ... this gaze is precisely the epiphany of the face as a face. The nakedness of the face is destituteness. To recognize the Other is to recognize hunger. To recognize the Other is to give. (76)

To give what is "mine," to give a hand, to give food, to give shelter, to give protection, to give "my" world, which can no longer be simply or inalienably mine:

> The conceptualization of the sensible arises already from this incision in the living flesh of my own substance, my home, in this suitability of the mine for the Other, which prepares the descent of the things to the rank of possible merchandise. This initial dispossession conditions the subsequent generalization of money. Conceptualization is the first generalization and the condition for objectivity. Objectivity coincides with the abolition of inalienable property—which presupposes the epiphany of the other.... The generality of the Object is correlative with the generosity of the subject going toward the Other, beyond the egoist and solitary enjoyment, and hence making the community of the goods of this world break forth from the exclusive property of enjoyment. (*TI* 76)

To encounter the Other is not simply to give what one no longer wants or needs but to give the bread from one's own mouth: "giving only has meaning as a tearing from oneself despite oneself," Levinas writes, as a tearing of oneself from "the complacency in oneself characteristic of enjoyment, snatching the bread from one's mouth" (*OTB* 74).

To encounter a face is to receive a rhetorical imperative that drops me into response-only mode, subjecting me to the scandal of obligation, to a responsibility that I can neither comprehend nor ignore, and in which my "joyous possession of the world" is called into question (*TI* 75, 76). In the encounter with the Other, which takes place *over* the world of things that I can possess, I am dispossessed of *my* self and *my* stuff—of my *world*—which is, when I turn and speak, given over to the establishment of "community and universality": "I" am/is a subject to the extent that I am the one "who finds the resources to respond to the call," Levinas writes (*EI* 89). And when I turn to the other and speak, I respond to this rhetorical imperative by *giving* world—naming, signifying, asserting, describing. "Language," Levinas writes, "offers things which are mine to the other. To speak is to make the world common, to create commonplaces" (*TI* 76). According to him, my welcoming of the other, before any conscious choice, is "the ultimate fact" that communication communicates: "The relationship between the same and the other, my welcoming of the other, is the ultimate fact, and in it the things figure not as what one builds but as what one gives" (*TI* 76–77).

What is significant (what is ethical) in my response has nothing to do with *what* "I" may end up saying to "you" and everything to do with the fact *that* I respond to you: "the essential is the interpellation, the vocative," Levinas says (*TI* 69). Before the face, it is necessary to speak of something—the weather, the game, the time. My first actual word to you ("bonjour") is before anything else a *response* to an address, a demonstration of solidarity that precedes understanding. And when I address you, even if only abusively to thematize you, I nonetheless invoke you as an interlocutor: I speak *to* you and therefore *face* you, respecting your alterity:

> The other is maintained and confirmed in his heterogeneity as soon as one calls upon him, be it only to say to him that one cannot speak to him, to classify him as sick, to announce to him his death sentence; at the same time as grasped, wounded, outraged, he is "respected." The invoked is not what I comprehend: he is not under a category. He is the one to whom I speak—he has only a reference to himself. (*TI* 69)

"The word that bears on the Other as a theme" attempts to contain the Other, Levinas explains, but if it is said to the Other as an interlocutor, if it is said in the "facing" position, then the Other irrepressibly "quits the theme that encompassed him, and upsurges inevitably behind the said" (*TI* 195).

The difference between ragging on you to someone else and ragging on you to "you," according to Levinas, is an ethical difference, in his particular sense of that term, because when I address you for any reason ("nice shoes," "beautiful day," "you piece of shit!"), I face you and thus am exposed both to my own exposedness and to yours: "In discourse [conversation] the divergence that inevitably opens between the Other as my theme and the Other as my interlocutor, emancipated from the theme that seemed a moment to hold him, forthwith contests the meaning I ascribed to my interlocutor." The address is both a response and a letting go—to greet is not to grasp. In conversation, the Other breaks with all thematizing form, overflowing and so interrupting my powers of comprehension; conversation names a relation with what remains irreducible to me, irreducible to cognition. "For the ethical relationship which subtends discourse is not a species of consciousness whose ray emanates from the I; it puts the I in question. The putting in question emanates from the other" (*TI* 195). And it is only inasmuch as this conversation remains a conversation—that is, it's only inasmuch as the other is addressed as an interlocutor, rather than talked about as a theme or concept, that it is ethical speech and not murder.

To Kill; Or Aiming at the Indestructible that Can Nonetheless Be Destroyed

The relation with the Other, "which dawns forth in his expression," Levinas writes, is anterior to all recognition and comprehension. As a phenomenon, the other presents him/herself to me within the context of the world we share, but as a face, the Other "breaks with the world that can be common to us." This is why Levinas insists that "speech proceeds from absolute difference" (*TI* 194). Conversation does not appropriate that difference but exposes it, holding me in relation with "what remains essentially transcendent" (*TI* 195). And significantly, Levinas insists that this relation with absolute alterity is originarily peaceful: the Other's resistance to my powers of comprehension is nonviolent, without force; its structure is not negative but ethical. In contradistinction to the Hobbesean-Kantian notion that peace results from the (temporary) cessation of war, Levinas proposes that all violence presupposes peace. There could be no violent reaction to an alterity that has not first been welcomed, that has not first been extended a kind of radical and unconditional hospitality—a hospitality that is extended before "I" can decide to do so. ("Whether it wants to or not, whether we realize it or not," as Derrida puts it, "hostility still attests to hospitality" [A 50]). The saying of the face first of all exposes me to my exposedness, to my relation with an inassimilable alterity, a peaceful relation outside the realm of power, which defies even my capacity for power. Peace, for Levinas, is "the unity of plurality . . . and not the coherence of the elements that constitute plurality" (TI 306).

As long as I face the Other, I am exposed to my predicament of exposedness and subjection. In conversation, I am the Other's addressee, not a speaking I but a responding you: "an I stripped of the illusion of being the addressor of phrases," as Jean-François Lyotard puts it, "grabbed hold of upon the addressee instance, incomprehensibly. The obligation is immediate, prior to any intellection, it resides in the 'welcoming of the stranger,' in the address to me, which does more than reverse a preexisting relation, which institutes a new universe" (D 111). In conversation's universe, ego loses its illusion of first-person status: "I" am only inasmuch as I respond to the Other. In speaking to or with the other, any derivative enjoyment of a for-itself ego is eclipsed by a being-for-the-other, Levinas tells us, by an obligation to respond that precedes all intentionality and egoity: in conversation, "I" am/is passively delivered over to the Other's command, stuck in response-only mode, deprived of spontaneity. "I" am/is a subject without the power of the subject; that is, I am a subject to the precise extent that I am subjected (host and hostage) to the Other.

The only specific content Levinas ever attributes to the saying of the face is a "No" that comes through, along with an invitation to speak, as an interdiction against murder. It comes in as a command, an order, "as if a master spoke to me," Levinas says (EI 89). Interestingly, it is at the very instant when my powers of comprehension are interrupted that I am also commanded not to kill, neither in the figural nor the physical senses of the word (and the former is the condition for the latter). In the instant that I turn away, I refuse the responsibility that holds my violence in check: I respond to the saying of the face by refusing it. The imperative still pressures, squeezes; it takes some willpower to ignore it—I have to force my attention elsewhere, toward the ground, the trees, someone else, my magazine, my music, or onto another passage in a text that "signifies a face" (PN 4). It's a conscious effort with which you are no doubt familiar: who has not been here, playing the perp in this murder scene? No longer in the "facing" position, I instantly refigure—and recover, if I'm lucky—smoothing over the disturbance, reducing the Other once again to a masterable concept, effacing his/her alterity while preserving enough of him/her for my use. That is, in turning away from a more originary peace, I am "free" to speak *about* the other rather than *to* the Other, having reinstated a sense of power and spontaneity by appropriating the otherness of the other: "Thematization and conceptualization, which moreover are inseparable, are not peace with the other but suppression or possession of the other" (*TI* 46).

It is because the face's expression remains unmasterable, because its saying remains irreducible to any said, because its nonviolent resistance defies ego's compulsion to know, to grasp, to master, that there is the temptation to murder: "As soon as the presence of the other in *autrui* is not received by me as the movement through which the infinite comes to me, as soon as this presence closes around *autrui* as a property of *autrui* established in the world, as soon as it ceases to give rise to speech," Blanchot writes, "the earth ceases to be vast enough to contain at the same time *autrui* and myself" (*IC* 61). Still, if the face's vulnerability, nudity, and powerlessness invites murder, its one and only command simultaneously prohibits it. This prohibition— "You shall not kill," or simply "No"—is at the same time a description: you *cannot* kill (the Other). The infinity expressed in the saying of the face paralyzes my power, not by opposing it with greater force but by *transcending* all force, Levinas tells us. Mistaking death for simple nothingness, murder aims to take out the Other, the ungraspable enigma, the radical alterity that interrupts all power and possibility. But it only ever manages to get at the other, the sensible, visible phenomenon. Murder, in other words, runs up against a founding impossibility, one that Shakespeare, for example, explores in *Hamlet* and *Macbeth*: the one I kill is never quite dead enough. There are hauntings and visitations that undermine the ultimate dichotomy: being *or* nothingness.

"The Other cannot present himself as Other outside of my conscience" to begin with, Levinas reminds us, and the "movement of annihilation in murder is therefore a purely relative annihilation, a passage to the limit of a negation attempted within the world. In fact, it leads us toward an order of which we can say nothing, not even being, antithesis of the impossible nothingness." (*TI* 232–33). Murder can change *Autrui* into an absence, Blanchot observes, but it cannot *touch* him/her because *Autrui* is already a sort of specter, a haunting visitor whose presence "slips away from every grasp" (*IC* 61). Here's Levinas:

Murder exercises power over what escapes power. It is still power, for the face expresses itself in the sensible, but already impotency, because the face rends the sensible. The alterity that is expressed in the face provides the unique "matter" possible for total negation. I can wish to kill only an existent absolutely independent, which exceeds my powers infinitely, and therefore does not oppose them but paralyzes the very power of power. The Other is the sole being I can wish to kill. (*TI* 198)

Jill Robbins observes that "the one who murders is caught in a substitutive structure; he is like a man who must aim at his target (infinity) over and over again and always misses it. (That is why he cannot kill his victim enough times)" (66). And it is why Blanchot writes that "man is the indestructible that can be destroyed" (*IC* 130). Neither "total annihilation" nor murder by figuration delivers me from my exposedness to radical alterity, from my vulnerability, affectability, susceptibility to an absolutely inappropriable exteriority—nor, therefore, does it deliver me from my obligation, my responsibility to respond, which precedes and makes possible any idea of freedom.

Face On: The Rhetoric of Ethical Speech

Don't get me wrong: even in the most ethical speech murder circulates. First, because the gift of speech offered to the Other in conversation is the gift of world, of figured things and concepts. But also because even in the facing position, face on, there is ultimately no letting up of the compulsion to know, to grasp, to make sense of the Other. So it's not quite correct to suggest that there is a speech/murder alternative, "as if it were a matter of choosing once and for all between good speech and bad death," as Blanchot puts it. What is required instead, he proposes, is a "grave speech" that is capable of maintaining "the movement of this *either* . . . *or*. . . . To speak is always to speak from out of this interval between speech and radical violence, separating them, but maintaining each of them in a relation of vicissitude" (*IC* 62). To speak in a way that puts murder off, even as "the speech of death" is allowed to circulate, requires a "plural speech," in which the speech that attempts to grasp, to negate, to oppose the Other, goes down in the facing position, keeping the murderousness in check. Ethical speech—conversation—is a discourse in which the said is not permitted to detach from the saying.

There is, then, an indissociable rapport between the ethical relation and rhetoric. Levinas tries to keep them separate, but his own investigations betray, at the very least, their interdependence. And it is almost impossible not to go further: What does Levinas end up showing, after all, if not that the ethical relation *is* the experience of an underivable rhetorical imperative, an obligation to respond to the other? This imperative announces itself in a saying (as pure affective appeal) that comes to interrupt the already said (as figuration and representation), an "event" involving two interconnected rhetorical operations. Throughout his oeuvre, Levinas situates rhetoric on the side of the said (*le dit*) and ethical language on the side of the saying (*le dire*). Unsurprisingly, however, he can't get the opposition to stick.[25] Rhetoric is (indissociable from) ethics not (simply) because it involves the sharing of meaningful figures in intersubjective dialogue, but because it involves the disfiguring of those figures in conversation. What Agnes was not quite in a position to understand is that "self-understanding"—if we must call it that—could only come by way of the *other's* face, by way of a rhetorical imperative issued by (or as) the face of the Other, which obligates me and so calls "me" into question.

It is only from within the context of the figured face that one can experience the epiphany of the face. Levinas insists that its saying is not an effect of the play of the signifier but is instead the latter's very condition of possibility. In other words, what's at stake in this discussion, the experience of the ethical relation, comes down neither to the semantic power of the trope nor to the endless proliferation of meaning that any trope may engender. And yet, this experience registers for consciousness only as a *disturbance* in the tropological field and so as an *interruption* in cognition. A persuasive force, an unlocatable yet undeniable obligation to respond, comes through in the instant of disfiguration. What Levinas shows without saying is that the ethical relation owes everything to the fact that there can be what he calls face *in* figure, which may transform the very meaning of figuration. Indeed, in her reading of Levinas, Robbins poses an interesting and possibly urgent question that it may be the responsibility of rhetorical studies to take up: "What is figure, if there can be a face in it?" (68). Or, put more generally for our purposes: what is rhetoric if it is not, after all, indissociable from hermeneutics?

3
Hermeneutics

Teaching is not reducible to maieutics; it comes from the
exterior and brings me more than I contain.

Emmanuel Levinas, *Totality and Infinity*

There is always the matter of a surplus that comes
from an elsewhere and that can no more be assimilated by me,
than it can domesticate itself in me. A teaching that may part ways
with Heidegger's motif of our being able to learn only what we already
understand—when does learning take place? what do we already
understand?—the Conversation belongs, as ethical relation,
to the effort of thinking the infinite, the transcendent, the Stranger.
None of this amounts to thinking an object.

Avital Ronell, *Dictations*

From *Rhetorical Power* to *Disciplinary
Identities* Steven Mailloux has brilliantly performed and explicated a "rhetorical hermeneutics" that demonstrates the "practical inseparability of interpretation and language use and thus of the discourses that theorize those practices,
hermeneutics and rhetoric" (*RH* 3). Many rhetoricians have challenged the
specifics of Mailloux's various arguments and have more generally objected
that "rhetorical hermeneutics" leans too far toward the hermeneutical, reducing rhetoric to an analytic or critical art and giving its productive (political)
function the squeeze.[1] Yet, within these lively debates very few have challenged
his basic premise that rhetoric and hermeneutics are inextricably intertwined:
the question has not been whether they are indissociable but which side of the
production-reception coin rhetorical studies ought to emphasize.[2] Michael
Leff, for example, flipped Mailloux's adjective-noun relation to spotlight pro-

duction, promoting a "hermeneutical rhetoric" that focuses more on political than literary texts; nonetheless, he agrees that "all interpretive work involves participation in a rhetorical exchange, and that every rhetorical exchange involves some interpretive work" ("Hermeneutical" 197–98). Rosa Eberly goes further in *Citizen Critics*, offering a hermeneutical rhetoric that is less interested in "already-written discourses" than in spotlighting "rhetoric's power as an art productive of discourses and subjectivities for the present and the future" (34). Yet Eberly, too, affirms Mailloux's basic premise, which was nudged in the direction of conflation in the introduction to the 1997 collection entitled *Rhetoric and Hermeneutics in Our Time*, in which the editors, Walter Jost and Michael Hyde, note in passing that their title can "be understood as virtually tautological" (xii).

And there is of course no doubt that rhetoric has a hermeneutic dimension; or, more carefully, that rhetoric *constitutes* the hermeneutic dimension. If "hermeneutics" indicates "the art of understanding," as Friedrich Schleiermacher wanted, then interpretation clearly depends upon production.[3] "Rhetoric not only has its place within the sphere of objects surveyed by hermeneutics," as Werner Hamacher puts it, "but also constitutes an integral component of every hermeneutic operation. Every step in an interpretation corresponds to a rhetorical—or grammatical—figure" (70). Put more bluntly: intelligibility, including self-intelligibility, is a tropological product; cognition itself is a trope that can in no way be secured. Hermeneutics—as it is defined by Schleiermacher and by Mailloux—is completely dependent on, even absorbed by rhetoric.[4] I have no problem with this. Nor with Mailloux's suggestion that the reverse is also true:

> In some ways rhetoric and interpretation are practical forms of the same extended human activity: Rhetoric is based on interpretation; interpretation is communicated through rhetoric. Furthermore, as a reflection on practice, hermeneutics and rhetorical theory are mutually defining fields: hermeneutics is the rhetoric of establishing meaning, and rhetoric the hermeneutics of problematic linguistic situations. (*RH* 4)

I don't disagree: As the production and appropriation of meaning, rhetoric and hermeneutics are an indissociable team; together, they strive to complete understanding's circle. I take this as a given.

However, there is also a *non*hermeneutical dimension of rhetoric not reducible to meaning making, to offering up signs and symbols for comprehension.

This one is subsumable neither by figuration in the standard sense nor by what typically goes by the name persuasion; it counts on a certain reception, but not on the appropriation of meaning. Preceding and exceeding hermeneutic interpretation, it deals not in signified meanings but in the address itself, in the exposure to the other (*autrui*); it deals not in the said (*le dit*) but in the saying (*le dire*). The said indicates the realm of conceptual forms, themes, ideas (signified meaning); it thus offers itself up to interpretation. The saying, by contrast, indicates a nonreferential performative intrusion, an address that necessarily unsettles what is congealed in the already said. Most specifically for our purposes, it shatters the conceptual image that "I" have interiorized of "you," which takes us both out, "essentially." When you address me, you break through your own "plastic essence," Levinas writes, slipping from my appropriative grasp, holding me in relation with what "puts me into question," with what "empties me of myself, and does not let off emptying me" ("Trace" 350, 351).

Let me repeat that we are not talking simply about the "play of the signifier" here. What gets said diffracts into an endless proliferation of possible meanings, but it also, therefore, endlessly *invites* interpretation. I can and even must interpret who you are and what you say from within a given rhetorical and sociohistorical context. However, in the language relation called conversation, a gap opens between the "you" I can attempt to know and understand within the context of a particular speech act and the engaged "you" who (or that) *addresses* me, calls to me, obligates me. "The Other, in the rectitude of his face, is not a character within a context," Levinas writes (*EI* 86). When you address me, you both give a said to be interpreted and, simultaneously, withdraw from the interpretive context; Levinas says you "break with the world that can be common to us," putting me into relation with what remains radically inassimilable (*TI* 194). "The subject in saying approaches a neighbor in expressing itself," Levinas writes, "in being expelled in the literal sense of the term, out of any locus" (*OTB* 49). Express: to speak, but also to force out by pressure, to squeeze or press out as one would express the juice from a fruit. "Ordinarily," Levinas writes, "one is a 'character': a professor at the Sorbonne, a Supreme Court justice, son of so-and-so, everything that is in one's passport, the manner of dressing, of presenting oneself. And all signification in the usual sense of the term is relative to such a context: the meaning of something is in its relation to another thing" (*EI* 86). When you are safely *over there,* I attempt to know who you are and what you represent by assessing your relations within a particular context. But when you address me, "you" are ex-pressed from the tropological field, from the world we can know and share. Sending me a greeting from the "outside," you communicate more than I can comprehend, a "surplus" of alterity that I can neither appropriate nor abdicate, announcing, prior to and as the condition for all determinate meaning, "the proximity of one to the other," as Levinas puts it (*OTB* 5). The saying names the site of my encounter with and exposure to the other *as* other (as *autrui*), which by definition leaves my hermeneutic aspirations in the dust.

Don't get me wrong: Levinas famously *rails* against rhetoric, locating it quite unceremoniously on the side of nonethical language. "Not every discourse is a relation with exteriority," Levinas writes in *Totality and Infinity*, and rhetoric clearly doesn't make the (ethical) cut. Approaching the other at and with an angle, it refuses the *other*'s approach: "Rhetoric approaches the other not to face him, but obliquely," he says; inasmuch as it goes toward the other only to "solicit his yes," rhetoric is "preeminently violence," already murder.[5] According to Levinas, though rhetoric is "absent from no discourse," it "resists discourse," blocking the *opening* toward the other (70). However, it's the address that provokes the opening, and what is rhetoric but addressed language? The address *as such* is interruptive: it names a saying that disturbs the very movement of comprehension, opening a nonappropriative rapport with the other. If rhetoric intersects with ethics at all, it is right there, in the rupture of the "circle," in the interruption and depropriation catalyzed in the address. What the address announces, over and beyond any semantic meaning, is both the exposedness to the other and the obligation to respond, which is called responsibility.

Michael Hyde points up the interruptive nature of the address in *The Call of Conscience*, but according to his descriptions and examples, this "rhetorical interruption" is instigated by the "eloquence" or "truly moving" nature of *what* is said rather than by the saying itself, which is sans all eloquence.[6] That is, Hyde depicts the saying as an interruption in one appropriation (or habit) of meaning by the articulation of another, rather than as an interruption *of* the appropriation of meaning as such. Immediately reducing the saying to the said, he reaffirms the indissociability of rhetoric and hermeneutics: as a rhetorical pragmatist, he sets out to offer us a rhetorical hermeneutics or a hermeneutical rhetoric, a goal that necessarily delimits his discussion of the saying. So though there is no question that Hyde's work is significant, what we will attend to here is precisely what *The Call of Conscience* cannot abide. My aim is to offer a rhetoric of the *saying*, an elaboration of rhetoric's explicitly nonhermeneutic, ethical dimension.

In a light and particularly accessible essay called "Making Comparisons," Mailloux analyzes an episode of *Star Trek: The Next Generation* to illustrate the way in which "rhetorical hermeneutics" can blaze trails of communication across very different cultures, and his meticulous hermeneutic analysis necessarily effaces what I'm trying to expose. So I'll start by offering an explication of Mailloux's essay that I hope will demonstrate why I'm calling rhetorical hermeneutics (but also hermeneutical rhetoric) a rhetoric of the said. Then I'll offer another reading of this "first contact" narrative that zeroes in on the saying, pointing up the nonappropriative (ethical) encounters evoked in this "text." The goal is to spotlight not only the differences between a hermeneutic and nonhermeneutic rhetoric, but also what's at stake in those differences.[7]

First Contact, Take One: The Appropriative Relation

In the Darmok episode, the *Enterprise* crew is sent into the El-Adrel System to make first contact with "an enigmatic race known as the Children of Tarma" (119). "Enigmatic" because each of the seven Federation vessels to encounter a Tarmarian ship in the past hundred years has failed to establish relations—no one has been able to communicate with them. The last Federation captain to encounter the Tarmarians called them "incomprehensible," and all other accounts have been comparable. Star Fleet, for once, is flabbergasted. "But Captain Picard is optimistic," Mailloux notes; he remains confident that "communication is a matter of patience and imagination," and he thinks his crew has a sufficient supply of both. When contact is made, the Tarmarian captain appears on screen and very earnestly utters a string of incomprehensible phrases: "Rai and Jiri at Lungha. Rai of Lowani. Lowani under two moons. Jiri of Ubaya. Ubaya of crossed roads. At Lungha. Lungha, her sky gray." A moment of bewildered silence on the *Enterprise*. Picard turns to Counselor Troi and then to Data for insight and a possible translation, but this time even the empath and the android are clueless. So Picard goes to "Plan B," taking a step forward and addressing the Tamarian captain: "Captain, would you be prepared to consider a mutual non-aggression pact between our two peoples, possibly leading to a trade agreement and cultural interchange?" Bewildered silence on the other end. The Tarmarian captain shakes his head and utters a disappointed "Shaka, when the walls fell."

At this point, the Tarmarians go to "Plan B," too, suddenly transporting Picard without his consent to the surface of a nearby planet and blocking the

Enterprise's capacity to beam him back. The Tarmarian captain, Dathon, also beams down to the planet's surface, and with the words "Darmok and Jalad at Tenagra," he tosses Picard one of his two daggers. Picard figures he wants to fight, says no, and pitches the dagger back to him. Dathon: "Shaka, when the walls fell." They temporarily give up and make separate camps, but in the morning, a giant beast attacks, forcing the two captains to fight together to survive. As they battle the beast, Picard realizes that the Tarmarian is communicating by citing example, by metaphor, and this prompts Dathon to utter a joyful "Sokath, his eyes uncovered!" Mailloux notes that "Picard's patience pays off as he uses his imagination to produce a rhetorical theory to make sense of the Tarmarian's actions and sounds" (120). Meanwhile, back on the *Enterprise*, Data and Councilor Troi do some research of their own and come up with the same basic rhetorical theory:

> DATA: "The Tarmarian ego structure does not seem to allow what we
>   normally think of as self-identity. Their ability to abstract is highly
>   unusual. They seem to communicate through narrative imagery, a
>   reference to the individuals in their mytho-historical accounts."
> TROI: "It's as if I were to say to you 'Juliet on her balcony.'"
> DR. CRUSHER: "An image of romance."
> TROI: "Exactly. Imagery is everything to the Tarmarians. It embodies
>   their emotional states, their very thought processes. It's how they
>   communicate and how they think."

The crew deciphers something like the grammar of the language, but without the vocabulary, as Data puts it. Without the historical "narrative from which the Tarmarians draw their imagery," the crew is still out of luck. As Dr. Crusher points out, if you don't know the story of *Romeo and Juliet*, then the phrase "Juliet on her balcony" communicates nothing to you. Picard, however, does have some luck on this score: after the beast mauls Dathon and disappears again, the two captains hold a kind of one-on-one tutoring session on Tarmarian mythology, and Picard picks up enough of it to express something of their experience at El-Adrel. Dathon dies from his wounds, the two star ships start blasting each other, and Picard is beamed back to the *Enterprise* just in time to save the day. "Darmok and Jalad at Tenagra," he says to the on-screen image of the Tarmarian first officer. Translation: "your captain and I fought together in solidarity." Stunned silence on both ships. Picard continues: "Darmok and Jelad . . . on the ocean." Translation: "we would have left together, too, if he had survived." The Tarmarian gasps, "Sokath, his eyes opened!" and he offers a new "first contact" *topos*: "Dathon and Picard at El-Adrel." With that, the *Enterprise* is off again to "boldly go where no one has gone before."

Mailloux suggests that this episode illustrates his own, along with Richard Rorty and Donald Davidson's, position that "there is no absolute incomprehensibility between alien cultures. . . . With every community that we recognize as a community, our form of life always overlaps significantly," Mailloux writes, "for it is only against such a background of commonality that we can perceive radical difference." Quoting a familiar passage by Rorty, Mailloux notes that it's this "overlap" that "reduces the intercultural case to an intracultural one—it means that we learn to handle the weirder bits of native behavior (linguistic and other) in the same way that we learn about the weird behavior of atypical members of our own culture." The "we" evoked by both Mailloux and Rorty is the product of hermeneutical understanding, an "overlap of sameness" from which difference can then be discerned. The encounter with the other is staged here not in terms of one infinitely finite singularity addressing another infinitely finite singularity but rather as a somewhat (culturally or cross-culturally) unified "we" attempting to tolerate and accommodate its weirdos. "This is exactly the way the *Enterprise* crew figures out the rhetorical acts of the Tarmarians," Mailloux writes. They employ the skill of "a cultural rhetorician, using a rhetorical vocabulary and theory from within their own culture to make sense of a foreign language and to enable them to translate it (at least partially) into their own idiom." The result, he says, is a "successful communication" (120–21).

The Obligation to Share

Or, so it seems. Mailloux admits, however, that Lyotard's account of the Cashinahua in *Just Gaming* implies the possibility of another interpretation of this intergalactic contact case, one "that questions both Picard's confident understanding of his communicative success and [Mailloux's] own Davidsonian explanation of that success." Picard seems to me much less confident of his success than he seems to Mailloux, but more on that below. The Cashinahua communicate via storytelling, and when someone tells a (male) Cashinahua a story, he is obligated to retell it. Mailloux notes that if the Tarmarians were actually more like the Cashinahua than the *Enterprise* crew, then perhaps they were simply telling stories "for the sake of telling a story," "to fulfill their obligation to share," and not for the purpose of achieving "some later goal," such as establishing "diplomatic relations, mak[ing] economic and cultural treaties, etc." (121–22). Now, I'm not sure what this "obligation to share" suggests to Mailloux—he passes over it very quickly—but it seems to me that this extraordinarily *ordinary* obligation, an obligation inherent in all communication, signals precisely what's at stake for us here. Lyotard tells us that the Cashinahua narrator assumes an "I" only inasmuch as he repeats the story that has been told to him, only inasmuch as he responds to the other's address by offering an address in (re)turn. But these storytellers are anything but faithful to the narrative they're repeating, which suggests that the narrative itself is not what matters; what matters is the bearing of it, the address, the saying. The (performance of a) response *is* the message, which doubles as an address, a return call. What is communicated in this response is not first of all semantic meaning but communicability as such: both a shared exposedness, a "we" that precedes and exceeds hermeneutic understanding, and an attendant rhetorical imperative, a responsibility to respond.

Nonetheless, Mailloux returns us instantly to rhetoric's hermeneutic dimension. Noting that even the Cashinahua demonstrate "hermeneutic ethnocentrism" when they interpret Brazilian traders across their own Inka mythology, he reiterates that "ethnocentrism is unavoidable in cross-cultural comparisons" (122). According to him, there is no way to encounter a cross-cultural other without translating this other into one's own cultural presumptions; or, to bring it down again to an intracultural case: there is no way to encounter the other *as other* at all. One has no choice but to approach the other as an alter ego, another subject, just like me—except, of course, for any of his or her weird-ass habits. Understanding the other, as Dilthey's hermeneutic theory proposed, means rediscovering the I in the thou, rediscovering the same in the other, who is therefore the same. It's the search for confirmation, in the other, of one's own structures of understanding. One has understood almost everything once one has detected, in the other, an overlap of sameness; all the rest amounts to a maieutic (or Maillouxtic?) exercise: a coming to grips with what one already knows or is preprogrammed to assimilate.

There has to be overlap if there is to be an encounter, Mailloux writes elsewhere, because "a completely other would be unintelligible" (*RH* 15). It's thanks to this stabilizing overlap that we are able to "reweave our webs of beliefs to take account of the other" (16). This reweaving, which takes place "through interpretation and persuasion," Mailloux writes, is "what constitutes learning"

(17). Learning, then, leads in each case to new knowledge; it's the progressive accumulation of "accounts" of the (not completely) other within one's own field of experience. The learner, according to Mailloux's descriptions, is enormously stable: s/he weaves and reweaves, emerging from the pedagogical scene without suffering any abrupt *unravelings*—any massive interruptions in interpretive progress, any rips in the fabric of the weave.

Indeed, Mailloux presents a Picard who is never not in charge of himself; a kind of hermeneutic action hero, he is always busily weaving, making sense, using his own "ethnocentric web of beliefs" to gain "interpretive purchase" on his "object of attention" (*RH* 14)—in this case Dathon, the captain of the Tarmarian ship. In Mailloux's description, Picard's structures of understanding are never challenged by his encounter with this singular other; the scene of learning doesn't amount to any kind of effraction at all. Like everything else, Dathon is taken as a problem that needs to be solved, and the solution lies in Picard's ability to appropriate this other as fully as possible. According to Mailloux's depiction, learning takes place inasmuch as Picard is able to reweave his web of beliefs in way that accounts for this new appropriation.

Levinas describes learning quite differently: if it's really learning, he says, then it is necessarily a trauma, a shattering of self and world, not an appropriation but an experience of depropriation and alteration from which there is no return. Learning, in Levinas's lexicon, takes place via an encounter with the other, who, in addressing me, exceeds my thematizing powers and "brings me more than I contain" (*TI* 51). This could not be further from the process of homogenization and accretion that Mailloux describes, a process which grows the learner's world while simultaneously shielding him/her from any outside encroachment. Learning only what s/he already knows or is preprogrammed to assimilate, the rhetorical hermeneut makes sense of others by running them through his or her own structures of understanding. And there is, of course, no other way to make sense: hermeneutic interpretation is grounded in preunderstanding, in what Heidegger describes as a tripartite "fore-structure": fore-having (*Vorhabe*), fore-sight (*Vorsicht*), and fore-conception (*Vorgriff*) (*BT* 150–53). I want to be clear that I am not challenging this. What I'm suggesting, rather, is that preunderstanding is precisely what's shattered in the address, which announces its *own* sense, an unmasterable surplus irreducible to semantic appropriations. The instant that the other addresses me, all forestructuring's bets are off. The address—the encounter, the saying—is the specifically rhetorical gesture that "rhetorical hermeneutics" effaces, and what one "learns" in the face of it is not the effect of an appropriation.

Mailloux suggests that one knows otherness only by judging it across an overlap of sameness, and I am in complete agreement with him there; however, he concludes that it would therefore be impossible to encounter any other as other, and that's where we disagree. The encounter takes place in the "face of the Other," but one can only *undergo* it, and to undergo is not the same as to know. "To undergo an experience with something," Heidegger writes, "means that this something befalls us, strikes us, comes over us, overwhelms and transforms us. When we talk of 'undergoing' an experience, we mean specifically that the experience is not of our own making; to undergo here means that we endure it, suffer it, receive it as it strikes us and submit to it" (*OWTL* 57). If understanding has to do with power and possibility (with being-able, in Heidegger's parlance), undergoing has to do with neither but instead names a kind of not-being-able-to-be-able, a passivity and an impossibility that "befalls" you. Indeed, it may be that even this sense of "undergoing" is too strong, too cognitive an experience and transformation to describe the encounter with the Other. Inasmuch as the Other is not a phenomenon but an "enigma," the experience of the encounter is not a positive event that you could later grasp but a withdrawal of meaning, a "disturbance" in cognition, as Levinas puts it.

Cognition itself is eclipsed in the encounter with the Other, whose approach, says Lyotard, is precisely what "announces the insufficiency of knowledge" (*D* 110). Momentarily disabling my conceptual grids and "prejudgment structures," the encounter with the Other profoundly affects me without granting understanding, putting me into relation with what I can neither grasp nor relinquish, neither appropriate nor refuse. Here, learning operates according to an entirely different protocol of ethical attunement: it amounts to a depropriation that takes *me* out, leaving an "I" without a me, or better: leaving an "I" sans appropriating ego. But the disturbance in cognition prompted by an encounter with the Other is not itself forceful or powerful; as a withdrawal of cognition, it offers an interruption from which ego often immediately recovers:

> [D]isturbance disturbs order without troubling it seriously. It enters in so subtle a way that unless we retain it, it has already withdrawn. It insinuates itself, withdraws before entering. It remains only for him who would like to take it up. Otherwise it has already restored the order it troubled—Someone rang, and there is no one at the door: did anyone ring? . . . [D]isturbance is possible only through an intervention. A stranger is then needed, one who has come, to be sure, but left *before* having come, ab-solute in his manifestation." ("Phenomena and Enigma" 66, 68)

I could "retain" this fragile teaching experience, "take it up" in a way that will forever influence (or "transform") my modes of thinking and being, or I could let it go and move on as if nothing ever happened. Either way, however, "I" have encountered inassimilable otherness; I have been exposed to a relation that precedes and exceeds understanding.

In *The Infinite Conversation*, Blanchot describes three ways of relating to the other. The first is appropriative, cognitive, in which one works "to reduce everything to the same, but also to give to the same the plentitude of the whole that it must in the end become" (66). The second relation is fusional, in which one loses oneself in or to the other via certain secular and religious participatory rituals. Both of these relations are unifying. The "relation of the third kind," by contrast, is (un)founded on "the *strangeness* between us," Blanchot writes (68), and it is in play whenever existents enter into "conversation" (*entre-tien*). Outside conversation's rapport, everything stabilizes; I operate with apparent spontaneity, and (or because) I understand you. But when you address me, you withdraw from my appropriative grasp, opening a *relation* that calls both my understanding and my sense of spontaneity into question: "The relation with the other presupposes an infinite separation," Derrida writes, "an infinite interruption, where the face appears" (*A* 9). Or, as Ronell puts it, "[t]he greeting first establishes a distance so that proximity can occur" ("Sacred Alien" 208).

There are (at least) two terms, "I" and "you," involved in the language relation, and for conversation (the relation) to continue, these terms must by necessity remain separate. Conversation's odd rapport takes place in the between of the I and the you, holding an "us" together only by keeping this I and you apart, exposing *within* an experience of profound intimacy an infinite distance, an uncrossable abyss. This is why Blanchot can suggest that the language relation is neither a means of knowledge nor a way of seeing but is instead the interruption of both knowledge and sight; it is "the relation whereby the one whom I cannot reach becomes present in his [or her] inaccessible [and] foreign truth" (*IC* 63). So long as "we" are engaged in conversation—written or spoken, it doesn't matter[8]—I can't get a fix on you. You remain both unbearably close and inaccessible.

Though I can neither appropriate nor fuse with you, however, I must *respond* to you, orient myself toward you with seemingly boundless generosity. Not because I'm a figure of exemplary politeness; this generosity doesn't come from me as if it were simply my choice. Rather, when you address me, no matter what you say to me, you expose in me a readiness to respond (a response-ability) that precedes both desire (for recognition) and will. For, as long as I am conversing with you, opening toward you, I remain your addressee, which means, strictly speaking, that I am/is ejected from the addressor slot: "It is the scandal of an I displaced onto the you instance" Lyotard writes (*D* 110). In the relation called conversation, my "I" has no nominative form—it *is* only inasmuch as it responds to the other's call, inasmuch as it is both host and hostage to the other, as Levinas puts it. That's why conversation's "we" never attains anything resembling equality: because I always owe(s) you exorbitantly.[9]

There is nothing weirder or more depropriating than conversation's apportionment, and only one who witnesses it without being engaged in it could mistake it for a tranquil and equalizing dialogue between already constituted subjects. A language relation that precedes and exceeds intellection, conversation takes place *as* an interruption in my spontaneity that calls me to my response-ability. Any empirical address also gives a said, of course, and the said can, even must, be interpreted. But before anything else the saying gives a *relation* with the other, with what remains "radically out of my reach," as Blanchot puts it, beyond my grasp (*IC* 68). This nonappropriative rapport, which Blanchot also calls "friendship," is not a bond, not even a bond *of* friendship; it is rather the experience of an "infinite imminence," a "common strangeness that does not allow us to speak of our friends but only to speak to them," he writes (*Friendship* 290–91). Conversation designates "a modality of approach to the other person," which introduces into interpretation the surplus of "sociality," as Levinas puts it, a surplus in excess of any knowledge about the other ("Everyday" 141–42). What the address initiates is a *relation* rather than an appropriation or assimilation, a "we" that is not a function of interpretation and that is not reducible to commonality, reciprocity, or equality.

First Contact, Take Two: The Relation Without Relation

There are two "approach" scenes in this *Star Trek* episode in which Picard appears, maybe, to experience this nonappropriative relation—and significantly, Mailloux doesn't mention either one. Given that both involve the trauma of depropriation, a lapse in the power to appropriate, they may simply fly too low for interpretive scanners (and interests) to pick up. But the interruption as such demands a reading—it's where all the (ethical) action is. What comes through as an interruption in the movement of comprehension is something like an "Ethical Scream," which the hermeneutic machine itself massively and

perpetually interrupts.[10] And what's at stake in attending to rhetoric's interruptive function, to the address—that is, what's at stake in offering a rhetoric of the
saying—is an affirmation of the ethical relation itself.

Let me be clear that this rereading of the episode does not offer itself as a
"counterreading," nor does it oppose itself to Mailloux's interpretation; it simply tries to read what is left unread in Mailloux's reading. In other words, it
tries to read something *else* in the "text" of the episode—not its narrative (and
narratable) line but that which no narrative mode can accommodate: its interruption, an "anachronic" disturbance in the representable/synchronizable. As
Judith Butler puts it in *Giving an Account of Oneself*: "the structure of address is
not a feature of narrative, one of its many and variable attributes, but an interruption of narrative . . . a rhetorical dimension that is not reducible to narrative
function" (62). How to read the interruption as such? This is also Levinas's
question. We'll try here to catch a trace of the traumatic and depropriative encounter with the other, to risk mediating a trace of the immediate in order to
show that the *condition* for Picard's struggles to understand, to know, to assimilate, is an irreparable exposedness and an irremissible obligation—which indicates that his appropriations are both necessary and impossible. The point is
not to show that Picard could or should have responded differently but to show
that he can only respond, that the most appropriative and colonizing response
is still a response, that response-only mode is the sole option for any subject,
even (the gods help us) for a Jean-Luc Picard.

The first of these two scenes takes place after Picard declines Dathon's dagger and the two captains make separate camps. Night is approaching, the tem-
perature is dropping, and Picard can't get a fire going. Dathon's fire, however,
is blazing, and Picard watches him warily: "What now, captain?" he whispers
to himself. "Will you attack me in my sleep? If I don't freeze to death first. . . ."
But Dathon unexpectedly takes a burning stick from his own fire and tosses it
to Picard. A gift of fire, we could say, but the fire is not the *gift* in the strictest
(Derridian/Levinasian) sense of that term; the fire is only the present/pres-
ence through which the gift announces itself. The gift—which has nothing to
do with a subject who "intends-to-give something to someone," Derrida writes
(*Given Time* 10)—is the address itself, the saying or greeting, the generosity
of an approach that communicates communicability as such.[11] When Dathon
tosses Picard the burning stick, it signifies, before any hermeneutic meaning,
the exposedness of the one to the other, an extreme proximity and vulnerabil-

ity. Picard, however, scrambles to maintain his interpretive posture in the face of the gift, the generosity of which therefore doesn't arrive right away:

DATHON (having tossed the fire to Picard): "Temba."
PICARD: "Temba? What does that mean? Fire? Does temba mean fire?"
DATHON: "Temba, his arms wide."
PICARD: "Temba is a person? His arms wide . . . because he's . . . holding
   them apart in . . . in generosity? In giving? In taking?"
DATHON: "Temba, his arms wide."

No big hermeneutic breakthrough, here. Picard's incessant questioning, his demand for immediate answers, calls to mind the intimate connection between speech and violence, indicating that he has not yet begun to question. However, in the next moment, unexpectedly, the interrogation breaks off—there is an uncomfortable hesitation, an interruption in hermeneutic demands. Here, perhaps, conversation begins. Dropped by the address into response-only mode— or more carefully, exposed by this address to the fact that he may have no other mode—Picard appears for the first time vulnerable, desituated, prompting a pause, however brief, in his hyper-hermeneutic disposition. The discernable stumble is marked by an instant of silence, a suspension in the interrogation, a shift in countenance, and then: a hoarse "thank you." This barely audible expression of gratitude for the present (the fire) is also the gift of a response, a return call, which both affirms and repeats the sharing that "we" are, prior to any hermeneutic understanding. In this instant, in the untimely time of the saying, Picard does indeed seem more like the Cashinahua than a Federation captain.

In *What Is Called Thinking?*, Heidegger notes a provocative etymological connection between thinking and thanking (139), both of which involve an experience of declension that affirms the thinker/thanker's radical non-selfsufficiency.[12] This may be one reason Derrida suggests that "nothing is more difficult to accept than a gift" (*Given Time* 14). It's probably also why Heidegger says it's possible that we are still not thinking. According to him, thinking is not (the same as) knowing—it doesn't "bring knowledge" or "produce usable practical wisdom"; it "solves no cosmic riddles," nor does it "endow us directly with the power to act" (*WCT* 159). Thinking, for Heidegger, doesn't even certify existence, as it does in Descartes's *cogito ergo sum*; rather, it puts the "I think" itself into question because thinking is only able to take off when all my preunderstandings fail and my knowing trips on an aporetic snag.[13] The address is the snag that catches the weave of Picard's spontaneity, tripping him up, interrupting his presumed self-sufficiency and exposing him to his exposedness. At this instant—or rather, in this syncopation, this caesura—Picard is both inside and outside himself; which is to say that he is both obliged to respond (no one else can take his place) and/but that his "prejudgment structure" has been temporarily knocked off-line. We're talking here about an intermission of sorts, an interruption in the myth of intersubjective dialogue by the communication of communicability as such: Picard's scramble to make sense of the other's address is put on hold as he undergoes this address *as* sense, as a call to responseability. His interrogation of what Dathon *means* to say to him is interrupted by his experience of the fact *that* this other addresses him and that a response is required from him, that there is an obligation to respond. The communication that takes place here is not an appropriative understanding but a depropriative interruption. The other is encountered as other in the interruption of my illusion of spontaneity, in the address as such, which shares the fact of "our" nonappropriative sharing.

After a good night's sleep by the fire, however, Picard awakes with a renewed sense of self-determination, as if the previous evening's lapse in spontaneity has sparked a backlash. Dathon is away from his camp, and Picard seizes the opportunity: "Forgive the intrusion, captain," he says to himself, "but I need some answers." Kicking on the interpretive scanner, he snoops through Dathon's log book and other personal items. Dathon returns to camp to find Picard poking around, and the Tarmarian announces *right then* the approach of the beast. The timing of its appearance makes it possible to read the beast as an allegory in the allegory, as a figure for Picard's hermeneutic machine, which must by necessity kill off the other in order to make sense of him, to turn him into a masterable concept—to ditch the "we" that locks him in response-only mode. The absolutely other would be incomprehensible, as Mailloux says, and when the hermeneutic disposition encounters the incomprehensible, Hamacher observes, it "takes the only path that the blockage of the aporia leaves open: a path back to itself" (9). Certitude is purchased by retreating in the face of a fundamental aporia: faced with the inappropriable (approaching) other, understanding swerves back around, toward itself, toward what it already knows and is already programmed to assimilate. It's not nothing that Picard is trapped in the *Enterprise's* transport beam for the precise duration of the beast's attack on Dathon. As the interpretive machine *grasps* the other, Picard is already on his way back "home," back to himself, beating the retreat inherent in hermeneutic self-affection. This autohermeneutics may manage to understand something along the way, as it scrambles from the other back to the self, but Hamacher reminds us that it understands only "by turning away from that which, as incomprehensible," sets understanding in motion to begin with (9).

Understanding can only have *understood* by fleeing in the face of what it can't grasp, by fleeing in the face of the very alterity that it is its job to approach. Indeed, understanding "breaks off," Blanchot observes, at the instant it "ceases to be the approach toward what rules out any understanding" (*SL* 198). And because "only those things that are not alive and have thus departed from the 'structural connectiveness' of life can be grasped," as Hamacher notes (24), Picard's hermeneutic machine must annihilate its "object of attention" (Dathon in his infinite singularity), must fix him in a theme or a concept that can be known and represented. Dathon's death figures his installment into an immanent (and therefore identifiable) identity, which grants Picard a sense of mastery that clears the way for identification, for a seizing of this other's position—specifically, it allows Dathon to be reduced to a kind of alter ego onto which Picard projects an image of himself. Once Dathon is gone, Picard respectfully positions the Tamarian captain's remains and confidently asserts that he has understood: "I understand your sacrifice, captain." It's the identification that grants the understanding: I understand you because you are nothing other than (an analogue of) myself; you are none other than me, I am none other than you. Picard's reference to sacrifice is already a budding epideictic rhetoric poised to declare this death a beautiful and necessary one, a *meaningful* one, which Picard, as he says, understands.

Interestingly, however—and this is the second "approach" scene—just when understanding seems to have landed and Picard is leaning over Dathon's corpse, the beast shows up again, fighting mad and roaring as loud as ever. This hermeneutic kickback, *after* Dathon has been safely fixed within a masterable identity, is perhaps due to the fact that, strictly speaking, Picard has just identified with (what is now) a *dead* man, death being the ultimate alterity, the Unmasterable. The place of the dead one (*der Tote*) cannot be occupied or seized: death sets the absolute limit on identification, and so on understanding. Dathon's death may be justifiable and meaningful from a certain abstract perspective; it may even be readable as the figure for a purifying transformation, as Burke might say. But the *singular* death is not finally sublatable; it cannot be turned into a work of meaning because it names precisely the withdrawal of all meaning. The identification backfires; it's an appropriation that leaves him face-to-face with what is absolutely inappropriable: his own death, his own dying (*le mourir*), his finitude—which is to say his non-selfsufficiency, his exposedness, his inability to master or even to be equal to himself.

So, on the one hand, Dathon's death figures his murder by figuration. As long as Dathon is alive, he keeps calling, approaching, holding Picard in a relation with infinite strangeness to which language can only attest. "Language is spoken," Levinas observes, "where the common plane is wanting or is yet to be constituted. It takes place in transcendence. Discourse is thus the experience of something absolutely foreign, a *pure* 'knowledge' or 'experience,' a *traumatism of astonishment*" (*TI* 73).[14] "We" don't speak to each other because we share a "common plane," in other words; we speak to each other because we don't, because this we names a *relation* rather than an appropriation or assimilation: "speech proceeds from absolute difference" (194). Language does not close the abyss in the between of the "I" and the "you," which is what keeps the conversation going. It is only by turning away from him, by ending their conversation and hanging a U-turn, that Picard becomes "free" to obliterate Dathon's singularity, reducing him once again to an interiorized image or knowable concept. Death shuts Dathon up, in other words, ending his capacity to approach, detaching him from the "structural connectiveness of life," and installing him within an immanent identity that Picard can know and master. By killing him off, Picard effaces Dathon's radical alterity while nonetheless preserving the discernable part, the overlap: Dathon was a man, a starship captain, a subject and citizen of his society, and so on. *Just like Picard.* It is only when Dathon is detached from his infinite singularity that the violence of identification becomes possible, and this identification grants Picard's sense of understanding. Picard understands Dathon's sacrifice because Dathon, in death, is reduced to (an analogue of) Picard, to an overlap of sameness.

Simultaneously, however, and on the extreme other hand, death pulls Dathon *away* from himself, away from his knowable, culturally defined self, drawing him into an absolute alterity that refuses to be effaced by any presumption of immanence. Picard's hermeneutic machine kills off Dathon in order to get a fix on the ungraspable singularity that interrupts understanding's power and possibility—but in the process, it lands Picard face-to-face with a *founding* impossibility, the one that is explored, again, in Shakespeare's *Macbeth* and Freud's *Totem and Taboo* no less than in the texts of the New Testament and on every analyst's couch: the one I kill is never quite dead enough. S/he never stops calling me, addressing me, demanding a response. Death, as it turns out, does not shut Da-thon ("Dathon") up; it neither ends their conversation nor springs Picard from response-only mode. What withdraws in this death is precisely Dathon's cultur-ally assigned identity, precisely the overlap of sameness that invites the illusion of immanence. And when that goes, only an utterly incomprehensible and exceed-ingly lively opacity is left—an opacity that is figured here by Dathon's corpse.

Escaping all conceptual categories, the corpse is not really the living per-son anymore, but it's not anyone or anything else, either. So even when it's right before me in all its weighty materiality, Blanchot observes, it is also never quite *here*, establishing "a relation between here and nowhere" (*SL* 256). Its appeal—a pure appeal that comes through without content (a saying without a said)—effects an interruption that is all the more brutal because it is inescap-able: I cannot elect to end a conversation with one who is no longer simply here, with one whose incessant and unbearably amplified address comes in via an intercom from *nowhere*. The withdrawal of any sense of immanence catalyz-es an altogether different experience of identification: the dead one with whom Picard inexplicably finds himself identified is not an alter ego; it is *no* ego. That is, Picard finds himself identified with (a) *no one*, with an other Other in which/whom he precisely does *not* recognize himself. Unable to be himself alone, he finds himself in relation with, opened to, inhabited by precisely what he had hoped to annihilate: an Ultimate Alterity that he can neither own nor master.

This experience of "community" takes place in or as a lapse, a break, the sort of intermission that Levinas calls *l'entre-temps* or "the meanwhile."[15] As Picard is positioning Dathon's remains, confident that their conversation is over, an ap-peal comes in, comes in from *nowhere* and from (a) *no one*. Now, we have to imagine that this address provokes a massive depropriation, putting everything that Picard hoped to settle back into play, and so flipping his hermeneutic ma-chine back to "ON." Having done in Dathon only to be confronted with an other Other, with an absolutely unsublatable alterity that won't stop calling, the beast is pissed, exasperated by this endless deferral of certitude and self-mastery. An inner struggle ensues between the exposed Picard, who is undergoing identity's withdrawal, and Picard-the-hyperhermeneut, who demands certainty and sta-bility. When the beast attacks Picard, it analogizes the internal scuffle, and to pull himself together, to regain his sense of spontaneity, Picard must find a way to close his ears to the saying, to turn away from the incomprehensible.[16] He suc-ceeds, temporarily (the battle is never over), as the *Enterprise* crew manages this time to beam him back to the ship, to return him "home" (to himself).

Still, after Picard's exchange with the Tarmarian first officer, Riker asks: "New friends, captain?" and Picard's response demonstrates uncertainty: "I can't say, Number One, but at least they're not new enemies." Note that the goal of uniting the two cultures in pacts and trade agreements is deferred, perhaps indefinitely. Picard doesn't even mention it, and the two ships go their separate ways. This encounter, then, has led neither to economic gain nor to practical understanding. And yet, there is peace. There is peace without understanding, or better: there is peace despite profound nonunderstanding. This suggests that understanding is not a prerequisite for peace, that a radically hospitable welcoming of alterity precedes both cognition and volition. But here's the point: if Picard's only real contact with alterity takes place in/as a (non)experience of depropriation, in/as a deselfing "conversation" that cannot offer itself up to narrative assimilation but can show up only as an interruption in the representable, then what's missing from Mailloux's otherwise compelling account of this intergalactic first contact narrative is *the other*. What Mailloux's narrative details is Picard's contact with himself, with his own structures of understanding, and Mailloux describes this self-contact as "successful communication." Levinas would call it "the play of the Same."

Taking It Up: Rhetorics of the Saying

I think they're both right. But again, what's on the line here, in this play of the Same that we are content to call "successful communication," is any affirmation of the ethical relation. Rhetoric's hermeneutic dimension allows subjects to get things done in the world, and this work is of course imperative. But this work, by definition, requires appropriation and assimilation; it can account only for the other that overlaps with the Same, which means that it *cannot* account for the Other at all, cannot attend to radical alterity—it can at best suffer it as an interruption, a rupture in the tropological field. This is why there is an ethical imperative to engage a rhetoric of the saying, to attend to the interruption itself. There is no said without the saying, no hermeneutic understanding without this address which, in obligating me to respond, holds me in relation with an inassimilable other, exposing me to my irreparable exposedness, my radical non-selfsufficiency.

Of course, the said also demands our attention; as Friedrich Schlegel reminds us, "There is a hermeneutic imperative."[17] Mailloux's essay focuses on the possibility and the necessity of making cross-cultural comparisons, and I agree that there is no getting around the charge to interpret and compare. I am doing it here. But for me the extreme and devastating difficulty of this charge arises from its inherent impossibility, from the fact that it is a command to compare incomparables. "There must be a justice among incomparable ones," Levinas writes (*OTB* 16), and that means that the challenge is to compare without completely effacing the incomparableness of the "we" that is exposed in the simple fact of the address; that is, the challenge is to refuse to allow the said to detach from the saying, to keep hermeneutic interpretation from absorbing the strictly rhetorical gesture of the approach, which interrupts the movement of appropriation and busts any illusion of having *understood*.

I want to reiterate that my disagreement with Mailloux is not over whether or not to remain open to the other, as if one had the freedom to choose.[18] "I" come into being only inasmuch as "I" *respond* to the other, who was welcomed before I got the chance to decide. Inasmuch as this impossible responsibility both gives one to be and makes one an effect of the other's affection/alteration, it indicates the simultaneous constitution and deconstitution of "the subject," who "is" only inasmuch as s/he responds. The priority of the other, then, is not a matter of the subject's choice but of its inescapable predicament. In Levinas's lexicon, ethics is not some predetermined "proper" response but an obligation to respond prompted by the interruption *of* the self by the other, each time, in which "the I loses its sovereign coincidence with itself, its identification" ("Trace" 353).

My disagreement with Mailloux is over the implications of this irreparable opening for the field of rhetorical studies—and specifically for hermeneutic approaches to rhetoric. Though "I" cannot stop welcoming the other, scholarly endeavors may or may not elect to attend to that predicament, to "take it up," as Levinas puts it; thus far, rhetorical studies have mostly elected not to. In proposing that there is an ethical imperative to do so, I am advocating for a kind of foreign policy in the field, a particular style of scholarly approach that attends not simply to the said but to the saying, to the address as such. And if I risk labeling the terrain of this imperative "ethical"—rather than, say, political, even if it is also, no doubt, political—that's because it invites and involves an *interruption* in presumptions of sovereignty and (so) in postures of certitude. It involves an interruption, that is, in the fantasy of spontaneous agency.

4

Agency

It is through the condition of being hostage that there
can be in the world pity, compassion, pardon, and proximity—
even the little that there is, even the simple "After you, sir."

Emmanuel Levinas, *Otherwise than Being*

We don't need another hero. We don't need to know the way home.

Tina Turner, "We Don't Need Another Hero"

If ethics involves a *relation*, an approach in which I turn toward an other who is not simply an object, toward an other who may also turn toward me, it first of all implies that neither I nor the other is an enclosed entity but that both are already exposed, posed in exteriority, radically non-selfsufficient; it implies, then, an originary (or preoriginary) relation with alterity—a relation that precedes the apparently self-sufficient self. Emmanuel Levinas focuses on this preoriginary relation, offering not an ethics in the sense of "laws or moral rules" but an "Ethics of Ethics," as Derrida puts it, a rigorous inquiry into the conditions of possibility for acts that put the other before the self ("Violence" 111). Levinas doesn't preach self-sacrificing generosity; he simply acknowledges that it takes place, every day, in both small and spectacular acts—from the simplest gestures of politesse (the "after you") to putting one's own life on the line to save another's. And he proposes that the very fact that such acts take place challenges Western philosophy's ontological presumptions about the originariness of the for-itself ego. There could be no acts of inexplicable generosity and sacrifice in a world consisting only of competing freedoms and desires. Generosity is possible, Levinas says, only because at the heart of subjectivity is not a sovereign ego but what he calls "the one-for-the-other," a preoriginary "substitution." The "subject" (in his radically

revised sense) is ethically *structured* so that it has already taken up responsibility for the other before it has the chance to choose. This is why—to jump ahead
just a bit—there are no heroes in Levinas: for him, responsibility is grounded
in the passivity of the host-age and not in the freedom of a spontaneous or self-
determining agent capable of resolute choice.

Responsibility, according to him, precedes and exceeds the realm of consciousness, so any conscious sense of the freedom to choose would already be
an effect of this exorbitant responsibility and not the other way around. After
Levinas, it becomes necessary to rethink the subject's readiness to be-for-the-
other, to say "Here I am" in the service of the other, in terms of belatedness, as
"a slow resumption of what has already taken place," as Ronell puts it (*S* 211).
This is a radical reversal of most contemporary discourses on ethics, which are
grounded in the phantasm of the free and willing agent. I don't have to tell you
that this phantasm is alive and well in rhetorical studies, often circulating under the name "rhetorical agency," and very frequently pegged as the fragile link
between rhetorical practice and civic responsibility. Indeed, at the Alliance of
Rhetoric Societies (ARS) meeting in 2003, the three working groups deliberat-
ing over the question "How ought we to understand the concept of rhetorical
agency?" consistently pinned any hope for "being efficacious in the world," as
Michael Leff puts it, to "the exercise of individual agency through language"
(Leff and Lunsford 62). Cheryl Geisler's report on the ARS agency discus-
sions documents the pervasiveness of this presumption, which—unless I'm
delusional—dominated the conversation. There was, of course, some notable
dissent, which was about as quickly dismissed in my working group as it was in
Geisler's report.[1]

In their thorough response to this dismissal, Christian Lundberg and
Joshua Gunn challenge the "habit of reducing agency to a transparent human
agent" (87) and of positing agency as this agent's possession (89); they argue
instead that agency (the production of effects) possesses and constitutes the
"agent" rather than the other way around, "casting the problem of rhetorical
agency as a rhetorical affect, instead of as a point of origin for rhetorical effect"
(97–98). To the presumption that there must be a free and willing agent who
chooses to act responsibly, they propose alongside Derrida that responsibility
is, first of all, "'response'-ability," that "every action, discursive or otherwise, is
only born of an engagement with the set of conditions that produced it." This
means that "any call for normative doctrines of responsibility determined by
the agential choices of the subject paradoxically entails a *deferral* of responsi-

bility" (96). Lundberg and Gunn name three of the major post-Heideggerian exemplars whose thinking resists this deferral and challenges the givenness of the human agent: Jacques Derrida, Jacques Lacan, and Michel Foucault. Heidegger's thought is deservedly situated as a turning point and inspiration for future posthumanist (and postontotheological) reflections. There is no mention of Emmanuel Levinas.

What I will propose here, however, is that Levinas's extraordinarily concrete explications of an always prior responsibility offer a nonheroic notion of rhetorical agency that challenges even the ethical consciousness assumed by the authentically individuated Dasein that Heidegger describes in *Being and Time*. Now, Levinas is not always a generous reader of Heidegger, and these two thinkers are very often more aligned than Levinas seems willing to acknowledge. Still, it's crucial to maintain a certain distinction because what Levinas struggles endlessly to articulate (or to evoke through the reduction of the said to the saying) is at the very least effaced in Heidegger's *early* work, specifically in the language of *Being and Time*. All ungenerous readings, language barriers, and discrepancies in vocabulary aside, the "resolute choice" names a point at which these two thinkers share (*partagé*) a real *différend*. Here, we'll examine carefully this *différend* as a way to begin to rethink both rhetorical agency and its relation to responsibility.[2]

Let me note first, though, that Michael Hyde has taken pretty much the opposite approach in his award-winning book, *The Call of Conscience: Heidegger and Levinas, Rhetoric and the Euthanasia Debate*, emphasizing instead the overlap in Heidegger and Levinas's notions of conscience in order to develop his theory of rhetorical heroism. Hyde reads these two thinkers together, proposing that Levinas makes little sense without a prior understanding of Heidegger, but also that Heidegger is dangerous without certain Levinasian adjustments.[3] Given both the much deserved prominence of Hyde's book in rhetorical studies and this present work's oddly parallel (though opposite) trajectory, it seems necessary to begin by acknowledging that Hyde's reading both opens and closes the site that we will here attempt to excavate. Indeed, at one point, Hyde directs the reader's attention precisely to the *différend* we'll be tracking but for practical purposes takes Heidegger's side, reading Levinas through a Heideggerian lens and so silencing the irreconcilable difference to which we will try to give voice.

Acknowledging that in Levinas the existent is ethically structured, always already for-the-other, Hyde nonetheless does not accept that an existent could engage in ethical *practice* sans the authentic individuation and resolute choice that Heidegger describes. So, in the name of pragmatics and in the face of Levinas's insistence that "no one is good voluntarily" (*OTB* 11), Hyde reframes via the privileged Heideggerian appropriation: "Even if one accepts Levinas's description of how human existence is structured as a being-for-others," he writes, "it is still the self, in a moment of authenticity, that must put this 'goodness' into practice. Helping others presupposes the action of a self assuming the ethical responsibility of freedom of choice" (105). But again, Levinas: "We can see the formal structure of nonfreedom in a subjectivity which does not have time to choose the Good and thus is penetrated with its rays unbeknownst to itself" (*OTB* 11).[4] By forcing Levinas's language into a Heideggerian vocabulary, Hyde litigates the unlitigable, silencing the *différend* we'll be tracking by applying a rule of judgment that is equitable for one side only. According to Levinas, being-for-the-other does not come down to an authentic self's freedom of choice, neither in the existential realm nor in the pragmatic one. Rather, an immemorial obligation "provokes this responsibility against my will, that is, by substituting me for the other as a hostage" (*OTB* 11).

This present work acknowledges the significance of Hyde's project, which of course has its own purpose, audience, and constraints. But it is necessary to go further: what's at stake in distinguishing between a heroic theory of agency and Levinas's agency of the host-age is the ethical relation itself. Any affirmation of the resolute choice, any conflation of the saying and the said, any perpetuation of the myth of the hero will cover over what seem to me to be Levinas's most significant contributions to philosophy, to ethics, and—potentially—to rhetorical studies. The field's "habit" of grounding ethical agency in the freedom of choice effaces what Levinas, much more clearly than the early Heidegger, gives us to think: a nonspontaneous and thoroughly rhetorical notion of agency. After Levinas, if there is something like an ethical task for rhetoricians, if there is, it would need to involve the deconstruction of heroics, and even perhaps the exposition and affirmation of a radically nonheroic but ethical agency that takes the subjection of the subject all the way to substitution. Not in order to grind all ethical discourses to a halt—on the contrary—but to call into question any effort to turn the privilege of the other into a function of *my* efforts, *my* decisions, *my* choice. As if an originary freedom came first, as if it were *I* who grants the other her privilege, *I* who takes responsibility or rejects it. In *Alterity Politics*, Jeffrey Nealon mocks this sort of ethical hubris with a Barry Manilow tune: "And by the way, *I* write the songs that make the whole world sing" (168).

To pull the notion of a nonspontaneous rhetorical agency into tighter focus, we'll examine carefully the *différend* that separates (the early) Heidegger from (especially the later) Levinas. We'll begin with Heidegger—very specifically with the Heidegger of *Being and Time*, the language of which, it should be noted, he later determined to be insufficient for his thought. Still, as he observes in *What Is Called Thinking?*, you can't just call off a text as if it were a game; texts have their own destiny and destinations, and once they're out there they're out there, stirring up trouble in your name (51). This one in particular, *Being and Time*, was both a theoretical grounding for Hyde's widely acclaimed book and the target of some of Levinas's most powerful critical passages.

Authentic Individuation: Being-Toward-Death

In *Being and Time*, Heidegger revolutionized the occident's thinking about both singularity and solidarity by naming "being-with" (*Mitsein*) the very condition of possibility for "being-there" (Dasein), positing a "togetherness" that precedes the *cogito* and turns any sense of intentional consciousness into the product of a more originary sharing. Heidegger is clear that Da-sein names (a) being that is first of all in-the-world and with-others—"world," for Heidegger, being always a "shared world" (*Mitwelt*). Dasein is constituted in and as its sharing of this world, a world that is perpetually coming into being and putting Being into play. And Heidegger's ethic of care is built on the notion that "concern-for" the other (*Fürsorge*) is an existential function of this originary sharing (121–22). Proposing that there is no being that is not already being-with, Heidegger posits an originary sociality, a structure of exposedness from which he insists any sense of authentic individuality—and so any sort of ethical consciousness—would have to be extracted.

The early Heidegger's irreconcilable difference with Levinas hinges on this presumption that Dasein is able to assume ethical consciousness only by pulling itself together, embracing an existentiell sense of individuated wholeness uncut by "the Others." In a certain sense, Levinas agrees with Heidegger that "Dasein, as everyday Being-with-one-another, stands in subjection to Others. It itself *is* not; its Being has been taken away by the Others" (126). However—again, in a certain sense—he does not agree with Heidegger that this situation, this substitution, "deprives the particular Dasein of its answerability" (127). I say "in a certain sense" because for Levinas it is not first of all "the Others" to whom Dasein "stands in subjection" but "the Other." We'll carefully unpack the basis for this fundamental disagreement below, but for now, back to Heidegger:

Dasein's everyday possibilities of Being are for the Others to dispose of as they please. These Others, moreover, are not *definite* Others. On the contrary, any Other can represent them. What is decisive is just that inconspicuous domination by Others which has already been taken over unawares from Dasein as Being-with. One belongs to the Others oneself and enhances their power. "The Others" whom one thus designates in order to cover up the fact of one's belonging to them essentially oneself, are those who proximally and for the most part "*are there*" in everyday Being-with-one-another. The "who" is not this one, not that one, not oneself, not some people, and not the sum of them all. The "who" is the neuter, *the "they"* [*das Man*]. (126)

As "everyday Being-with-one-another," Dasein remains lost in the "they," a sort of massive "levelling down" that "dissolves one's own Dasein completely into the kind of being of 'the others,'" Heidegger writes (126–27).

According to him, this is a problem because "[i]n Dasein's everydayness, the agency through which most things come about is one of which we must say that 'it was no one'" (127). The ethico-political predicament leaves Heidegger with much the same problem that we saw Freud facing in chapter one: how to theorize the necessary rise out of an originary identification in which "[e]veryone is the other, and no one is himself" to a particular Dasein capable of responsible responsiveness (128). Heidegger responds to this predicament by proposing that there are, in fact, *two* modes of being-with-others in-the-world, one authentic and the other inauthentic. Predictably, the inauthentic mode consists in being lost in the "they." The authentic mode, on the other hand, consists in Dasein recovering its ownmost potentiality for Being, which was, from the start, "taken away by the Others."

All beings are thrown beings, Heidegger tells us, thrown into a "world" they have neither made nor chosen. And yet, Dasein is *essentially* in-the-world and of the world, fundamentally conditioned by and dependent upon the web of relations that *gives it to be*. World is not optional for Dasein; rather, being-in-the-world with-others *is* the being of Dasein and not some accidental restriction or limitation to be transcended. Tossed into the world, Dasein typically just follows along, assuming the interests and investments dictated by the "they." But Heidegger insists that even those Daseins who rage against conformity and cultivate their "individuality" are fundamentally determined by their average everyday being-with-others—by an inauthentic mode of "Being-among-one-another [*Untereinandersein*]" (128). Whether it takes the form of conformity or nonconformity, this "everyday absorption in the 'world'" is Dasein's canny comfort zone. Dasein's most comfortable and familiar mode of existence is a "they-self" in which its answerability is given over to "the Others" (129): "The everyday publicness of the 'they' . . . brings tranquillized self-assurance," Heidegger writes, a feeling of "Being-at-home" (189).

Heidegger's task is to distinguish this "they-self" from "the *authentic Self*— that is, from the Self which has been taken hold of in its own way." The inauthentic self is lost in the "they," but the authentic Self takes hold of itself, finds itself: "As they-self, the particular Dasein has been dispersed into the 'they,' and must first find itself" (129). The state of mind or "mood" that grants Dasein the chance to "find itself" beneath all the disguises, concealments, and obscurities, to lift itself out of its inauthentic mode, is anxiety (*Angst*), which Heidegger distinguishes from fear. Fear has a specific object, a definite, localized threat coming from within-the-world (you fear *that* someone will break into your home, *that* you will fail an exam, *that* someone will hurt your child, and so on). But anxiety has no discriminate object; Heidegger tells us that the threat doesn't come from the world and so is not nameable or objectifiable: "what threatens" in anxiety "is *nowhere*," and yet "it is so close that it is oppressive and stifles one's breath" (186). Anxiety amounts to a radically generalized fear, fear for one's own being, one's own being-able-to-Be, and the suffocating force that oppresses Dasein in anxiety turns out to be Da-sein itself, calling in as the voice of conscience from its future authenticity. Heidegger insists that this call "does not come from someone else who is with me in the world" (275) but instead that "[i]n conscience, Dasein calls itself." Authentic Dasein pursues lost Dasein through the "call of conscience," which prompts the mood of anxiety.[5]

This "call" from "me" to "me" is not some peaceful soliloquy but comes in unexpectedly, from out of nowhere, "from afar unto afar" (271). I haven't "planned" or "prepared" or "voluntarily performed" this call; rather, "'it' calls, against [my] expectations and even against [my] will." The call, Heidegger says, "comes *from* me and yet *from beyond me and over me*" (275). Strictly speaking, then, Dasein does not simply call itself, either; rather "It" (*Es*) calls from *within* Dasein; the caller is an internal alterity that remains radically inappropriable: "The caller," Heidegger writes, "maintains itself in conspicuous indefiniteness" (274). "I" am called, then, by no one, by an addressor who is none other than "me," but a "me" that does not coincide with me, that is not even in the same time zone with me. The call consists not of signifying content but solely in an interruption in the chatter of the "they," a syncopation that disturbs my at-homeness in the world.

When this silent and silencing call comes through, anxiety strikes, ripping me from my everyday absorption in the world and granting me a certain escape hatch from "the Others": "But in anxiety there lies the possibility of a disclosure which is quite distinctive; for anxiety individualizes. This individualization brings Dasein back from its falling, and makes manifest to it that authenticity and inauthenticity are possibilities of its Being" (191). When the call interrupts the "they's" idle chatter, all the world's points of reference withdraw and Dasein is no longer capable of understanding itself through the activities, necessities, and "ready-to-hand" causes that it never authentically chose and/but that give it its sense of purpose and significance. In anxiety, this sort of "everyday familiarity collapses" (189), exposing the "world" in its "empty mercilessness," drained of significance and concernful solicitude (343). In anxiety, world stops worlding, in other words, ready-to-hand gives way to "present-at-hand," leaving Dasein to face its being *as such*, the sheer fact *that it is* and that, for it, "to be" at all is to be outside itself, *in*-the-world: ekstatic.[6] What "anxiety is anxious about," Heidegger assures us, "is Being-in-the-world itself" (187), which is another way of saying: Being-without-shelter. Anxiety, a fundamental mode of Being for Dasein, boots Dasein from its "tranquillized self-assurance," its feeling of "Being-at-home," and exposes it to itself as a being that is outside itself, "*not-at-home*," leaving it face-to-face with the uncanny "in" of its Being-in-the-world.

Importantly, "that kind of Being-in-the-world which is tranquillized and familiar is a mode of Dasein's uncanniness, not the reverse. *From an existential-ontological point of view, the 'not-at-home' must be conceived as the more primordial phenomenon*" (188–89). Uncanniness, then, is the "basic kind of Being-in-the-world," but when anxious Dasein recognizes itself, in a flash, as sheer uncanniness, it freaks. Nostalgic for the comfort and safety of what it thought was home, it often flees what it's anxious about, flees in the face of the "not-at-home," scrambling toward the "at home," toward "entities within-the-world," alongside which Dasein and its concern might dwell again "in tranquillized familiarity" (186–88). This fleeing, Heidegger tells us, is a "falling," falling (back) into the "they," into its inauthentic mode of Being-in-the-world with-others.

Nonetheless, it is in anxiety that Dasein (re)discovers "itself as the thrown being that it is and that [it] in existing has to be," as Christopher Fynsk puts it (*Heidegger* 37). "Thrownness" (*Geworfenheit*), Fynsk explains, "is an experience of nothingness or 'nullity,' and Heidegger calls this experience 'guilt'—a radical impotence regarding the conditions of the 'there' in which one finds oneself thrown and a powerlessness to become anything other than what one is" (*Heidegger* 38–39). The withdrawal of "world" brings Dasein into contact with the Nothingness or the Void that is both its past and its future, both its "origin" and its destiny; it gives Dasein an experience with "death" then, with death in life: with the possibility of the impossibility of existence. But it is also from here that Dasein discovers the very possibility of the meaningful world, as well as the possibility of its own existence in that world. Indeed, the call calls Dasein to *assume* its thrownness, to take it up *as* a possibility. When anxiety strikes and Dasein rediscovers its thrown being, it may choose authenticity, snapping to its "ownmost potentiality-for-Being" and so turning this death scene into a scene of (re)birth in which it resolutely chooses the life and world into which it has been tossed.

In choosing its life, in taking up an "*authentic resolution to repeat itself*," Dasein responds to the call of conscience, returning to itself authentically by throwing itself back into the factical possibilities that already have been disclosed to it (308). Authentic Dasein is not given the chance to choose *another* life but becomes "free" to choose the life it has been dealt—it becomes free, in more Nietzschean terms, to *amor fati*, to love its fate. The resolute choice involves Dasein choosing to repeat itself, Heidegger tells us, so that Dasein "hands down to itself" the possibilities that have been there (384). Or, as Fynsk puts it, Dasein hands down to itself the possibilities "that Dasein has come down to in its being thrown." In *choosing* the fate it has been dealt, Fynsk notes, "Dasein gives itself its fate" (*Heidegger* 46) and so triumphs over its original impotence and therefore over the nothingness from which it came and toward which it's headed. Anxiety signals a generalized fear *for* Being, for one's own Being, but "being-toward-death" names an authentic response to anxiety, a mode of Being in which Dasein chooses its life while facing its death (its nullity) and thus prevails over it.[7]

What I want to draw out and spotlight here is that, according to Heidegger, death is from the start a possibility for Dasein; in fact, it's *the* possibility that opens it to all its other possibilities. Dasein's authentic potentiality-for-Being lies in its capacity to live its life while facing its death, to exist in the mode of being-toward-death—and not toward some abstract notion of death but toward its *own* death: "by its very essence," Heidegger writes, "death is in every case *mine*, in so far as it 'is' at all" (240). No one else can die for me; I am all alone in death.[8] So Heidegger proposes that when Dasein experiences death in life and takes up its "uttermost not-yet" as a possibility, Dasein is individuated, rising out of the dictatorship of the "they" and gaining the potential for resolute choice:

> Death is a possibility-of-Being which Dasein has to take over in every case. With death, Dasein stands before itself in its ownmost potentiality-for-Being. This is a possibility in which the issue is nothing less than Dasein's Being-in-the-world. Its death is the possibility of no-longer-being-able-to-be-there. If Dasein stands before itself as this possibility, it has been *fully* assigned to its ownmost potentiality-for-Being. When it stands before itself in this way, all its relations to any other Dasein have been undone. This ownmost non-relational possibility is at the same time the uttermost one. (250)

When Dasein takes up its death *as* its "ownmost non-relational possibility," the "they" falls away and Dasein is *individualilzed*, "*fully* assigned to its ownmost potentiality-for-being."

The key to Dasein's individuation—and so to its ethical consciousness—is the conceptual closure of its existential structure, its capacity to take up its "uttermost not-yet" as "the *possibility* of the measureless impossibility of existence" (262).[9] "Since anticipation of the possibility which is not to be outstripped discloses also all the possibilities which lie ahead of that possibility, this anticipation includes the possibility of taking the *whole* of Dasein in advance [*Vorwegnehmens*] in an existentiell manner; that is to say, it includes the possibility of existing as a *whole potentiality-for-Being*" (264). This "constancy of Self" (322), as Heidegger puts it, this existentiell sense of individuated wholeness is the ground for meaningful, authentic existence, and (so) of the resolute choice. Facing its own death in anticipatory resoluteness, Dasein is individualized "down to itself," which is what grants Dasein the "virginal integrity" of an authentic self, as Ronell puts it in *The Telephone Book* (49), and this integrity is necessary to its freedom. (There is no freedom of choice for the existent who remains dominated by the suggestive chatter of the "they"). Being-toward-death is a mode of being in which *anxious* Dasein gets its mortality in its sites in an understanding way and so achieves power over it—Heidegger's definition of understanding, it should be noted, is "being-able."[10]

It is this presumption of power that Levinas and others rightly challenge. "We glimpse here one of the oldest and greatest ruses of philosophy," Fynsk writes, "an appropriation of the very event of disappropriation, an overcoming of the most radical form of otherness and negativity in the essentially tragic gesture of confronting death. Death has become a possibility" (*Heidegger* 38).

What Heidegger accomplishes by making death an aspect of Dasein's understanding is the closure of its circle. And, as Werner Hamacher observes, with
that, "there is nothing more that could withdraw from understanding, oppose
itself to understanding as something exterior, or determine it from the outside"
(33). If Dasein has "always already enabled its own not-being-able," Hamacher
writes, "then it never stops understanding itself and understanding itself as understanding. . . . So death as a possibility and a capacity of Dasein is the absolute of its self-appropriation" (33). According to Heidegger, it's only from this
scene of "authentic" individuation that Dasein becomes capable of authentic
solicitude.

Dasein demonstrates a resolute concern-for-others only by first pulling itself
together, embracing itself as a "constancy," a wholeness or totality uncut by the
Others. In "Shattered Love," Jean-Luc Nancy observes that, despite everything,
Heidegger's "concern for" starts "from an 'I' or from an 'identity' that [then]
goes toward the other" (104). The question is whether such a sense of integrity
is available to Dasein, and therefore whether resolute choice is ever an option
for it. Hamacher, for example, notes that if Dasein's possibility stretches out and
touches impossibility, and if it does this from the outset, originarily, then this
possibility is always already wrecked, having crashed into impossibility:

> If finite Being is comportment toward the end of Being, then it is comport-
> ment toward the impossibility of this very comportment. Understand-
> ing—since it means being-able—must be structured as an understanding of
> the non-understanding of this understanding itself. It can understand itself
> only as possible non-understanding, and since this possibility does not remain
> exterior to it but rather determines it from the outset, it can understand itself
> likewise only by not understanding itself—and by not understanding itself
> understanding. . . . [N]on-understanding must still "belong" to the most au-
> thentic and "the most primordial" understanding. And this affects every pos-
> sibility of Dasein, including the possibility of ontology, phenomenology, and
> hermeneutics. (33–34)

If Dasein comports itself toward its own end, which is its uttermost impossibility, then this impossibility/noncomprehension already contaminates all possibility, all comprehension. Nonunderstanding becomes the simultaneously
enabling and disabling ground for any understanding—and Dasein, presuming
that it understands, understands nothing, perhaps least of all itself. The sense

of wholeness and authenticity that Heidegger has so laboriously constructed is thus shattered, taking with it the figure of the resolute choice.[11]

The *il y a:* Inextinguishable Existence

There is no comparable figure in Levinas, who famously reverses Heidegger's definition of death, proposing instead that death signifies "the impossibility of every possibility"—and this flip changes everything. One of Levinas's central arguments in *Time and the Other* is that Dasein's rapport with death is an instance of radical nonunderstanding that "cannot take place in the light." When it comes to death, he says, Dasein finds itself "in relationship with what does *not* come from itself. We could say it is in relationship with mystery" (70, my emphasis). So what in Heidegger is Dasein's "ownmost non-relational possibility" becomes in Levinas the existent's *relation* with alterity. And because there is no understanding, because this alterity is not appropriable, the existent's relation with it cannot be a determinate one—it would instead take the form of what Levinas calls a "rapport *sans* rapport." Being-toward-death, the mode of being that Heidegger describes as authentic, strikes Levinas as too cocky and sure of itself, presuming a "supreme lucidity and hence a supreme virility" (70). Dasein, in its being-toward-death, comes off as a kind of cowboy of the Nothing. What this heroics of the void effaces, Levinas writes, is that death is "absolutely unknowable . . . foreign to all light, rendering every assumption of possibility impossible, but where we ourselves are seized" (71). Death is a nocturnal force that *remains* nocturnal, unknowable, outside all possibility. According to Levinas, death *un*-powers me and is in *no* case mine—even when it's "mine," even when it's happening to "me."

Because death is resolutely foreign and ungraspable, Levinas proposes that "it marks the end of the subject's [supposed] virility and heroism. The now is the fact that I am master, master of the possible, master of grasping the possible. Death is never now. When death is here, I am no longer here, not just because I am nothingness, but because I am unable to grasp. My mastery, my virility, my heroism as a subject can be neither virility nor heroism in relation to death" (72). "I" cannot experience death as my uttermost not-yet (*la mort*) or take it upon myself as an accomplishment or an achievement because when death arrives, "I" am/is already gone: "Perhaps death is an absolute negation wherein 'the music ends,'" Levinas writes, "(however, one knows nothing about it)"

(*EI* 49). I can only experience death as coming, as an imminent "menace" that is always approaching; I experience(s) death only as an interminable dying (*le mourir*) that is at the very heart of existing. Rather than being the subject of my death, I undergo it in utter passivity, in the way, for example, that I undergo aging. It happens in a manner that excludes the self "from mastery and from its status as a subject (as first person)" (Blanchot, *WD* 23). In *Totality and Infinity,* Levinas elaborates:

> My death comes from an instant upon which I can in no way exercise my power. I do not run up against an obstacle which at least I touch in that collision, which in surmounting or in enduring it, I integrate it into my life, suspending alterity. Death is a mystery that approaches me as a mystery; its secrecy determines it—it approaches without being able to be assumed, such that the time that separates me from my death dwindles and dwindles without end, involve[ing] a sort of last interval which my consciousness cannot traverse, and where a leap will somehow be produced from death to me. The last part of the route will be crossed without me; the time of death flows upstream; the I in its projection toward the future is overturned by a movement of imminence, pure menace, which comes to me from an absolute alterity. (234–35)

Death, as "the impossibility of every possibility," Levinas writes, is a "stroke of *total* passivity alongside which the passivity of the sensibility, which moves into activity, is but a distant imitation" (235). The "total passivity" that one suffers in-relation-to-death is in no way the decision of a Decider who could, if she chose to, reverse the charges and bust a move.

Heidegger suggests that the call of conscience brings Dasein face-to-face with the void, the sheer nothingness out of which Dasein arises and to which it ultimately will return. Being-toward-death is the mode of being that signifies a certain mastery over the nothingness that bookends Dasein's existence. Levinas, on the other hand, redescribes the void itself as a "plenitude," an "inextinguishable" existence that precedes and exceeds figuration and phenomenalization (all substantives). Underpinning the tropological field, the representations and thematizations that make up "world," Levinas tells us, is the yawning abyss of the *il y a* (the *there is*): existence as such, raw materiality, the indeterminate *heap* that "world" covers over.[12] "For where the continual play of our relations with the world is interrupted we find neither death nor the 'pure ego,'" Levinas writes, "but the anonymous state of being. Existence is not synonymous with the relationship with a world; it is antecedent to the world" (*EE* 8). A testament to the weakness of the negative, the *il y a* is what there is, as Blanchot has put it, "when there is no more world, when there is no world yet" (*SL* 33). What bookends the existent's being-in-the-world, according to Levinas, is not nothingness, which from his perspective would be a comfort, but the *il y a*, "the fatality of irremissible being" (*EE* 57). When the world withdraws and the existent encounters the *il y a*, he says, s/he is overcome not with anxiety (generalized fear *for* being) but with horror (generalized fear *of* being) (*EE* 58).

Whereas Heidegger describes being in general, *es gibt*, as the exorbitant generosity of being, the giving of world, Levinas describes the *il y a* as sheer horror. In contradistinction to the silent emptiness of the void, the *il y a* names not only an "existence without world" but also an existence "without existents"— for, when the existent ("the appearance of the substantive" [*EE* 83]) encounters the *il y a* from which it emerged, it experiences resubmergence, depersonalization, depropriation.[13] "In horror," Levinas writes, "the subject is stripped of his subjectivity, of his power to have a private existence"; the subject "loses this private character and returns to an undifferentiated background" (*EE* 56). Even "nausea" doesn't quite cut it as a descriptor since nausea, still "a feeling for existence, is not yet a depersonalization," Levinas writes; "but horror turns the subjectivity of the subject, his particularity qua *entity*, inside out" (*EE* 56). The real kicker for Levinas is that there is no way out. Fleeing into the world will not shelter the existent from this irremissible existence: "It is a participation in the *there is*, in the *there is* which returns at the heart of every negation, in the *there is* that has 'no exits.'" There is no chance of opting out the other way, either, since this existence is, "if we may say so, the *impossibility of death*, the universality of existence even in its annihilation" (*EE* 56; my emphasis).

According to Levinas—who penned most of *Existence and Existents* while a prisoner of war in a Nazi prison camp—the existent encounters its abyssal ground, the brute and brutal fact of irremissible being, especially in times of weariness and fatigued isolation. He offers as an example the inescapable vigilance of insomnia when "sleep evades our appeal" (*EE* 61). One cannot will oneself to sleep: inasmuch as it fastens consciousness to the night, insomnia introduces the subject, each time, to its vulnerability, its subjection, its inability to retreat into itself and so to master its "own" existence. In insomnia, there is consciousness without a subject. "Attention," Levinas writes, "presupposes the freedom of an ego which directs it; the vigilance of insomnia which keeps our eyes open has no subject" (*EE* 62). The night that the insomniac suffers is not the reassuring partner of the day, Levinas tells us—and what insomniac would disagree?—but the restlessness of indeterminate being, of impersonal, anonymous subsistence unconditioned by the negative (by figuration): existence without world:

> We could say that the night is the very experience of the *there is*, if the term experience were not inapplicable to a situation which involves the total exclusion of light.
>
> When the forms of things are dissolved in the night, the darkness of the night, which is neither an object nor the quality of an object, invades like a presence. In the night, where we are riveted to it, we are not dealing with anything. But this nothing is not that of pure nothingness. There is no longer *this* or *that*; there is not "something." But this universal absence is in its turn a presence, an absolutely unavoidable presence. It is not the dialectical counterpart of absence and we do not grasp it through a thought. It is immediately there. . . . *There is*, in general, without it mattering what there is, without our being able to fix a substantive to this term. *There is* is an impersonal form, like it rains or it is warm. Its anonymity is essential. The mind does not find itself faced with an apprehended exterior. The exterior—if one insists on this term—remains uncorrelated with an interior. It is no longer given. It is no longer a world. (*EE* 52–53)

In insomnia, irremissible being locks onto the exhausted body, which seeks in vain some form of relief from this indeterminate "presence," this ghostly invasion that just keeps coming. "Insomnia thus puts us in a situation where the disruption of the category of the substantive designates not only the disappearance of every object," Levinas reiterates, "but the extinction of every subject" (*EE* 64). There is no escape, no exit from this haunted house of Being. The *il y a* names a "nocturnal space," Levinas says, but not an "empty space" because "[d]arkness fills it like a content; it is full, but full of the nothingness of everything" (*EE* 53).

This loss of perspective "becomes an insecurity"—not because we can no longer see whether the scary things of the day are approaching but precisely because "nothing approaches, nothing comes, nothing threatens," save this "mute, absolutely indeterminate menace." In horror, "there is no determined being, anything can count for anything else." And in an encounter with "this obscure invasion," Levinas tells us, "it is impossible to take shelter in oneself, to withdraw into one's shell. One is exposed. The whole is open upon us. Instead of serving as our means of access to being, nocturnal space delivers us over to being" (*EE* 53–54). And daylight doesn't necessarily bring shelter, since the nocturnal space of the *il y a* can come at you any time, day or night, sucking you into what Blanchot calls the "other night" (*SL* 170).[14] Its darkness, "as the presence of absence, is not a purely present content," Levinas reiterates. "There is not a 'something' that remains. There is the atmosphere of presence, which can, to be sure, appear later as a content, but originally is the impersonal, non-substantive event of the night and the *there is*. It is like a density of the void, like a murmur of silence. There is nothing, but there is being, like a field of forces" (*EE* 59).

In this "obscure invasion," world dissolves, taking my power and virility out with it: "What we call the I is itself submerged by the night, invaded, depersonalized, stifled by it. The disappearance of all things and of the I leaves what cannot disappear, the sheer fact of being in which one participates, whether one wants to or not, without having taken the initiative, anonymously" (*EE* 52–53). The *il y a*: not the empty stillness of a nothing that would be Being's opposite but the incessant murmur of the no-thing that *there is*, that there *still* is, each time world dissolves. Each time "I" dissolve(s). There's no way to master this *other* night, this spectral "encounter" that can neither be lit up and known nor triumphantly faced and overcome. What the existent learns from its encounters with the *il y a* is that *la mort*, one's uttermost not-yet—the sweet relief of nothingness—is not a *possibility* for it. One cannot choose nothingness anymore than one can choose sleep: Being offers no exits. "'And it is over with,'" Levinas writes, "is impossible" (*EE* 57).[15]

Blanchot, who is with Levinas on this issue, writes about Heidegger: "when a contemporary philosopher names death as man's extreme possibility . . . he shows that the origin of possibility is linked to the fact that he can die, that for him death is yet one possibility more, that the event by which man departs from the possible and belongs to the impossible is nevertheless within his mastery, that it is the extreme moment of his possibility" (*SL* 240). But how can I assimilate my death within my horizon of understanding, Blanchot asks, when its nothingness is forever outside my grasp? "Even when, with an ideal and heroic resolve, I decide to meet my death," Blanchot writes, "isn't it still death that comes to meet me, and when I think I grasp it, does it not grasp me? . . . Do I myself die, or do I not rather die always other than myself, so that I would have to say that properly speaking *I* do not die?" (*SL* 98).[16] In a sense, the average everyday understanding of death, the banal realization that "everyone dies," Blanchot suggests, may be a more "authentic" understanding of it than the one Heidegger so painstakingly teases out. In fact, Blanchot observes that death is "that which never happens to me, so that never do I die, but rather 'they die.' Men die always other than themselves, at the level of the neutrality and the impersonality of the eternal They" (*SL* 241). In Heidegger being-toward-death names the mode of existence through which one succeeds in extracting oneself from the "they," but in Levinas and Blanchot, the relation with death is precisely what reduces one to this anonymous neutrality. Strictly speaking, death is impossible—"I" don't get to die, but rather "one" dies in my place, an anonymous, neutral one.

Death, according to both Levinas and Blanchot, marks the "measureless impossibility" of my *every* possibility: If I can't own my own death, if "I" can have no proper closure, no sense of wholeness, then I—as an authentic entity or totality—am/is impossible. Death holds me in *its* grasp while remaining absolutely unassimilable. I am always already dying, aging helplessly and—despite all my skincare products—passively. Though I can never face it or get it authentically in my sights, I am exposed to and affected to the "core" by this inappropriable alterity—which means, precisely, that I can have *no* core, no "virginal integrity," and therefore no heroic potential, no possibility for the triumphant overcoming that Heidegger describes. What the existent's rapport with death demonstrates to Levinas is that a radical impossibility shakily "grounds" all my possibilities: it demonstrates the nonsubstantial and inessential nature of identity and, therefore, the *farce* of the resolute choice, which turns out to be about as effective, in terms of self-mastery, as my overpriced moisturizers.[17]

According to Levinas, it is only because the existent *cannot* be "individualized down to itself," only because "I" am preoriginarily opened to the other's affection/alteration/inspiration, that there can be any generosity in the world, even the little that there is (*OTB* 117). Up against the recurrent theme of "gathering" in Heidegger, and specifically of self-gathering, Levinas offers a relentless inquiry into a nonthematizable welcoming that would be the *condition* for any gathering up of being. Being-for-the-other, he proposes, is not an option that "I" could choose and should choose but a responsibility that "comes from the hither side of my freedom, from a 'prior to all memory'" (*OTB* 10). In contradistinction to the early Heidegger, Levinas's thesis is that there is no "being-there" that is not already the function of being-for, that an undeniable obligation to respond is the condition for any ethical "choice" (which is therefore never resolute), and that any sense of the freedom to choose is already an effect of this excessive responsibility. From his perspective being-for-the-other is not heroic; it is ethical. And the ethical relation is not a choice but a nearly existential and thoroughly rhetorical predicament: "no one is good voluntarily." There are no heroes in Levinas; there are only hostages with assignments. And that is (the) Good.

Assignation: Nonspontaneous Agency

Levinas describes the field of representation and thematization as resting uneasily atop the sheer horror of being in general, which both calls for figuration and quietly (through its constant murmur) disturbs it. Between the yawning abyss of the *there is* and the totalizing synchrony of figured world, Levinas situates an event, "the upsurge of an existent in existence," "an *existent* for which to be," Levinas writes, "means *to take up being*" (*EE* 25). In his very early work, particularly in *Existence and Existents* (1947), Levinas described this event in terms of a spontaneous self-positing: "an existent arises in impersonal Being, through a hypostasis" (*EE* 12, 3). "In the midst of the anonymous flow of existence, there is stoppage and a positing," Levinas writes (*EE* 23). This positing does not come from the world and is not a function of nominatives or substantives. The *il y a* is "pure verb," and the "apparition of an existent" is the effect of a "transmutation of a verb into a substantive" (*EE* 83, 102). The hypostasis, Levinas explains, is "the event by which the act expressed by a verb became a being designated by a substantive. Hypostasis, the apparition of a substantive, is not only the apparition of a new grammatical category: it signifies the suspension of the anonymous *there is*, the apparition of a private domain, of a noun. On the ground of the *there is* a being arises" (*EE* 83). Existence takes up a place, a position, a base from which a consciousness arises and takes up existence.

The apparition of an entity emerges, "a subject of the verb *to be*," who thus "exercises a mastery over the fatality of Being, which has become its attribute. Someone exists who assumes Being, which is henceforth *his* being" (*EE* 83). Birth of the intending ego. "To be conscious is to be torn away from the *there is*, since the existence of a consciousness constitutes a subjectivity, a subject of existence that is, to some extent, a master of being, already a name in the anonymity of the night" (*EE* 55). As master of its existence, the subject enjoys its world. But Levinas is quick to point out that already "in the hypostasis of an instant—in which a subject's mastery, power, or virility are manifested as being in a world . . . —we can discern the return of the *there is*." Underpinning the appearance of "mastery, power, or virility," Levinas insists, is the *il y a*: "The 'I' always has one foot caught in its own existence." Ego, in all its mastery, is still an existent (a self) chained to irremissible and impersonal being. I do have the freedom to take a little distance from my self—perhaps, if I'm lucky, to drift off to sleep—but this freedom is not really a liberation, Levinas insists; rather "it is as though one had given more slack rope to a prisoner without untying him." Existing, he continues, "is the impossibility of getting rid of oneself" (EE 89).

The only glimmer of hope, Levinas proposes—and we are still in *Existence and Existents*—the only escape from this interminable existence to which "I" am irrevocably chained, is the other; not an other just like me, but the other *as* other (*autrui*), the other "par excellence."[18] To reach for the other, he says, involves "on the ontological level, the event of the most radical breakup of the very categories of the ego, for it is for me to be somewhere else than my self: it is to be pardoned, to not be a definite existence" (EE 85–86). To approach the other is to be ripped out of being and planted elsewhere, between being and nonbeing, in the *autrement qu'etre*. In this very early formulation, which also shows up in *Time and the Other* (1948) and perhaps to some extent in *Totality and Infinity* (1961), there is first the conscious existent (ego) stuck with its self, and then there is the other, who breaks in, offering the existent a temporary escape not from nothingness but from the irremissibility of existence.[19]

By the time *Otherwise than Being* is published in 1974, however, Levinas has radicalized this already radical thesis, proposing now that the relation with the Other precedes and is the condition for the emergence of ego. This time the hypostasis—the "stoppage" and "positing"—is already a *response*: the existent (noun), rather than being the effect of a spontaneous self-positing instead emerges from impersonal existence (pure verb) in response to a "non-thematizable provocation," a "preoriginal saying" that is "prior to every memory," a signification that "precedes essence" (OTB 10–13).[20] This is not to say that some divinely intentioned being sends out a message that prompts the hypostasis; significantly, there is no subject of the address in Levinas's account.[21] Nor is there an intended addressee, since there is not yet any "one" there when the address goes out. We are not in the realm of beings sending and receiving messages here but of materially exposed creatures, affected, moved to response prior to cognition. Levinas's thinking begins not with the consciousness of a subject who recognizes itself but with "proximity," contact at the level of "a materiality more material than all matter" (108). If he insists that both the provocation and the response remain in "a past more ancient than every representable origin, a pre-original and anarchical *passed*" (9), it is because this "signification" is irreducible to conceptualization and thematization—it is immediate and so already past/passed by the time a consciousness could begin to grasp or (re)present it.

According to him, material incarnation (anterior to any *concept* of "body") is the site of a passivity more ancient than the active/passive dichotomy; it is the very condition for the subject's exposure, susceptibility, vulnerability. And the immediate contact associated with "proximity," Levinas tells us, is already a call,

> already a summons of extreme urgency, an obligation that is anachronistically prior to every engagement. An anteriority older than the a priori. This formulation expresses a way of being affected that can in no way be invested by spontaneity: the subject is affected without the source of the affection becoming a theme or re-presentation. The term obsession designates this relation which is irreducible to consciousness. ("Substitution" 81)

Proximity, structured as provocation and response, Levinas suggests, is the "assignation of me by another" (*OTB* 100). "It is in the passivity of obsession, or incarnated passivity, that an identity individuates itself as unique . . . in the impossibility of evading the assignation of the other" (112).

There is no way to grasp or analyze this rhetorical situation in the present; however, the priority of the other who assigns me before I am around to refuse (or to represent anything to myself) is *signaled*, a posteriori, Levinas tells us, in the everyday hostage scenes of responsibility: even, for example, in the "after you, sir," which is said to an other before an open door. This simple and extraordinarily ordinary instance of politesse involves a *"responsibility that is justified by no prior commitment"* ("Substitution" 82), a scene of obligation in which "all my inwardness is invested in the form of a despite-me, for-another," and in which the "response answers before any understanding" (*OTB* 11–12).

According to Levinas, (in) the beginning (*my* beginning, my *archē*) was the response. He uses phenomenology in order to indicate that which exceeds phenomenological reach: the immediate relation with the other in the absolute passivity of material incarnation. What he proposes, working backward from everyday instances of self-sacrificing generosity, is that it is the response to an underivable address that *institutes* the dissociating association in which both self and other are posited as substantives. This positing necessarily grants a "sense of 'oneself'" but only as an *effect* of response-ability, as an "accusative that derives from no nominative" (11).[22] What Levinas is proposing is that a responsibility to respond, a preoriginary *rhetorical* imperative, is the condition for any conscious subject rather than the other way around. This relation with and obligation to an alterity that precedes (and exceeds) any sensible or given being is antecedent not only to the apparition of ego but also therefore to any relation ego could have with self.

According to him, it is thanks to this preoriginary responsibility that there is consciousness and so the emergence of ego, which is now "free" to enjoy all the pleasures and pitfalls of being-with-others-in-the-world, including drive-based psychodramas, class warfare, gender troubles, and racial struggles.[23] But ego, immersed as it is in all its worldly investments, encounters a trace of its immemorial obligation in the "face" of the "neighbor." It is in the expression of the face that a trace of the Other breaks through, an enigma in the phenomenon, interrupting both ego's sense of spontaneity (its "mastery, power, or virility") and the smooth ordering of its world. That is, it is in the encounter with the face that the obligation to respond becomes a *conscious* experience.[24] In turning to face—and not marching side by side, *Mitsein* style—"I" am exposed to the trace of a relation that precedes "me," a relation that is irreducible to the contemporaneity of being-with and that carries with it an obligation that exceeds cognition. This inappropriable excess, which puts me into relation with what I can neither assimilate nor abdicate, is the creaturely saying that issues the rhetorical imperative. Ego's relation to the Other is a relation to the trace, which is not a relation that I *have* but one that gives me to be. (Levinas: "The great 'experiences' of our life have properly speaking never been lived" ["Phenomenon" 68].) The encounter with the face, each time (each "recurrence"), is a trauma, a "blow of affection" that contests me without submitting to cognitive scrutiny. To encounter *l'visage d'Autrui* is to be torn up from myself, "returned" to a native land (*terre natale*) that owes nothing to birth—not to another mode of being but to the *autrement qu'etre*.

Whereas Hyde argues that "helping others presupposes the action of a self assuming the ethical responsibility of freedom of choice" (105), Levinas suggests close to the opposite: a subject engaging in an act of generosity or sacrifice is obsessed and possessed, compelled by an obligation that is the very condition for its being. "Like the anonymity of the *there is*," Michael Marder observes, the face of the Other "forces me to turn inside out, this time not only in a confirmation of my anxiety that I will be stripped of my power 'to have private existence,' but because of the dynamics of signification, in which I am the-one-for-the-other" (par. 34). To encounter a face, its signifyingness or expression, is to be torn-up-from-oneself-*for-another*. The difference between the depersonalizing force of the *il y a* and the depersonalizing force of the face is that the latter *charges* me with subjectivity as response-ability, assigning to me a uniqueness *in* anonymity. In *le visage d'Autrui*, "I" am utterly depersonalized, deprivatized—and yet no one can replace me. It is in facing the face of the Other that I am (re)called to my responsibility to respond. This "despite me, for-the-other," Levinas says, is the "very fact of finding oneself while losing oneself" (*OTB* 11).

In response to Heidegger's insistence that no one can die for me, that death is "in every case mine," Levinas shows that to die for the other is not to die in the other's place, as if death were transferrable or transmittable, but to give up one's being, one's place in being, for-the-other, *l'un-pour-l'autre*, not by "choice" but by something like rhetorical structure:[25]

> The neighbor assigns me before I designate him. This is a modality not of a knowing, but of an obsession, a shuddering of the human quite different from cognition. . . . In an approach I am first a servant of a neighbor, already late and guilty for being late. I am as it were ordered from the outside, traumatically commanded, without interiorizing by representation and concepts the authority that commands me. (*OTB* 87)

The Other's command is something "I" suffer in the mode of an obsession rather than something I know and understand in the mode of a cognition: it is an extraordinary instance of persuasion without a rhetorician, "command without tyranny" ("Freedom" 18). This obligation to respond gives "me" to be; it therefore exceeds any possible commitment I could consciously and presently make. For, the "blow of the [other's] affection makes an impact, traumatically," Levinas reminds us, "in a past more profound than all that I can reassemble by memory, by historiography, all that I can dominate by the a priori—in a time before the beginning" (*OTB* 88). The obsession with or possession by the other, the situation of being hostage, indicates a responsibility prior to any free commitment and a self "outside all the tropes of essence." It indicates not a responsibility to assume *my* freedom through resolute choice but—and this is completely different—a "responsibility for the freedom of others" (*OTB* 109). The "paradox" of responsibility is that "I am obliged without this obligation having begun in me, as though an order slipped into my consciousness like a thief, smuggled in, like an effect of one of Plato's wandering causes. But this is impossible in a consciousness, and clearly indicates that we are no longer in the element of consciousness" (*OTB* 13).

I am a subject to the precise extent that the ungraspable Other has already inspired "me" in the most fundamental sense, to the precise extent that "my" material incarnation is already, *to the core*, both host (*TI*) and hostage (*OTB*) to an Other that commands and assigns me. Even my generosity does not come from me, as Ronell notes in *Dictations*, but amounts instead to a "command performance issued by some unknown force that [I] can only welcome" (xiv). At the very core of me you'll find a trace of the Other (an "inspiration"), and my most profound inner experience will turn out always already to be a *relation* with inassimilable exteriority. Even before I accomplish acts of "social" or "symbolic" identification, Levinas suggests, I am/is *occupied*, already responding to alterity's prior command. The subject as host and hostage is *substituted* for the other, but this being-one-for-the-other is on the "hither side," as Levinas likes to say, of the self-conscious identity that would be for-itself. To be means to be under assignation, to be obligated, to be at the service of the other, to be hostage: "The word *I* means *here I am*, answering for everything and everyone" (*OTB* 114).

And yet, "I" is not simply a figural vacancy for the other to occupy—in which case I would be home free, shielded from all blame and responsibility. Pace Heidegger, who insists on Dasein's ecstatic structuring (its being outside-itself-in-the-world), Levinas argues that, due to the Other's recurrent invocation, the existent is, each time, *riveted* to an identity that it cannot escape: "There is an assignation to an identity for the response of responsibility," he writes, "where one cannot have oneself replaced without fault. To this command continually put forth only a 'here I am' (*me voice*) can answer, where the pronoun 'I' is in the accusative, declined before any declension, possessed by the other" (*OTB* 141). "I" names an occupied, inspired, and assigned subject, always already obligated, in response-only mode, denied first-person status. This irreparable subjection to the immediate command of alterity is the ungrounding ground of what Levinas calls the subject. My very subjectivity is an effect of "my" subjection to and assignation by the Other:

> The passivity of the exposure responds to an assignation that identifies me as the unique one, not by reducing me to myself, but by stripping me of every identical quiddity, and thus of all form, all investiture, which would still slip into the assignation. The saying signifies this passivity; in the saying this passivity signifies, becomes signifyingness, exposure in response to ... being at the question before any interrogation, any problem, without clothing, without a shell to protect oneself, stripped to the core as an inspiration of air, an ab-

solution to the *one*, the one without a complexion. It is a denuding beyond the
skin, to the wounds one dies from, denuding to death, being as a vulnerability.
(*OTB* 49)

So much for freedom, for mastery and virility, for heroic being-toward-death.
"This passivity is not only the possibility of death in being, the possibility of
impossibility," Levinas writes. "It is an impossibility prior to that possibility, the
impossibility of slipping away, absolute susceptibility, gravity without frivolity.
It is the birth of a meaning in the obtuseness of being, a 'being able to die' subject to sacrifice" (*OTB* 128).

In *Being and Time* the other never *really* closes in on you, which is why you
remain free and can emerge in all your triumphant authenticity. According to
Levinas, however, you are first of all, *preoriginarily*, the site of an unconditional
hospitality. "Responsibility for the other, going against intentionality and the
will," Levinas writes, "signifies not the disclosure of a given and its reception,
but the exposure of me to the other, prior to every decision. There is a claim
laid on the same by the other in the core of myself, the extreme tension of the
command exercised by the other in me over me, a traumatic hold of the other
on the same, which does not give the same time to await the other" (*OTB* 141).
This claim laid on me by the other possesses and commands me before "I" have
the chance to be for-myself. Levinas calls this claiming of the same by the other
"the psyche," which signifies an "inspiration, beyond the logic of the same and
the other, of their insurmountable adversity. It is an undoing of the substantial
nucleus of the ego that is formed in the same, a fission of the mysterious nucleus of inwardness of the subject by this assignation to respond, which does not
leave any place of refuge, any chance to slip away, and is thus despite the ego, or,
more exactly, despite me" (*OTB* 141).

Whereas in *Existence and Existents* and *Time and the Other* the existent is
stuck with itself due to its contract with Being, in *Otherwise than Being* the existent is assigned and riveted, each time, to an identity stripped of "every identical quiddity" *for-the-other*. The psyche amounts to:

> [A]n alteration without alienation or election. The subject in responsibil-
> ity is alienated in the depths of its identity with an alienation that does not
> empty the same of its identity, but constrains it to it, with an unimpeachable
> assignation, constrains it to it as no one else, where no one could replace it.
> The psyche, a uniqueness outside that of concepts is a seed of folly, already a
> psychosis. It is not an ego, but me under assignation. . . . Here I am—is a say-

ing with inspiration, which is not a gift for fine words or songs. There is a constraint to give with full hands, and thus a constraint to corporality. (141)

In Heidegger, Dasein—who is never shown to be hungry, Levinas notes
(*TI* 134)—gets its authentic and triumphant sense of wholeness by pulling
itself together, shedding relations in the face of death; but in Levinas the existent is riveted to an *assigned* identity, already for-the-other and because of the
Other: host and hostage. From this Levinasian perspective, "I" marks a site of
extreme surrender, a passivity beyond passivity that precedes and exceeds any
active/passive choice. The one who responds is not a self-sufficient ego but a
psycho "psyche": it is me under assignation, me deprived of first person status—"*moi sans moi*," as Blanchot puts it in *The Writing of the Disaster*, or "*moi
comme autre que moi*" (me as other than me). There are no action heroes in
Levinas; there are only radically exposed existents infinitely subject(ed) to the
other's inspiration, alteration, assignation.

It is *because* "I" am riveted to an identity that is already assigned, because
"my" subjectivity names a structure of irreparable exposure and a site of ethical substitution (being-for-the-other) which *bars* me from mastery or control,
that "I" must bear responsibility for everyone and everything. And according
to Levinas, nothing lets me off the hook. What individuates "me" is not that no
one can *die* for me but that no one can *respond* for me, no one else can take my
place: "the way in which my 'I' is an I is something utterly singular in the world.
And therefore *I* am responsible, and may not be concerned about whether the
other is responsible for me. The human, in the highest, strictest sense of the
word, is without reciprocity." There is no way to dump this obligation; the other's "unimpeachable assignation" offers me no sleep or slack but instead operates as an obsession (*OTB* 87).

None of this implies, obviously, that "I" will always or even frequently respond generously. "[I]f no one is good voluntarily, no one is enslaved to the
Good," Levinas writes (*OTB* 11). Ego, while "founded in this responsibility
and substitution" (*OTB* 120), enjoys its sense of mastery and protects it. "Murder, it is true, is a banal fact," Levinas explains, "one can kill the Other; the ethical exigency is not an ontological necessity. The prohibition against killing does
not render murder impossible, even if the authority of the prohibition is maintained in the bad conscience about the accomplished evil—malignancy of evil"
(*EI* 87). One can take out the other, but inasmuch as the originary liability remains operative, one cannot take out the Other, which is otherwise than being,

beyond vision's adequation, already spectral. The experience of bad conscience, as much as any act of self-sacrificing generosity, points to the unremitting responsibility, which is "presupposed in all human relationships. If it were not that," Levinas continues, "we would not even say, before an open door, 'After you, sir!' It is an original 'After you, sir!' that I have tried to describe" (*EI* 89). "Bad conscience," "conversation," the "after you" are all expositions (signals) of an always prior responsibility, and "the appearance in being of these 'ethical peculiarities,'" Levinas writes, "is a rupture in being. It is significant, even if being resumes and recovers itself" (*EI* 87). What Levinas shows without seeing is that this underivable obligation to respond that is the condition for any ethical action whatsoever amounts to a preoriginary *rhetorical* imperative.

An Ethical Task for Rhetorical Studies

What all of this suggests, at least for our purposes here and in the context of Levinas's work, is that "I" am/is no hero, that there can be no heroes. There are only hostages. However, and contrary to one's everyday sense of things, Levinas writes, "the unconditionality of being hostage is not the limit case of solidarity but the condition for all solidarity" (*OTB* 117). Being hostage, being *claimed* by the other prior to all freedom, is the condition for determinate ethical and juridical practices (laws and moral rules) as well as for all determinate forms of solidarity. After Levinas, the most pressing ethical task, it seems, would not be to recognize one's freedom to choose but to affirm that it is already too late to pose the issue of responsibility in these terms. According to him, "ethical consciousness" is not a "variety of consciousness" that one is free to take up and should choose to take up; rather, it names "the concrete form of a movement more fundamental than freedom" ("Philosophy" 58). It's always already too late for *my* spontaneity, *my* choices, *my* heroism. Will, initiative, interpretation, Levinas proposes, all trail behind my being-*for*-the-other, which is not a decision I make but a predicament that gives me to be. And not as a being-for-itself, nor even as a being-*with*-others, but as response-*ability*, as an "I" who can be, who is "able," only inasmuch as "I" respond(s). Lundberg and Gunn are surely correct that "every action, discursive or otherwise, is only born of an engagement with the set of conditions that produced it" (96). But what Levinas never stops demonstrating is that this engagement is itself prompted—no matter what the conditions, constraints, or particular cultural norms—by an always prior *obligation* to respond, an underivable rhetorical imperative.

Rhetoricians at the ARS agreed, Geisler writes in her report, "that rhetorical inquiry should make a difference in the world" and that this ethical objective is tied tightly to the field's "educational mission" (14–15). "What shall we, as teachers, say to our students," she asks, "about their potential and obligations with respect to becoming rhetorical agents? What shall we, as critics, say to our fellow citizens about their potential and obligations with respect to being rhetorical agents?" (16). Rhetorical studies can hardly have "a mission to educate rhetors to have agency," she warns, if we cannot "assent to the role of the rhetor in producing efficacious action" (13). If "agency is illusionary," Geisler continues, then both these questions and rhetorical inquiry itself are "irrelevant" (16). The presumption grounding this commonly articulated concern is that there is an unbreakable link between efficacy and autonomy—a link which is unceremoniously snapped in Levinas's work. And that is part of what we rhetoric teachers and critics might want to say to our students and fellow citizens: responsibility is not a matter of freedom; your capacity (and desire) to effect change is already a function of your inescapable responsibility, and not the other way around. You are obligated to respond in the way that you are obligated to age. An irrevocable passivity underpins your active decision to speak or not, to moisturize or not. You are responding, either way; aging, either way. This infinite responsibility does not make rhetorical practice irrelevant—it makes it both possible and necessary.

If rhetoric has a specifically ethical task today, it surely would not involve revving the engines of virility and mastery all over again. Perhaps it would involve the deconstruction of heroic thematizations and the exposition of exposedness, the nonheroic ethical structuring of subjectivity. Of course, after Levinas we'll also need to rethink our sense of what it means to assume a task. In *The Writing of the Disaster*, for example, Blanchot suggests that the passivity antecedent to any active/passive binary should itself be understood as a "task," not as something one consciously takes up but something one "non-dialectically" undergoes, suffers (27). A task, then, is not only something that you pursue; it is also something that pursues you, that you fulfill irrepressibly, like aging. Inasmuch as rhetoric names a language *relation*, an approach to the other, an address, it is always already exposing you to your assignation, to the obligation to respond, and therefore to the "surplus of sociality" that always already "is." This task pursues you relentlessly, aggressively . . . mercifully.

Still, if there is an ethical task that rhetoricians could take up in the name of making a difference, a task that would not simultaneously efface the structure of exposure that grants the very possibility for "pity, compassion, pardon, and proximity—even the little that there is"—perhaps this would be it: to approach speaking and writing, any form of the address, not simply or firstly as the *means* of communication (as servants of the said), but *as* communication itself, as modes of the saying, expositions of an ethical relation that precedes identity, intellection, and intentionality. To take up such a task would not be to suggest (absurdly) that meaning is insignificant or that the subject has no agency. On the contrary, it would be to acknowledge that agency is always already for-the-other: it is not spontaneous or self-determined or heroic but thoroughly rhetorical, responsive, assigned. Rhetorical agency, before it can involve symbolic action, requires an extra-symbolic signification, a saying, and the responsibility to respond. "The status of 'autonomy' cannot be stabilized in this subject who acts," as Ronell puts it ("Confessions" 270), but the subject is nonetheless charged with acting: s/he is not a free agent but an assigned agent, an agent on assignment, infinitely responsible for responding to the call of the Other(s).

5
Judgment

It is then not without importance to know
if the egalitarian and just State in which man is fulfilled
(and which is to be set up, and especially to be maintained)
proceeds from a war of all against all or from the irreducible
responsibility of the one for all.

Emmanuel Levinas, *Otherwise than Being*

An individual—indivisible and spontaneous—would be another story. But as a singularity, finite and exposed, "I" come into being only inasmuch as "I" respond to the other, and this preoriginary obligation to respond is called "my" responsibility. Responsibility, from this Levinasian perspective, is not something a self-sufficient subject chooses to take up; rather, "the subject" is ethically structured *as* response-ability: "the subject" *is* the response to alterity, a first response to the saying, each time, and all of the "saids" are granted on the basis of this response, including the appropriations and identifications that constitute "self" and "ego." The priority of the other is not a matter of the subject's choice (if it were, let's face it, the other would be toast) but of its inescapable predicament. "Ethical responsibility for the other is prior to subjectivity," Ronell explains, and "it's only through this ethical relationship that a subject can emerge." Thanks to an undeniable rhetorical imperative, "there is something like originary liability: you are liable prior to any empirical evidence of guilt. . . . You are already marked by this being-for-the-other—that is, you are indebted, kind of guilty, kind of ready to assume responsibility prior to anything else" ("Confessions" 269–70).

This obligation to respond that is prior to any freedom and through which your being is given is exposed and confirmed in the language relation: each time the other addresses me, "I" am/is demoted to a "you," a subject without nominative capacity, reduced to response-only mode. I am/is ousted from the addressor slot, "stripped of the illusion of being the addressor of phrases," as Lyotard puts it, and "grabbed hold of upon the addressee instance, incomprehensibly" (*D* 111). The obligation to respond "is immediate, prior to any intellection," Lyotard continues, preceding "any commentary upon the nature of the other, of the request, of my freedom" (*D* 111).

Aristotle proposes that practical wisdom (*phronêsis*) involves understanding and experience, which together with intuitive reason give some "men" the capacity for "equitable judgment" (1143^a). But responsibility, this extraordinarily ordinary obligation played out in any conversation, reverses the Aristotelian order of things: the "response answers before any understanding," Levinas writes (*OTB* 11–12). Response involves action before understanding and before judgment, turning the response into the *condition* for understanding and judgment. So long as it is only me and the other to whom I am responsible, this responsibility is not a question and is not in question. If it were only me and the other (the neighbor, the addressor, the first one on the scene) to whom I am responsible, both Levinas and Derrida insist, there would be no problem: my responsibility for the other is prior to all questioning, so I would owe the other, imprudently, without question, without comprehension, without the expectation of reciprocity—without the need for justice or judgments.

The problem that arises right away, however, the specifically political problem—the problem of the political—is that you, an assigned agent infinitely responsible for responding to the call of the other, are never not faced with *more than one other*. If that were not the case, if the radical exposedness constitutive of your singular existence were somehow limited or limitable, there would be no moral or political problems, and so no need for rhetorical reasoning. "There are only moral and political problems, and everything that follows from this," Derrida writes, "from the moment when responsibility is not limitable" ("Remarks" 86). It is because agency is nonspontaneous, because my "I" is granted only in and as response to the other, that "I" am/is responsible to and for the other, infinitely—and not only to *this* other but to all the other others. Alongside Levinas and in contradistinction to Hobbes and Locke, as well as to Rousseau and more recent social contract theorists such as John Rawls and David Gauthier, Derrida proposes that if I did not owe myself infinitely to "each and every one," and to the stranger as much as to the neighbor, the *question* of responsibility would never arise.

However, Levinas proposes that this immediate ethical relation (the rhetorical relation, the infinite obligation to respond to the other) is interrupted and becomes conflicted when a third party approaches:

> If proximity ordered me only to the other alone, there would have not been any problem, in even the most general sense of the term. A question would not have been born, nor consciousness, nor self-consciousness. The responsibility for the other is an immediacy antecedent to questions, it is proximity. It is troubled and becomes a problem when a third party enters. (*OTB* 157)

This third party is also an unreachable alterity to whom I am infinitely obligated. My troubles begin here, in the face of the third party, who is "other than the neighbor, but also another neighbor, and also a neighbor of the other, and not simply his fellow." I now have to ask: "What then are the other and the third party for one another? What have they done to one another?" (157). And to whom am I most responsible? Interrupting the untroubled ethical immediacy of the "face to face," "[t]he third party introduces a contradiction in the saying whose signification before the other until then went in one direction," Levinas explains (*OTB* 157). With the approach of the third, the one-way street of my infinite responsibility is opened to multiple lanes of traffic. Derrida calls this "terrible contradiction of the Saying by the Saying, Contra-Diction itself" (*A* 30), a necessary betrayal of the immediate ethical relation provoked by the proximity of a (specifically) human plurality.[1]

The entry of the third party is both "the limit of responsibility," because my "I" cannot be donated to more than one other, "and the birth of the question: What do I have to do with justice?" (*OTB* 157). According to Levinas, and then Derrida, "the first question in the interhuman is the question of justice. Henceforth it is necessary to know, to become consciousness," Levinas writes ("Peace" 168). From the moment the third party arrives on the scene—which is right away, he says, the third party does not wait—there is a need for comparison, "contemporaneousness," "order," "thematization," "the intelligibility of a system," and "also a copresence on an equal footing as before a court of justice" (*OTB* 157). Justice is exercised through the state and its institutions, which are now inevitable and necessary. With the approach of the third, "I pass from the relation without reciprocity to a relation wherein, among the members of society, there is a reciprocity and an equality." And from here, "every excess of generosity that I should have in regard to the other is submitted to justice" (*Is it* 214).

This depiction of the birth of justice among singularities carries drastically different implications than those histories of justice woven around individual narcissi out to defend their property. For one thing, it indicates that everything begins with rhetoric, with a nearly existential rhetorical "situation" from which there is no exit. (The Burkean Parlor meets Hotel California: you can "check out" occasionally, but you don't get to "depart," not even when "the hour grows late."[2]) From the perspective of the singular existent—and not the individual entity or organism—the need for justice, and so for prudent judgments, is the *product* of a rhetorical predicament, an infinite imperative to respond that precedes and imprudently exceeds understanding. Following Aristotle, scholars in rhetorical studies tend to agree that civic subjects must engage in rhetorical reasoning through public deliberation to gain the understanding necessary for competent judgment. But the *condition* for this engagement, which the field has not addressed, is a different sort of rhetorical imperative altogether: an underivable and radically imprudent imperative that is not satisfied or silenced by acts of prudent judgment.

The relation between this imperative and the public sphere has not been addressed adequately outside rhetorical studies either. Key contemporary thinkers representing a diverse array of theoretical approaches—proponents of pragmatism, set theory, public sphere studies, post-Marxist political theory, and so on—share the suspicion that the notion of "infinite responsibility" explicated by both Levinas and Derrida has nothing to do with advocating for social justice. Richard Rorty, for example, claims in *Achieving Our Country* that this notion "may be useful to some of us in our individual quests for private perfection. When we take up our public responsibilities, however, the infinite and the unrepresentable are merely nuisances" (96–97). He confesses in *Deconstruction and Pragmatism* that he has "trouble with the specifically Levinasian strains in [Derrida's] thought," that he is "unable to connect Levinas's pathos of the infinite with ethics or politics." Rorty doesn't "find Levinas's Other any more helpful than Heidegger's Being—both strike [him] as gawky, awkward, and unenlightening" (41). Alain Badiou agrees, arguing that Levinas's notion of infinite responsibility to the Other is indissociably bound up with a "religious axiom," which annuls its philosophical aspirations in advance, and/but that any attempt to "suppress, or mask, its religious character" leaves us "with a pious discourse without piety," a gutted "spiritual supplement for incompetent governments." Any political discourse derived from Levinasian ethics, Badiou avers, is by definition devoid of both theological and philosophical heft, capable only of offering up ethical platitudes about recognizing the other, respecting differences, and affirming multiculturalism (*Ethics* 20–23). "No light is shed on any concrete situation by the notion of the 'recognition of the other,'" Badiou writes, adding that "the other doesn't matter"; what matters is the truth process through which the Same "comes to be" what it is (27).[3]

Jürgen Habermas contends that social justice is an effect of moral progress, which is itself a function of the rationally produced tolerance achieved in *symmetrical* dialogical relations. According to him, neither moral progress nor (therefore) the social justice implied by rational consensus could be moved along at all by the sort of *asymmetrical* relations connoted by "infinite responsibility." Such an exorbitant and (so) unreasonable solidarity could only be based on the "pre-political ethical convictions of religious or national communities" and not on the ideal of undistorted communication among free and equal citizens that he claims is the ground of modern liberal democracy ("Pre-Political Foundations" 27). Ernesto Laclau agrees with Derrida that the political, as "the process of *institution* of the social," involves "deciding within an undecidable terrain" that no universal rule can mediate; however, he does not see how "some kind of openness to the otherness of the other, to a primordial ethical experience, in the Levinasian sense . . . [could] be anything else than a universal principle that precedes and governs any decision." The passage from the undecidable to the decision "cannot have an ethical grounding," he insists; "I am definitely against contemporary currents which tend to an 'ethicization' of ontological levels. There are, in my view, no ethical principles or norms whose validity is independent of all communitarian spaces" (58).

I could go on. But what this diverse and somewhat representative sampling of contemporary political critiques of Levinas and the later Derrida share in common is a conviction that there is no legitimate place in the public sphere for appeals to "infinite responsibility" or for its attendant affirmation of a primordial ethical relation—which would not, by the way, be reducible to an "ethical principle," "norm," or "pre-political ethical conviction." By contrast, I would like to propose instead that if there is something like a "public sphere," even today, a realm of receptivity and responsivity that remains irreducible both to the "private sphere" and to the state and its institutions, a realm where rhetorical practice is necessary because opinion formation is not overdetermined by preexisting power structures or the law—if there is a realm of "genuine" decision or judgment (*krisis*)—it is opened by the impossible requirements of an infinite responsibility. What I am suggesting here, through a close reading of

Derrida, is that it is thanks to an experience of this rhetorical imperative, the infinite obligation to receive and respond, that both moral and political fields can be and remain open. An inessential and thoroughly rhetorical solidarity, which is not in itself limited or limitable, is the condition for any "truth process" as well as any political instantiation of social structure. This infinite responsibility is a "nuisance" in deliberative, juridical, and ceremonial discourses—wherever it is necessary to advocate for social justice—precisely because, being what *calls for justice* in the first place, infinitely, it is where all our moral and political problems begin. It is also where all our hope lies (a provocative double entendre that I may as well let stand).

Any thinking of this rhetorical imperative is foreclosed in advance by hermeneutical approaches to rhetoric every bit as much as it is by rhetorical approaches to hermeneutics; it is also the first casualty of rational-critical discourse, or at least of its a priori privilege, and of any approach to publics formation that starts with private individuals or symmetrical relations.[4] Our aim here will be to begin to articulate the relationship not only between this rhetorical imperative and the public sphere but also, more specifically, between this imperative and any practice, theory, or pedagogy of rhetorical reasoning and responsible advocacy.

The Contra-Diction

So the third party comes along and "henceforth, it is necessary to know," Levinas tells us. "Comparison is superimposed onto my relation with the unique and the incomparable, and in view of equity and equality, a weighing, a thinking, a calculation, the comparison of incomparables" ("Peace" 168). Justice transforms the irreducible other into a member of society and turns me into an other for the others. It "requires contemporaneousness of representation," Levinas writes. And "[i]t is thus that the [other] becomes visible, looked at, presents himself, and there is also justice for me"—finally, for me! Fashionably late, self-interest arrives on the scene. "The saying is fixed in a said, is written, becomes a book, law and science" (*OTB* 159). With the approach of the third party comes an interruption in immediate ethical responsibility by the necessity for political-juridical responsibility, an interruption of one responsibility by another. This sketch would seem to suggest that a just politics could be derivable from a more primordial ethics—this is what Laclau is objecting to above.

However, what Levinas is proposing (and Derrida's reading makes the point more pointed) is that no such derivation is possible. The rhetorical imperative, the infinite obligation to respond, comes through without instructions. The confusion Laclau evidences is double(d), so the response will be a backward two-step. First, Levinas emphasizes that the third party approaches already *in* the face of the other, in its epiphany: "It is not that the entry of the third party would be an empirical fact. . . . In the proximity of the other, all the others than the other obsess me, and already this obsession cries out for justice, demands measure and knowing, is consciousness" (*OTB* 158). In *le visage d'Autrui*, there where my "I" and its joyous possession of the world are interrupted, where a depropriating disfiguration leaves me in relation with an alterity that I can neither appropriate nor abdicate, where my "I" is donated, substituted in a despite-me-for-the-other—the third party shows up, shows up *already*, interrupting ethical immediacy, immediately. And in this immediate interruption a question is born, the question of justice, which grants ethical consciousness even as it puts it into conflict.[5] In the face of the other (*autrui*), "I" am/is obligated right away, immediately, both ethically *and* civically. There is no way to derive a politics from this so-called ethical grounding, then, since consciousness of ethical responsibility and the necessity for law and politics are effectively cooriginary: there is no ethical consciousness before the question of justice.

And yet—step two—Derrida adds that this question "is surely not first (it comes after the *yes* to the other and the *yes* of the other) though nothing precedes it. No thing, and especially no one" (*A* 31). Before the *question*, that is, the question born *in* the face of the other, there is nothing, no subject, no consciousness or knowledge—and so no conscious sense of responsibility, no ethics as such: no problem. There is, however—there must be—the *condition* for the question, a *pre*originary hospitality, an *an*archic receptivity and responsivity, the "yes" that grants the possibility for any conscious "yes" or "no." Before I can consciously welcome you or turn you away, in other words, "I" must already have welcomed you; the condition for my "yes" or "no" is a more radically fundamental hospitality, a "yes, come in" that is extended before "I" have the chance to choose.[6] Any "yes" is already a double "yes," a "yes, yes" in which the consciously chosen "yes" is preceded and made possible by a first "yes," a welcome before the choice, which is, again, constitutive of any singularity.

Ronell opens *The Telephone Book* with a now famous analogy of this predicament: you pick up the phone, and your first word is "yes?" Even if you say "hello?" it means "yes?" Before you can say, "yes, I will take your call" or "no, I won't take your call," you have taken the call, *in order* to get the chance to decide. Already in picking up, you have responded, welcomed the other in.[7] Indeed, even before you pick up, the ringing itself announces that the other is in, has already come in through the phone line or cable line or cell signal that runs into your home (or pocket) from the outside. The line or signal turns your home, the sovereign space in which you are at-home-with-yourself, into a structure of welcoming: "In order to constitute the space of a habitable house and home," Derrida writes, "you also need an opening, a door and windows, you have to give up a passage to the outside world. . . . The monad of home has to be hospitable in order to be *ipse*, itself at home" (*OH* 61). Constitutive violation of the supposedly inviolable: by the time the phone rings (or the SMS arrives on your screen), by the time you are presented with the option of answering, inviting, hosting, you have already welcomed the other, already offered your "yes, come in."

As a singular existent, "I" am anything but indivisible, inviolable. Levinas surely does suggest—Laclau is not mistaken—that "some kind of openness to the otherness of the other" precedes political decisions. However, this welcome takes place *before* any beginning, any *archē*—in an-*archē*—as the condition for both ethical and political consciousness. The "scarcely thinkable hypothesis" that Derrida draws from the final pages of *Totality and Infinity* is that, in and as the beginning, "there is no *first yes*, the *yes* is already a response. But since everything must begin with some *yes*, the response begins, the response commands. . . . It is necessary to begin by responding. There would thus be, in the beginning, no first word. The call is called only from the response" (*A* 24).[8]

The condition for ontology, for epistemology, for ethics *and* politics as such—is rhetoric, as the limitless and underivable imperative to respond, which is irreducible to any principle or norm.[9] Ethical and political consciousness and so a subject and its decisions emerge *in* the response to the other and not the other way around; this "I" *is faced* immediately with both an infinite response-ability (to more than one other) *and so* with the necessity for justice and its attendant instruments, law and politics. Simultaneously. And that is the problem. Justice demands that *le visage d'Autrui* become "visible, looked at," that the other become thematizable, comparable, a subject of politics. And yet, politics "hides what it throws light on," Derrida notes. "Giving the face to be seen, bringing or attracting it into the space of public phenomenality, it thereby renders it invisible" (*A* 98). In turning the incomparable into the comparable, law, politics, and normative ethics (morals) betray the immediate ethical relation, my infinite responsibility to the other and to all the others.

"But exhibiting the invisibility of the face is not the only way of dissimulating it," Derrida continues. "The violence of the political mistreats the face yet again by effacing its unicity in a generality" (98). Justice both requires and is simultaneously betrayed by this generality, this anonymous universality that motors politics, which cannot be "left to itself" and still have anything to do with justice. The thematizing and conceptualizing language of civic discourse, in other words, "rational-critical discourse," does not release me from my infinite responsibility—it does not cut me free—but instead *responds* to the "contradiction" internal to the saying where it is a "question of responsibility before the other, in the face to face or in attention to the third, in the very place where justice is," as Derrida puts it, "nondialectical contra-diction" (A 118). Derrida continues: "the illeity [radical otherness] of the third is thus nothing less, for Levinas, than the beginning of justice, at once as law and beyond the law, in law beyond the law" (A 29). "In law," because justice requires laws; "beyond the law," because no particular law or political formation can *embody* justice. Justice both requires and transcends the laws that serve it.

And this means that justice is never not terrible, never not tragic—it is always a betrayal of the other. Derrida describes it as an "initial perjury":

> If the face to face with the unique engages the infinite ethics of my responsibility for the other in a sort of *oath before the letter*, an unconditional respect or fidelity, then the ineluctable emergence of the third, and, with it, of justice, would signal an initial perjury [*parjure*]. Silent, passive, painful, but inevitable, such perjury is not accidental and secondary, but is as originary as the experience of the face. (A 33)

Inasmuch as justice requires law and politics, "[j]ustice would begin with this perjury," Derrida continues, and "justice commits perjury as easily as it breathes," betraying the "primordial word of honor" that I have always already given to the other. The "intolerable scandal" is that justice perjures and "swears [*jurer*] only to perjure, to swear falsely [*perjurer*], swear off [*Abjurer*], or swear at [*injurier*]" (33–34). Justice turns me into a liar and a deadbeat in the instant that it hails me as its subject—that is, right away, without hesitation.

Levinas and Derrida maintain this crucial distinction between the ethical subject and the civic one, but according to them, justice situates me in an inescapable tension between the two, which means that I will never be off the hook in either case: I'll never get a clear conscience, I'll never be just enough, I'll never be able to say, finally, that "I have acted responsibly." As Levinas puts it, "the better I accomplish my duty the fewer rights I have; the more I am just the more I am guilty" (*TI* 244). Nonetheless, justice demands decisions, which are only possible, as Derrida so beautifully demonstrates in "The Force of Law," in the face of the undecidable. "I" am charged with comparing incomparables but without ever effacing that incomparableness; "I" am charged with making judgments that engage rhetorical reasoning, with rigorously examining precedents, themes and concepts, the constative realm of the already said (because what else is there?), but always within the "context" of the saying that unmoors it, that both makes the said possible and simultaneously betrays it—and so, without ever imagining that my judgments are eternal, that I have truth on my side, that I'm on a mission from God.

Justice

Because the rhetorical imperative is not reducible to an ethical principle or norm, to use Levinas's descriptions of infinite responsibility in order to argue for any sort of determinate ethics or politics is to have missed the point. There is no way to "*deduce* from Levinas's ethical discourse on hospitality a law and a politics, some particular law or politics in some situation today, whether close to us or far away," Derrida writes (*A* 20). An *epoché* or hiatus separates infinite ethical responsibility from moral and civic responsibility. However, to use this *epoché* to justify an avoidance of adjudication altogether is to make things too easy for oneself, like Zarathustra's dwarf. Justice demands laws and judgments, which will necessarily betray it in order to serve it. It is both impossible *and yet* necessary, then, "to deduce a politics and a law from ethics," Derrida writes, but justice itself requires that:

> the political and juridical *content* thus assigned remain undetermined, still to be determined beyond knowledge, beyond all presentation, all concepts, all possible intuition, in a singular way, in the speech and the responsibility *taken* by each person, in each situation, and on the basis of an analysis that is each time unique—unique and infinite, unique but *a priori* exposed to substitution, unique and yet general, interminable in spite of the urgency for the decision. (*A* 115)

There is no decision and so no justice outside this tension between unconditional ethical responsibility and conditional political or moral responsibility.

Justice is not a "degradation of obsession," Levinas insists, not "a degenera-
tion of the for-the-other, a diminution, a limitation of anarchic responsibility."
What's so terrible, so traumatizing about justice is that it by definition *cannot*
neutralize my infinite responsibility. "Infinite responsibility" is a "nuisance" for
precisely that reason: it cannot be neutralized. Justice is not that easy, not that
simple or simplifying. "The contemporaneousness of the multiple is tied about
the diachrony of the two" Levinas continues: "justice remains justice only in
a society where there is no distinction between those close and those far off,
but in which there also remains the impossibility of passing by the closest.
The equality of all is borne by my inequality, the surplus of my duties over my
rights" (*OTB* 159).

Now, it's no secret that "society" barely even notices "the closest," as its able-
bodied professionals step over the destitute and the sick on their way to happy
hour. Responding by refusing to is always an option, and it's evidenced everywhere in the public sphere—you'd have to be unconscious or on crack to not
notice. It is on display, for example, in the continuous and unthinkable tolerance of abject poverty, hunger, sweat shops, domestic violence, homelessness,
hate crimes, and so on. Recently in this country, the willfully ignorant rants
by political leaders and pundits against universalizing health care—knotting it
up with "death panels" and such—could snap even the most somnambulating
"subject" to attention. We didn't need Levinas to tell us that no one is "enslaved
to the Good" (*OTB* 11), or that the "ethical exigency is not an ontological necessity" (*EI* 87). Still, this exigency, as exigency, does present itself everywhere,
in bad conscience, yes, but in the language relation too, in the unremitting responsibility to respond. The good news, for "you," is that infinite responsibility
is not up to "me." It is instead what makes *you* and *me* possible to begin with,
and if not for it, there could be *no* generosity in the world, not "even the little
that there is." If you are breathing, you are responding—Levinas defines death
as the scandal of "no response [*de non-réponse*]" (*God, Death, and Time,* 37)—
and the "ethical exigency" itself survives all the negative responses, all the *nos*
that follow its primordial *Yes.*

It is because this exigency is infinite, because "I owe myself infinitely to each
and every singularity," as Derrida puts it, that justice is necessary; and yet, justice immediately betrays that responsibility. There is no escape from this aporia,
which is the very space of any just judgment. Justice needs the state and its institutions, but they must always be held in check by my infinite responsibility. "This
means concretely and empirically" that justice is not some abstract or formal

legality designed to produce "social equilibrium" and harmonize "antagonistic forces," Levinas writes. "That would be a justification of the State delivered over to its own necessities. Justice is impossible without the one that renders it finding himself in proximity." The function of the judge "is not limited to the 'function of judgment,' the subsuming of particular cases under a general rule." The judge—inasmuch as she is just—cannot be "outside the conflict," says Levinas, but must be "in the midst of proximity" (*OTB* 159).

According to him, my infinite responsibility to the other is the condition for "[j]ustice, society, the State and its institutions, exchanges and work," and:

> This means that nothing is outside of the control of the responsibility of the one for the other. It is important to recover all these forms beginning with proximity, in which being, totality, the State, politics, techniques, work are at every moment on the point of having their center of gravitation in themselves, and weighing on their own account. (*OTB* 159)

Levinas had already expressed the same basic sentiment, along with a redefinition of "metaphysics," in *Totality and Infinity*:

> Metaphysics, or the relation with the other, is accomplished as service and as hospitality. In the measure that the face of the Other relates us with the third party, the metaphysical relation of the I with the Other moves into the form of the We, aspires to a State, institutions, laws, which are the source of universality. But politics left to itself bears a tyranny within itself; it deforms the I and the other who have given rise to it, for it judges them according to universal rules, and thus as in absentia. (300)

The relation with the Other is governed by a fundamental asymmetry; the two terms (the "I" and the "you") remain separate, irreducible to a mathematical equation ("I" + "you" = "we"). But with the entry of the third party, the contradiction issues a demand for equality and reciprocity; a "we" takes form, along with the necessity for the state, institutions, and laws.

The third comes along (immediately) and institutes the question, "but also, as a result, justice, philosophical intelligibility, knowledge, and even, announcing itself gradually from one person to the next, from neighbor to neighbor, the figure of the State," Derrida writes (*A* 31). The state and its institutions have no value "on their own account"; their "center of gravitation" lies in their service to justice, which holds me in the tension between ethics *as* hospitality and a politics *of* hospitality. This is why Derrida doesn't simply say "ethics is hospitality" but adds that "hospitality is culture itself" (*OCF* 16–17). Any culture is dynamically defined by its capacity to welcome the other, as one of its own or as foreign(er):

> One cannot speak of cultivating an ethic of hospitality. Hospitality is culture itself and not simply one ethic among others. Insofar as it has to do with the *ethos*, that is, the residence, one's home, the familiar place of dwelling, inasmuch as it is a manner of being there, the manner in which we relate to ourselves and to others, to others as our own or as foreigners, ethics is hospitality; ethics is so thoroughly coextensive with the experience of hospitality. (*OCF* 16–17)

Ethics and politics are heterogeneous but indissociable. An imperative to receive, to welcome, is their point of intersection, but the imperative is unconditional on the one side and conditional on the other. Justice is served (however imperfectly) so long as the "judge" remains in the impossible and irresolvable tension between the two. For "politics left to itself," an inhospitable politics, a politics exercised "outside the control of the responsibility of the one for the other" could deliver at best an "impersonal justice," Levinas explains, a "cruel" justice, an *in*justice (*TI* 300).

Judgment with an eye to justice could have no illusions of finality or universality; in Kantian parlance, it could no more allow itself to be dictated by categorical imperatives than by hypothetical imperatives. A judgment aiming for justice would necessarily take place as a tentative gesture, offering itself without clarity or certitude, both as a test and an invitation. Toward the end of *Otherwise than Being*, for example, Levinas writes: "This book interprets the subject as hostage and the subjectivity of the subject as a substitution breaking with being's essence. The thesis is exposed imprudently" (184). Derrida notes that for Levinas the thesis "is therefore not posed, it is imprudently and defenselessly exposed, and yet that very vulnerability is ('this weakness is necessary,' we will read a little later on) the provocation to responsibility for the other, it leaves a place for the other in a taking-place of *this* book where *this here* no longer shuts in upon itself, upon its own subject" ("At This Very" 31). As Avital Ronell puts it, "rather than flexing a thetic muscle that would buff up under the light of truth, Levinas offers a discourse vulnerable to its own sense of exposure, frailty and uncertainty" ("Sacred" 207–8). Offering up his imprudent thesis imprudently, as test and invitation, he advocates not only for the philosophical and political significance of the notion of "infinite responsibility" but also for an approach to advocacy that—in its very vulnerability, frailty, and uncertainty—aims for justice.

A just judgment, if there is such a thing, could not be taken on the basis of precedents (alone): that would be the definition of an *unjust* judgment, a decision reduced to the mechanistic deployment of a program, which would not, therefore, be a decision. As Lyotard has put it, "that which ought to be cannot be concluded from that which is, the 'ought' from the 'is'" (*Just Gaming* 17). Neither universal principles nor instrumental calculations are capable of attending to the one-for-the-other, which means that neither universal principles nor instrumental calculations alone can be the ground for a just judgment. Every decision is surely political, but the (non)ground on which any decision—as *decision*—is taken would have to be this aporetic tension between unconditional ethical responsibility and conditional civic or moral responsibility. There is no way to *decide* without facing this impossible contra-diction, without first undergoing this experience of radical *un*decidability. Any judgment aiming for justice would have to be taken in the face of this aporia, in a perjurious response to an infinite demand.[10]

The Faces of Hospitality

In *Of Hospitality*, Derrida asks: "Does one give hospitality to a subject? to an identifiable subject? to a subject identifiable by name? to a legal subject? Or is hospitality *rendered*, is it *given* to the other before they are identified, even before they are (posited as or supposed to be) a subject, legal subject and subject nameable by their family name?" (29).[11] Must hospitality come with certain limits and conditions or does the concept itself require that it be limitless, unconditional, that it precede and exceed the designation of subjects and objects, hosts and guests, guests and parasites? In response to this question, Derrida proposes that when it comes to hospitality, there are two "regimes of law":

1. There are "the laws of hospitality," the conditional and always plural rights or duties of hospitality that remain conditional and reciprocal, and that have been defined by the Greco-Roman and Judeo-Christian traditions, by law and philosophy from Kant to Hegel, by "the family, civil society, and the State." These rights of hospitality are offered to foreigners, to those who come from "abroad," equipped with a proper name and a family name, subjects in law, who assume certain obligations along with these rights (77).

2. And then there is "*the* law of hospitality." In the singular, the law commands that an unconditional and nonreciprocal hospitality, both exorbitant and hyperbolic—infinite—be offered to the "new arrival" prior to anticipation or identification; that it be offered "*to who or what turns up*, before any determination, before any anticipation, before any *identification*, whether or not it has to do with a foreigner, an immigrant, an invited guest, or an unexpected visitor, whether or not the new arrival is the citizen of another country, a human, animal, or divine creature, a living or dead thing, male or female" (77).

These two "regimes of law," one limited and conditional (prudent and political), the other limitless and unconditional (imprudent and ethical), Derrida tells us, exist in an "unsolvable antinomy" that is staged in a "strange heriarchy": *The* law is above the laws. The law is illegal in that sense, transgressive, a lawless law (*nomos anomos*), a law above the laws and outside the law (75, 77, 79). You experience the law, which is not drawn from any book or tradition, most acutely when you are attempting to respond responsibly but cannot finally complete your obligation. The punishing infinitude of the demand is dramatized in film, for example, at the end of *Schindler's List*, when Schindler, having plucked eleven hundred Polish Jewish refugees from Nazi death camps, anguishes over his failure to respond responsibly: he could have done more, should have done more. Infinitely more. Beyond rational or physical capacity, more; beyond all prudence and practical wisdom, more.

But where does it come from, this unreasonable and lawless law, this punishing law, which is neither "natural" nor prudent and which requires one to break all the laws, to ignore the physical, logical, political, and reciprocal conditions that limit the scope of hospitality? Derrida notes that it is "as though the categorical imperative of hospitality commanded that we transgress all the laws (in the plural) of hospitality," in its name (75). However, inasmuch as it commands one to break the laws, it by definition could not be a "categorical imperative" in the Kantian sense—nor, for that matter, could it be reduced to a "transcendental ideal." We are not in the realm of reason here, neither pure nor practical. Or else—or else, on the extreme other hand—we *are* in the realm of reason, as Levinas redefines it: reason as receptivity, as an experience of receiving and welcoming. To welcome the Other, to "receive from the Other beyond the capacity of the I," and so "to have the idea of infinity" amounts for Levinas to a "teaching" irreducible to maieutics, which "comes

from the exterior and brings me more than I can contain." And this teaching—analyzed by Aristotle, according to him—is constitutive of reason: "The
Aristotelian analysis of the intellect, which discovers the *agent intellect coming
in by the gates, absolutely exterior, and yet constituting, nowise compromising, the
sovereign activity of reason* [my emphasis], already substitutes for maieutics a
transitive action of the master, since reason, without abdicating, is found to be
in a position to *receive*" (*TI* 51).

Derrida reminds us that Levinas deduces "from the presence in my finitude
of the idea of infinity that consciousness *is* hospitality, that the *cogito* is a hospitality offered or given, an infinite *welcome*" (*A* 48). It's not just that consciousness arises in response to this always prior welcome; it's that consciousness *is*
this infinite welcome. And from here, even "intentionality" becomes a function
of hospitality. Here's Levinas:

> [W]here radical separation and relationship with the other are produced si-
> multaneously—we have reserved the term intentionality, consciousness of. . . .
> It is attention to speech or welcome of the face, hospitality and not thematiza-
> tion. Self-consciousness . . . thus accomplishes separation positively, without
> being reducible to a negation of that being from which it separates. But thus
> precisely it can welcome that being. The subject is a host. (*TI* 299)

Derrida spotlights the string of not quite synonymous substitutions here: "intentionality, attention to speech, welcome of the face, hospitality—all these are
the same, but the same as the welcoming of the other, there where the other
withdraws from the theme" (*A* 23). "Because intentionality is hospitality, it resists thematization," Derrida explains. Intentionality connotes for Levinas "an
act without activity, reason as receptivity, a sensible *and* reasonable experience
of *receiving*, a gesture of welcoming, a welcome offered to the other as stranger."
This means that "hospitality opens as intentionality, but [that] it cannot become an object, thing, or theme." Indeed, thematization "already presupposes
hospitality, welcoming, intentionality, the face" (*A* 48). Yes, yes.

So Levinas is not suggesting that, here or there, intentional experience could
involve this unconditional hospitality. "No," Derrida emphasizes, "intentionality opens, from its own threshold, in its most general structure, as hospitality,
as welcoming of the face, as an ethics of hospitality, and, thus, as ethics in general." Far from being "simply some region of ethics" or "the name of a problem
in law or politics," hospitality "is ethicity itself, the whole and the principle of
ethics" (*A* 50). Reason and intentionality become, after Levinas, functions of

a more originary obligation to receive and respond (and to respond by receiving): reason and intentionality become functions of a preoriginary *rhetorical* imperative. As response-ability, the subject is a host; this also means that the subject is a hostage. The host is by definition a hostage to the guest, to the one to whom hospitality is *owed*. And not in the sense of some potential secondary attribute but constitutively: "Responsibility for the Other is not an accident that happens to a subject," Levinas writes; rather, responsibility "precedes" any "essence" in the subject, taking hold prior to any sense of freedom or guilt (*OTB* 114). There could be no intentionality or "consciousness of . . ." that did not already obey *the* law of hospitality.[12] Intentionality already testifies to the an-archic "yes" that is the condition for your delibrative "yes" or "no."

And yet, in order now consciously to *say* "yes" to the law, to obey this law above and beyond the laws, one would have to break all the laws, transgress any and all conditions that would delimit "my" unconditional responsibility to the Other. The reverse is also the case: in order to say "yes" to the laws, to obey the laws, the duties, the rights of hospitality, one would have to transgress the law of hospitality, to institute conditions and limitations on what must (and does) remain unconditional and unlimited. "There is no hospitality, in the classic sense," Derrida writes, "without sovereignty of oneself over one's home, but . . . sovereignty can only be exercised by filtering, choosing, and thus excluding and doing violence." Only *some* others are granted the right of hospitality, only some are allowed in; otherwise my sovereign right to let them in would be compromised. No hospitality in the "classic" or conditional sense, then, without transgressing the law of unconditional hospitality. "Injustice, a certain injustice, and even a certain perjury, begins right away," Derrida writes, "from the very threshold of the right to hospitality" (*OH* 53).

To keep the law, you have to break the laws; to keep the laws, you have to break the law. But this radical antinomy is not an opposition, strictly speaking, nor does it allow for any Hegelian synthesis. The law and the laws are heterogeneous but indissociable. The law needs the laws and requires them to become effective, concrete, to enter into consciousness, and to serve justice. Without them, the law would remain at best abstract, utopian, illusory. So the unconditional law needs the conditional laws, which nonetheless betray, corrupt, and pervert it (79). It is only because the laws limit and pervert the law, only because they inscribe it by restricting it, that there is a *history* of hospitality, that it is experienceable by a consciousness: one experiences the law in or as the disappointment of its betrayal. The laws also need the law as a kind of "regulative idea" or inspiration: the conditional laws of hospitality would have nothing to do with hospitality if they were not guided, inspired, required by the unconditional law; they would be reduced instead to their utilitarian, "demographico-economic interests" (*OCF* 12).[13] If they are to be called laws, rights, or duties *of hospitality*, they must take as their aim and inspiration the law of hospitality. The law and the laws simultaneously pervert each other and make each other possible. Hovering between unconditional and conditional responsibility, justice names the *imperative to actualize the infinite demand in a finite way*, which will bring the former into being even as the latter betrays it.

Hostipitality

Hospitality in the "classic sense" requires that one have a home to offer, that one be owner and master of one's house, and the whiff of paternal/phallogocentric presumption is inherent to the concept: the master of the house, the sovereign host, is traditionally a father figure. "It's the familial despot, the father, the spouse, and the boss, the master of the house who lays down the laws of hospitality. He presents them and submits to them to submit the others to them in this violence of the power of hospitality" (*OH* 149). This hospitality requires sovereignty: "I want to be master at home (*ipse, potis, potens*, head of house . . .)", Derrida writes, "to be able to receive whomever I like there." And "anyone who encroaches on my 'at home,' on my ipseity, on my power of hospitality, on my sovereignty as host, I start to regard as an undesirable foreigner, and virtually as an enemy" (*OH* 53–55). However, because my home, any home, is constituted by its openings onto an outside, by its capacity for hospitality, it is never inviolable, and my sovereignty as host is never secure.

Inasmuch as "home" is constituted by its fields of access—not only by doors and windows (physical ports of entry) but also by landlines, cellular signals, cable lines, DSL, and so on—it is by definition violable. And once an uninvited "guest" (a parasite, then) makes its way in, announces itself inside, "every element of hospitality gets disrupted"; that is, all the dichotomies presumed by hospitality "in the classic sense" collapse: private/public, interior/exterior, self/other, host/guest. This is why, ironically, "one can become virtually xenophobic in order to protect one's own hospitality, the own home that makes possible one's own hospitality," Derrida writes (53). There is at the very least a supplement of xenophobia driving vigilant border watchers and their supporters (the Minuteman Project, Lou Dobbs, and the like), for example, who offer up what we could consider a hyper-prudent response to the ongoing threat.[14] The parasite is a parricide (or a patricide); it announces *from within* the death of the father as master of the house, as the sovereign host, and so the end of hospitality, "in the classic sense."

The difference between a guest and a parasite seems fairly straightforward, and yet Derrida notes that to make the distinction, "you need a law; hospitality, reception, the welcome offered have to be submitted to a basic and limiting jurisdiction." Without the "right to hospitality or the right of asylum . . . a new arrival can only be introduced 'in my home,' in the host's 'at home,' as a parasite, a guest who is wrong, illegitimate, clandestine, liable to expulsion or arrest" (*OH* 59–61). When Dobbs calls for "higher levels of legal immigration," but a crackdown on "illegal immigration," for example, he confirms the need to legislate a distinction, to institute laws that establish a firm division between the welcome guest, who presumably confirms the sovereignty of the host, and the parricidal parasite (8). The difficulty here, however, one of the difficulties, is that this dichotomy cannot hold: the guest, too, is implicated in a kind of parricidal structure.

It is the sovereign right and power of the host, as father/master/head of household, to invite a guest, to welcome a guest into his home. However, as soon as the guest is invited in, the host becomes the guest's hostage, the power of the host is converted into the vulnerability of the hostage. But that is not all: inasmuch as it is the invited guest who first *liberates* the power of his or her host, inasmuch as the power of the host requires the guest in order to take place at all—there is no sovereign host without an invited guest—this conversion happens right away, from the start, even *before* the invitation has been extended. "So it is indeed the master," Derrida writes, "the one who invites, the inviting host, who becomes the hostage—and who really always has been. And the guest, the invited hostage, becomes the one who invites the one who invites, the master of the host. The guest becomes the host's host. The guest (*hôte*) becomes the host (*hôte*) of the host (*hôte*). These substitutions make everyone into everyone else's hostage. Such are the laws of hospitality" (123–25). Whether we are talking about a parasite or a welcome guest, Derrida tells us, hospitality, "in the classic sense," involves hostility: "hospitality, hostility, hostipitality" (45).

This analysis also indicates once again, however, that sovereignty both is and is not a requirement for hospitality. Sovereignty is the condition for hospitality "in the classic sense"—no hospitality without a home to offer; but on the other hand, "pure" or infinite hospitality, if there is such a thing, would be what frustrates or circumvents all sovereignty. In her running commentary on his lecture, Anne Dufourmantelle cites Derrida to signal the aporia:

> "To offer hospitality," he wonders, "is it necessary to start from the certain existence of a dwelling, or is it rather only starting from the dislocation of the shelterless, the homeless, that the authenticity of hospitality can open up? Perhaps only the one who endures the experience of being deprived of a home can offer hospitality." (*OH* 56)

Perhaps only the one who is not *one*, the one who is from the start a function of the substitutive structure implied in infinite responsibility, can offer "pure" hospitality. In other words, perhaps hospitality is offered only by the one who is not so much free to offer up her place as she is originarily displaced, enjoying no home base but instead existing in the mode of giving way, somewhere between being and nonbeing, in the otherwise than being where (where?) hospitality *takes* place, without question and without sovereignty.[15] This sort of substitution does not come down to ability or aptitude, to duty or will, but to a fundamental structure of exposure, a preoriginary homelessness and vulnerability: it comes down to an inability simply to be in oneself or for oneself, an inability not to be infinitely responsible.

But again, the fact that the law is above the laws does not make the latter any less necessary. In the closing pages of *Of Hospitality*, Derrida turns to the biblical story of Lot and his daughters to point up the sort of perversion that becomes possible when the law is not held in check by the laws—when my infinite responsibility to the other is not checked by my (also infinite) responsibility to the "third," to all the other others. The brutal story is well known: The two angels who have come to destroy the city of Sodom agree to stay in Lot's home overnight, to become his guests. That night, as the New International Version puts it, "all the men from every part of the city of Sodom—both young and old—surrounded the house." The men demand that Lot send his guests outside so that they might "have sex with them." (The King James says, so "that we may know them.") What happens next is the demonstration of a most irresponsible, a most inhospitable hospitality: "In order to protect the guests he is putting up *at any price*, as family head and all-powerful father," Lot—who is himself a foreigner in Sodom, a guest there—"offers the men of Sodom his two virgin daughters. They have not yet been 'penetrated' by men" (151). Again, the New International Version:

> Lot went outside to meet them and shut the door behind him and said, "No, my friends. Don't do this wicked thing. Look, I have two daughters who have never slept with a man. Let me bring them out to you, and you can do what you like with them. But don't do anything to these men, for they have come under the protection of my roof." (Genesis 19)

Lot demonstrates infinite responsibility for the Other without consideration for the third party or the moral (politico-ethical) "obligations that link him to his relatives and family, first of all his daughters" (151), Derrida writes. When the law is not conditioned by rights and duties, by justice for all the other others, it morphs into its opposite.

But Derrida is not finished. "Sodomy and sexual difference: the same law of hospitality gives rise to an analogous bargaining," he continues, "a sort of hierarchy of the guests and the hostages, in the famous scene on Mount Ephraim in Judges." The scene of this impossible economics to which Derrida now refers occurs in Judges 23–30: A man agrees to host and give shelter to a pilgrim, his concubine, and his entourage for the night. But when they get settled in, "some wicked men of the city" show up, surround the house, pound on the door, and shout to the owner of the house: "Bring out the man who came to your house so we can have sex with him." The unthinkable bargaining on behalf of the law of hospitality begins again:

> The owner of the house went outside and said to them, "No, my friends, don't be so vile. Since this man is my guest, don't do this disgraceful thing. Look, here is my virgin daughter, and his concubine. I will bring them out to you now, and you can use them and do to them whatever you wish. But to this man, don't do such a disgraceful thing."

The mob doesn't listen, the pilgrim tosses out his concubine, and they rape and abuse her all night, releasing her at dawn. She crawls to the threshold of her master's host, and when the pilgrim finally wakes up, he opens the door and says "'Get up; let's go.' But there was no answer." He hoists her lifeless body onto his donkey, heads for home, and then cuts her into "twelve parts," sending them "into all areas of Israel."

When the infinite obligation to the Other is not checked by the infinite obligation to the "third party," and so is not submitted to justice, it becomes the alibi for a sacrificial exchange in which all the other others are substitutable: daughters for angels, a concubine for a pilgrim, Isaac for Abraham, a ram for Isaac ("a ram for a kid," as Ronell puts it somewhere), and so on. Without the rights and duties that are the conditions for hospitality, the *other* others (disproportionately constituted still today by women, kids, rams—but also, depending on who and where you are, by nonwhites, non-Christians, nonhets, nonjocks, nonhumans, and other "nons") face an unconditional *in*hospitality.[16] To become what it is, unconditional ethical responsibility requires conditional political/legal/moral responsibility; the law needs the laws. And vice versa: without the law of infinite hospitality, the laws serve only the rights of the strongest, the "demographico-economic interests" of the ones most capable of securing them. Justice requires that I keep both the law and the laws, which means, simultaneously, that I break both. Justice requires that I break the law and the laws in an effort to perfect the laws, to extend them and keep them, infinitely. An impossible a-poria: no way, no how.

The aporetic roadblock, however, does not grant me the luxury of couch potato paralysis or political quietism. It is, on the contrary, the opening of what is called the "public sphere"—the space of "genuine" decision, if there is any, where rhetorical reasoning is required. Justice demands decisions urgently, right away, here and now, and in the face of the undecidable, in response to its "No Passage" sign. Indeed, Derrida proposes that "this distinction [between the law and the laws] requires us to determine what could be called, in Kantian language [but with a million caveats] intermediate *schemas*," which would begin by asking: How can one give place to a situated ethics and politics dedicated to an infinite responsibility that remains inaccessible for "structural reasons"? How to intervene "in the condition of hospitality in the name of the unconditional" (*OH* 147, 149)? More specifically for our purposes, how to engage a rhetorical *practice* that embraces and affirms the rhetorical imperative? In "On Cosmopolitanism," the published version of his 1996 address to the International Parliament of Writers, Derrida performs one possible response to these questions. Examining it will allow us to contemplate the place of infinite responsibility in concrete agitations for social justice and so to promote an extended understanding of the "responsibilities of rhetoric."[17]

A Case of Responsible Advocacy

On May 26, 1993, the young Algerian writer Tahar Djaout was brutally assassinated by an Islamic fundamentalist group because, according to one of the assassins, he "wielded a fearsome pen that could have an effect on Islamic sec-

tors" (Mohamad 62). In rapid response to this tragedy, which was only the lat-
est in a shockingly barbaric series in Algeria, more than three hundred writers
from around the world responded by signing a petition supporting the establishment of the International Parliament of Writers (IPW). The IPW met for
the first time in Strasbourg on February 14, 1994—the fifth anniversary of the
fatwa against Salman Rushdie—to establish an executive branch of seven members, which included Rushdie, Jacques Derrida, Pierre Bourdieu, and Christian
Salmon. Its founding task was to create the Network of Cities of Asylum, each
city of which would take in and protect writers threatened by fundamentalist
or totalitarian organizations.

The *fatwa* against Rushdie in 1989, which commanded Muslims world-
wide to execute not only the author of *The Satanic Verses* but also all of those
involved in its publication—*wherever* they were found—had already exposed
the particular vulnerability of writers in a globalized society. Indeed, the IPW's
first two presidents, Rushdie and Wole Soyinka, were hunted for many years by
assassins from Iran and Nigeria, both of which are members of the United Nations. The harsh fact is that "we have gone from censorship of works to the persecution of authors," Salmon writes, "from censored texts to beheadings" ("Parliament" 11). And most chillingly, Salmon continues, censorship "no longer
targets political, religious, or ideological opinions but instead the whole area of
representation. A new crime haunts the night of orthodoxies: the crime of cre-
ating, of writing, or imagining. The crime of literature" (11). The "murderous
persecution" of writers and thinkers "does not constitute the simple violation
of individual rights to opinion and expression," he insists. "The target of such
persecutions is anything in writing that sketches out a different world, different
kinds of relations among people, giving form and voice to the invention of a
different democracy" (11–12).

The state is of almost no help in the face of such privatized targetings since,
as Derrida puts it, "[w]henever the State is neither the foremost author of, nor
the foremost guarantor against the violence which forces refugees or exiles to
flee, it is often powerless to ensure the protection and liberty of its own citizens
before a terrorist menace, whether or not it has a religious or nationalist alibi"
(*OCF* 6). International law, as Hannah Arendt warned decades ago, is also prac-
tically impotent in cases in which the threatening decree neither comes from a
national government nor is restricted to a national territory. Mostly limited to
"reciprocal agreements and treaties between sovereign states," international law
has no real authority over extra-national organizations that choose to ignore

interstate legislation (*Origins* 267–302). So it's about as much help to the endangered writer as it is to other casualties of the nation-state system: refugees, stateless persons, displaced persons. But rather than champion the establishment of some "sphere that is above the nations," a kind of "world government" to oversee and protect the specifically human rights that current international law cannot adequately enforce, the IPW pinned its hopes on the city.[18]

City Limits

Rushdie served as the IPW's first elected president, penning the "Declaration of Independence" that served as its charter and formalized its commitment to an extraordinary collective responsiveness. This "Declaration" is a powerful defense of what Kant had described as a universal cosmopolitan *right*, except that whereas Kant had argued that the "right to visit, to associate, belongs to all men by virtue of their common ownership of the earth's surface" (*Perpetual Peace* 118), Rushdie defends the right of all people to visit both actualized countries and *countries of the imagination*:

> Writers are citizens of many countries: the finite and frontiered country of observable reality and everyday life, the boundless kingdom of the imagination, the half-lost land of memory, the federations of the heart which are both hot and cold, the united states of the mind (calm and turbulent, broad and narrow, ordered and deranged), the celestial and infernal nations of desire, and—perhaps the most important of all our habitations—the unfettered republic of the tongue. (92)

According to Rushdie, writers deserve special protection because they hold open the doors to this heterogeny of countries. "Today, around the world," he writes, "literature continues to confront tyranny—not polemically—but by denying its authority, by going its own way, by declaring its independence." "Our Parliament of Writers," he continues, "exists to fight for oppressed writers and against all those who persecute them and their work, and to renew continually the declaration of independence without which writing is impossible; and not only writing, but dreaming; and not only dreaming, but thought; and not only thought, but liberty itself" (93).

Taking Rushdie's "Declaration" as its charter and its inspiration, the IPW established the International Board for the Cities of Asylum and, in collaboration with the Congress of Local and Regional Authorities of Europe, tasked it with:

drafting a Charter of Cities of Asylum; setting up and running the Network of Cities of Asylum; supplying a list of writers wishing to reside in a participating city to the IPW; and collaborating with the Council of Europe, the participating cities, and writers, to "push forward the analysis of new forms of citizenship, particularly citizenship based on residence, begun by the International Parliament of Writers" (Salmon, "Towards," 134–35).[19] The following year, 1995, the European Charter of Cities of Asylum, which specifies the legal and institutional framework for providing asylum to threatened writers, was adopted by the Council of Europe and approved by the European Parliament.

So both of these official charters were in place and operative when Derrida addressed the IPW in 1996, and yet he refers instead to "a new charter of hospitality." This "new charter," as Derrida describes it, both embraces the IPW's vision for the network and not so subtly challenges the limits and conditions inscribed in both of these official charters. What will interest us here, in this clash of the charters, is twofold: first, the way in which Derrida's call for actual, concrete shifts in the mission of the network affirms the rhetorical imperative, and second, the fact that the "new charter" for which he is advocating requires that the *cities* situate themselves within the tension between the law and the laws, there where decisions take place and so where justice is served (however tentatively and imperfectly).

Without explicit reference to Rusdie's "Declaration," Derrida describes the network's protection of threatened writers not as the end goal but as a path toward a more radically generalized hospitality, asking the IPW to "make an audacious call for a genuine innovation in the history of the right to asylum or the duty to hospitality" (4). Describing the protection of foreign writers as an imperative but preliminary goal of the Network of Cities of Asylum, he insists that its ultimate goal is *not only* to promote new forms of citizenship but to radically "reorient" nation-state politics so that it might eventually protect *not only* foreign writers but any inscriber of the foreign:

> Whether it be the foreigner in general, the immigrant, the exiled, the deported, the stateless or the displaced person, we would ask these new cities of refuge to reorient the politics of the state. We would ask them to transform and reform the modalities of membership by which the city (*cité*) belongs to the state, as in a developing Europe or in international juridical structures still dominated by the inviolable rule of state sovereignty—an intangible rule, or one at least supposed such, which is becoming increasingly precarious and problemantic nonetheless. This should no longer be the ultimate horizon for cities of refuge. (4)

Each of these cities, "when dealing with the related questions of hospitality and refuge," Derrida insists, must find a way to "elevate itself above nation-states or at least free itself from them, in order to become, to coin a phrase in a new and novel way, a *free city*," free to establish itself as a place to which one "could retreat in order to escape from the threat of injustice. Such might be the magnitude of our task," Derrida proposes, "a theoretical task indissociable from its political implementation" (9). Up against a backdrop of dwindling international support for the right to political asylum, he challenges the cities, then, with instituting a new cosmopolitics beyond the sovereignty of nation-states by exercising sovereign rights that they currently do not have in order, ex post facto, to bring those rights into being. Derrida asks the cities to become welcoming sites that operate as autonomously as possible while nonetheless remaining allied to each other according to "forms of solidarity yet to be invented" (4). The ultimate goal of the IPW, according to Derrida's explication of their "new charter," is to actualize a new cosmopolitan solidarity that would far exceed anything Kant could have imagined.

Remaining allied through, and only through, this common "charter of hospitality"—and thus breaking with the nation-state's determinate ties to territorial boundaries, to native soil, and to blood—the network's cities, Derrida proposes, will inscribe new communitarian realities, which it is "our task" to invent and articulate. But this task is no mere utopian fantasy, as the "theoretical or critical reflection it involves," he insists, "is indissociable from the practical initiatives we have already, out of a sense of urgency, initiated and implemented" (4). By 1996, several cities have joined the network; the organized political response to a very specific injustice is already successfully under way. And now, in response to this urgent and prudent response, Derrida calls for further revision and reorganization: in order to protect everything that "sketches out a different world, different kinds of relations among people, giving form and voice to the invention of a different democracy," as Salmon had put it, Derrida charges the cities with carving out such an inscription; he charges them with *becoming* what they are called to protect in order to protect it.

Rushdie's "Declaration" and the network's charter had charged the cities with preparing themselves to take in selected writers—by definition *famous* writers, exiled but identifiable foreigners. And Derrida embraces this charge. However, the victims of "the multiplicity of menaces, of acts of censorship [*censure*] or of terrorism, of persecutions, and of enslavements in all their forms" are "innumerable and nearly always anonymous," Derrida reminds his addressees.

Indeed, even "to cite the best known cases [of state and nonstate persecution] would risk sending the anonymous others back into the darkness from which they find it hard to escape, a darkness which is truly the worst and the condition of all the others" (*OCF* 6). So Derrida zooms in on the broader context of the network's purpose, the infinite responsibility both betrayed and actualized by the establishment of the network, and refuses the famous writer any position of privilege. He instead charges the cities of refuge with becoming cities of *refugees*, with preparing to welcome those "anonymous others" for whom no preparation is adequate.[20]

Formally limiting the hospitality practiced by the network's cities to famous writers who are chosen and invited already removes the "choice" from the realm of decision, and so from the realm of justice. It's in the tension—the unsolvable antinomy—between the conditional and the unconditional, Derrida proposes, that "responsibilities and decisions have to be taken in practice" (*Paper Machine* 66). And he situates the cities right there, in the terrible and traumatizing space of the decision—that is to say, in the space of the undecidable, where no "ultimate horizon," no existing law or precedent can dictate a proper response. Justice requires that one "[c]alculate the risks, yes," Derrida explains, and this calculation requires the public give-and-take of rhetorical reasoning. But it also requires that one not "shut the door on what cannot be calculated, meaning the future and the foreigner," that one not become deaf to the imprudent demand of infinite responsibility that serves as the inspiration for any prudent response: "that's the double law of hospitality. It defines the unstable place of strategy and decision" (67). Derrida's "new charter" calls on the network's cities to occupy this "place of strategy and decision," this place, then, of "negotiation"—which is to say this place of *no place*, since negotiation indicates "the impossibility of stopping, of settling in a position" (*Negotiations* 12). The radically democratic charge Derrida gives to the cities is to remain in a space of constant negotiation between the prudent and the imprudent, to be responsible for calculating and managing the risks, which are numerous and profound, while simultaneously resisting the urge to slam the door on the incalculable, the unmanageable, the foreign(er).

Advocating for Responsible Advocacy

The "new charter" articulates, as an exigency *within* the rhetorical situation, the infinite responsibility to the other(s) and (so) the contra-diction that is the condition for any political or ethical dilemma. Derrida does not call on the cit-

ies to throw open their doors to any and every newcomer but to affirm the limitless responsibility that any condition limits and betrays in order to actualize:

> It is a question of knowing how to transform and improve the law, and of
> knowing if this improvement is possible within an historical space which takes
> place *between* the Law of an unconditional hospitality, offered *a priori* to every
> other, to all newcomers, *whoever they may be*, and *the* conditional laws of a right
> to hospitality, without which *The* unconditional Law of hospitality would be in
> danger of remaining a pious and irresponsible desire, without form and with-
> out potency, and even of being perverted at any moment. (*OCF* 22–23)

What is necessary now, he proposes, is "experience and experimentation." The
experience of these cities "will not only be that which cannot wait, but something which calls for an urgent response, a just response, more just in any case
than the existing law. An immediate response to crime, to violence, and to persecution." However, Derrida also imagines "the experience of cities of refuge
as giving rise to a place (*lieu*) for reflection—for reflection on the questions of
asylum and hospitality—for a new order of law and a democracy to come to
be put to the test (experimentation)" (23). With continued experience and experimentation, perhaps, these "new cities that would be something other than
'new cities'" will contribute to another "idea of cosmopolitanism" (23). That is
the hope.

Occupying the space of strategy and decision, Derrida negotiates between
the conditional hospitality that the network has successfully established and
the unconditional hospitality that must remain its aim and inspiration. He performs a sort of responsible advocacy that, in this case, advocates for preserving the conditions for responsible advocacy: he advocates for exposing and affirming the rhetorical imperative, in the face of which decisions are made and
justice is served (however tentatively and imperfectly). Is it significant for our
purposes, then, that no mention of this "new charter" shows up in the literature
dedicated to the contemporary installations of the original network, that this
call was itself, in a certain sense, too incalculable, too unmanageable for the
IPW to accommodate?

Between 2003 and 2005, the original network was dissolved and reorganized
into two: the Cities of Refuge North America and The International Cities of
Refuge Network (ICORN), and the laudable humanitarian effort undertaken
by both is now formally limited to the threatened writer who applies and is accepted, a *known* foreigner, then, for whom the cities can prepare, and to whom

they can extend their gifts, their site, their shelter, and their cover.[21] What has slipped out of the new networks' charters, almost without a trace—almost—is precisely what Derrida had slipped in a decade before: infinite responsibility, the unconditional "face" of hospitality. Both contemporary networks have now formalized their calculations, inscribing into their founding charters the limits and conditions on which they base their acceptance of any "writer applicant," which indicates that the cities have not (yet) taken up the space of decision. They extend hospitality only to known writers around whom the city's residents can rally without troubling the current political hierarchies—and so without much chance of inscribing new communitarian realities or reorienting the politics of the state. What was once a radical vision has become an admirable and necessary but well-ordered and well-delimited program.[22] So are we to conclude that the notion of infinite responsibility is useless, even a hindrance, when it comes to concrete agitation for social justice? Or, on the contrary, would that be missing a level of potentiality that goes beyond a strictly hermeneutic interpretation of the content of the argument?

That the networks are still thriving today, a decade and a half later, mostly under the radar and despite the wholesale federal crackdowns on municipal hospitality associated with "the war on terror," indicates that they continue somewhat successfully to calculate the risks and negotiate the limits of state sovereignty. That they've managed to hold together in the face of the Patriot Act, the artificial elevation of color-coded threat levels, and the federal challenge to "sanctuary cities," for example, means that the "experience and experimentation" continue, even if the fragile hope associated with Derrida's vision is still in need of protection: the "theoretical task," destitute and vulnerable, awaits refuge in "political implementation." It is, however, alive. In its self-description, ICORN indicates that though it limits itself to "one writer at a time," that is a decision it has taken in the name of all the other writers, with "each writer representing the countless others in hiding, in prison or silenced forever" ("About"). So though "the writer" retains its privileged position, the decisions about which writers to accept are taken against the backdrop of an impossible number of other others, others the networks cannot currently accommodate but to whom, for whom, and in the name of whom they remain responsible. In this sense the "new charter" and Derrida's approach to advocacy were successful.

Responsible advocacy would not aim to prevent or even postpone decisions. By exposing the radical undecidability inherent in the contra-diction, it would aim to make decisions "possible," to rescue the name of decision—and so the future, the "to come"—from the overdetermined and prefabbed "options" delivered up through precedents, rational-critical discourse, and the putatively bounded constraints of any rhetorical context. It would aim to expose and embrace the rhetorical imperative, the infinite obligation to respond that is the condition for decision, and so for ethics and politics—for any public and any rhetorical practice. It is necessary for rhetoricians to study and teach argument and a vast repertoire of rhetorical principles and strategies. But these principles and strategies are dependent upon an altogether *other* sort of rhetorical "situation," which it is also our responsibility to study and to teach. The "responsibilities of rhetoric," involve both a determination to analyze and use the available means of persuasion *and* a willingness to attend—relentlessly, imprudently—to the inessential solidarity that makes rhetorical practice both necessary and possible.

P. S. on Humanism

> If I have a duty [*devoir*]—something owed before any
> debt, before any right—toward the other, wouldn't it then
> also be toward the animal, which is still more other than
> the other human, my brother or my neighbor?
>
> Jacques Derrida, *The Animal that Therefore I Am*

Despite my eagerness to wrap up and get out, I cannot not address directly Levinas's humanism, which is in many ways unique and compelling, but remains a problem nonetheless. According to Levinas, the address that opens the space of the ethical relation takes place—first of all, if not exclusively—among human "brothers." Neither "the animal" nor the "feminine alterity"[1] are capable of the ethical saying that Levinas describes: the former is too stupid to "universalize maxims and drives," and the latter is situated in a preethical zone that lacks the transcendence of language. It's possible to zoom in on Levinas's offensive depictions of both in order to dismiss his notion of ethics, along with the politics it appears to imply. And yet, as Derrida notes in several places, it is not necessary to conflate the "dimension of femininity" with an empirical human being of the "feminine sex" (*A* 44)—indeed in *Totality and Infinity*, Levinas explicitly asks us not to (157–58). The place of "feminine alterity" could be occupied by either partner, male or female, at the threshold of the dwelling place called "home."[2] Furthermore, though the language of E. L. demonstrates a consistent and disappointing allergy to the *elle*, as Derrida puts it in "At This Very Moment," it is not necessary to conclude that Levinasian ethics demonstrates that same allergy.

The question of "the animal" is more problematic, however, in that Levinas himself declares that his notion of ethics arises precisely in the "gap between the animal and the human" (*TI* 149), and he stakes his "entire philosophy"

("Paradox" 172) on the conviction that this "gap" is uncrossable. What exactly constitutes this all-important "gap"? Not the usual suspects. For him, it does not come down to reason or language or "spirit" or culture or the ability to deceive (to pretend to pretend, as Lacan puts it). What it *does* come down to is not nearly so clear in Levinas's texts. In a late interview, however, he leaves open the possibility for "a more specific analysis" of the ethical potential of "the animal," and we will take that as an invitation. Though it will be necessary to examine very carefully what he has to say about this "gap," the primary goal isn't to determine whether "Mr. Levinas" himself operated on certain anthropocentric presumptions (of course, of course); the goal will be to begin the "more specific analysis" that he invites in order both to explicate his conception of this gap and to challenge his conviction that the ethical exigency, the rhetorical imperative he so beautifully exposes, is limited to human relations.

My aim is not to *blur* the difference between "the human" and "the animal" but to point up again something Derrida articulated more than twenty years ago: that "drawing an oppositional limit *itself* blurs the difference, the *différance* and the differences, not only between man and animal, but among animal societies—there are an infinite number of animal societies, and within animal societies and within human society itself, so many differences" ("On Reading" 183). That is, to deconstruct this opposition is not to reduce all living creatures to an undifferentiated homogeneity but, as Geoffrey Bennington puts it, to allow "absolutely singular configurations" to become events (55). To that end, we'll embrace the *play of differences* that are effaced by this rude and crude dichotomy ("the human"/"the animal") and attempt to demonstrate that it is necessary for rhetorics of the saying to move beyond it.

"The last Kantian in Nazi Germany"

In an essay in *Difficult Freedom* called "The Name of a Dog, or Natural Rights," Levinas describes the dehumanization he and his seventy prisonmates suffered in forestry commando unit number 1492, a camp for Jewish POWs in Nazi Germany where Levinas was held captive from 1940–1945. The guards, along with "the children and women who passed by and sometimes raised their eyes," Levinas writes,

> stripped us of our human skin. We were subhuman, a gang of apes. A small inner murmur, the strength and wretchedness of persecuted people, reminded us of our essence as thinking creatures, but we were no longer part of the world.

Our comings and goings, our sorrow and laughter, illnesses and distractions, the work of our hands and the anguish of our eyes, the letters we received from France and those accepted for our families—all that passed in parenthesis. We were beings entrapped in their species; despite all our vocabulary, beings without language. Racism is not a biological concept; anti-Semitism is the archetype of all internment. Social aggression, itself, merely imitates this model. It shuts people away in a class, deprives them of expression and condemns them to being "signifiers without a signified" and from there to violence and fighting. How can we deliver a message about our humanity which, from behind the bars of quotation marks, will come across as anything other than monkey talk? (153)

Immediately following this provocative and heart-wrenching paragraph, Levinas introduces a small gift of hope and life, a gift the prisoners named "Bobby":

And then, about halfway through our long captivity, for a few short weeks, before the sentinals chased him away, a wandering dog entered our lives. One day he came to meet this rabble as we returned under guard from work. He survived in some wild patch in the region of the camp. But we called him Bobby, an exotic name, as one does with a cherished dog. He would appear at morning assembly and was waiting for us as we returned, jumping up and down and barking in delight. For him, there was no doubt that we were men. (153)

Simultaneously touching and offensive, this little story offers some sense not only of the scandalously crushing conditions the prisoners endured but also of Emmanuel Levinas's anthropocentrism.

Levinas's tender depiction of this "cherished dog" suggests that he is the sole creature willing to welcome "this rabble" without discrimination, the singular "existent"[3] willing to testify, enthusiastically, to the irreducible value of the other. And yet, Levinas reads Bobby's welcoming reception as confirmation of the very human/subhuman dichotomy that underwrites the tragic politics of the camp, as confirmation, that is, of a troublingly simplistic opposition between mere creatures and "*thinking* creatures" endowed with language. As John Llewelyn suggests, Levinas would consider it crucial to discern whether "Bobby merely barks or whether in doing so he can say *Bonjour*" (*Middle Voice* 56). And it seems clear that for Levinas, Bobby's greeting, which comes from "deep within a life called animal," as Derrida has put it (*Animal* 12), testifies not to an ethical responsiveness but to the fact that the prisoners are *men*—and not subhuman, like a "gang of apes," or a pack of dogs.[4] Levinas considers Bobby's "barking in delight" to be a kind of "monkey talk," not a true greeting but a citation of one (as if *"Bonjour"* were not itself, each time, already a citation). Despite his articulations of gratitude and affection, Levinas does not consider this canine refugee to be capable of an *ethical* relation in his particular sense of that term.

Instead, this exemplary relation between man and "the friend of man" confirms for him the inherently (and inestimably) higher value of the human (152), which seems for a second to be grounded in the capacity to cogitate:

> Perhaps the dog that recognized Ulysses beneath his disguise on his return from the Odyssey was a forebear of our own. But no, no! There, they were in Ithaca and the Fatherland. Here, we were nowhere. This dog was the last Kantian in Nazi Germany, without the brain needed to universalize maxims and drives. He was a descendent of the dogs of Egypt. And his friendly growling, his animal faith, was born from the silence of his forefathers on the banks of the Nile. (153)

The Kantian descriptor is significant and cuts both ways. Insisting on the moral duty of human kindness, Immanuel Kant concerned himself with neighborliness and the fundamental capacity of humankind to abide those of their own species—even, perhaps, to abide the inhabitants of different planets.[5] In any case, Kant introduced into philosophical contemplation a somewhat alien notion of moral law, which—despite Kant's own racism and sexism—challenges long-held prejudices by extending the status of moral agency to "all rational beings," perhaps welcoming even women into the moral landscape.[6] So to align Bobby with Kant in this way is to suggest, it seems, that this "wandering dog" displayed a similarly transcendent neighborliness. And yet, to propose in the second half of the very same sentence that Bobby lacks the brain power needed to "universalize maxims and drives" is to slap him (back) into alignment with the *mere* creatures, to situate him again on the wrong side of a devastatingly indivisible line that Kant leaves intact.

According to Levinas, this "cherished dog" both was and was not a Kantian. He greeted the prisoners with generosity and enthusiasm, in a way that attested to their existence and value, and yet he did so stupidly, as he himself was without the capacity for reason that grounds Kant's sense of ethical action.[7] You might object that Levinasian ethics is not reducible to Kantian ethics, and you would be correct to do so.[8] For Kant, ethics is a very conscious and purely reasoned obligation to other rational beings that depends upon an originary freedom (to do one's duty) and that requires the capacity to universalize maxims in order to arrive at categorical imperatives.[9] But for Levinas ethics does not depend upon a prior freedom (on the contrary), nor does it begin at the level of conscious decision or logical contemplation; it involves an expropriating (rhetorical) relation—an imperative to respond—that precedes comprehension and interrupts cognition. Levinas allows for no logical limits to the subject's responsibility for the other: "The debt increases in the measures that it is paid" (*OTB* 12). Nor does he allow for reciprocal limits: "[T]he way in which my 'I' is an I is something utterly singular in the world. And therefore *I* am responsible, and may not be concerned about whether the other is responsible for me." The absolute dissymmetry between the "I" and all the others is a "truth" Levinas acknowledges lifting from Dostoevsky. "It is his great truth: 'We are all guilty in everything in respect to all others, and I more than all the others.' This last 'I more than all the others' is the important thing here," Levinas writes, "even if it means in a certain sense to be an idiot" (*IR* 133). An idiot. So it may be tempting to consider Bobby's allegedly deficient brainpower a nonissue for Levinas; that, however, would be a mistake.[10]

Bobby vs. the Idiot

No one has explored the connection between responsibility and idiocy (or nonunderstanding) more poignantly than Dostoevsky does in *The Idiot*, and no one has explored Dostoevsky's explorations through a Levinasian frame more brilliantly than Avital Ronell does in the fourth chapter of *Stupidity*, "The Disappearance and Returns of the Idiot." Honing in on an excessive responsibility that exceeds intentionality and hovers close to the extinction of consciousness, Ronell reads Prince Myshkin as an exemplar of ethical substitution, of being-for-the-other. What will most interest us in this reading is the undeniable similarity between the prince and the pooch, specifically in their displays of sacrificial readiness. Myshkin, Ronell writes, demonstrates "a readiness of pure exposure" reminiscent of "Abrahamic sacrifice: the sheer 'Here I am' in response to the invasive demand. But Abraham answers to God, whereas the Prince will answer to anyone." Myshkin, like Bobby, stands ready to respond without discrimination, without contemplation, without calculation. "He stands as his own lamb, ever prepared for slaughter. He stands ready, a figure of latent presence" (211). This ready stance, furthermore, indicates a problem of timing, "of when this immemorial sacrifice could take place, at what time and in whose place."

Is it possible for readiness to adhere to a concept of belatedness, a slow resumption of what has already taken place? The slaughter for which the Prince
stands ready could occur only after the prime of sacrificial epochality, when
the dignity of the offering is nearly lost on everyone and can hardly be made
in tribute to the big Other. Stripped of sacrificial grandeur, the sacrificial readiness has been somehow discounted, which is why we are faced with an idiot
and not a prophet, or a poet, or even a philosopher (the gap is admittedly closing). (211)

The difference between the "Here I am" of Abraham and the "Here I am" of
Myshkin is one of dignity and self-possession. Whereas the prophet restricted
his sacrificial responsiveness, holding out for the Almighty's command, the
Idiot offers himself up to anyone, anywhere, as if the sacrifice has always already occurred, without economic exchange (no ram shows up) and immemo-
rially—as if the best he can do is to testify to it with an unchecked exuberance
roughly analogous to "jumping up and down and barking in delight."

Significantly, neither Bobby's nor Myshkin's extraordinary responsiveness
can be attributed to the stamina that accompanies great health. On the contrary, Bobby is shelterless and "wandering." And Myshkin is chronically ill,
acutely aware of the irreparable claims body has upon him: "there is no phase
of attestable overcoming," Ronell writes, "for the disease, experienced in the
mode of silent chronicity, is always with the Idiot, even where it refrains from
proposing signs and symptoms or ceases to substitute itself for perception and
mime consciousness." An epileptic, "he walks about, ever in anticipation of an
attack." Ronell proposes that "idiocy and epilepsy reinforce each other in the
novel, as if to emphasize the impossible separation of domains, notably, where
the body ends" (182–83). However, his illness is not the point so much as the
pointer: "illness, if that is what it is, exhorts the body to reveal something of
itself," Ronell writes. Her analysis articulates a significant insight about the corporeal constraints of cognitive prowess: where body starts, knowledge stops,
desists, leaves off. That is to say, body, the animal life upon which any capacity
for knowing would depend, is also the end of knowing, where "knowing" encounters it abysses. Nonknowledge defines body, any body, even "your" body.

It's necessary to read this in at least two ways. First, that you cannot know
"your" body: "there is no epistemological stronghold, no scientific comfort or
medical absolute by which to grasp your body once and for all, as if it were
ever merely itself, once and for all" (S 180). And second, from the flip side,
that body does not operate on knowledge. As Nancy puts it in "Corpus," "the

body does not know; but it is not ignorant, either. Quite simply, it is elsewhere. It is from elsewhere, another place, another regime, another register, which is not even that of an 'obscure' knowledge, or a 'pre-conceptual' knowledge, or a 'global,' or 'immediate' knowledge" (199). Though body may think (and thinking may *be* a body) Nancy muses, "thought does not belong to the order of knowledge" (201).

So though "[i]diocy materializes itself in a kind of negative corporeal stylization," Ronell writes, "it points to the generality of a human predicament: idiocy has something to do with the nearly existential fact of being stuck with a body" (*S* 180). Your material incarnation is the site of a passivity more ancient than the active/passive dichotomy; it's the condition for your exposure, your susceptibility, your vulnerability—and therefore for your responsivity. This is Levinas's singular insight: it is precisely to the extent that you are a bodily creature that you are both an ethical subject and "in a certain sense an idiot." Ethics involves "a responsibility not resting on any free commitment," Levinas writes, "that is, a responsibility without freedom, a responsibility of the creature; a responsibility of one who comes too late in being to avoid supporting it in its entirety" ("Substitution" 91). Once again, Levinas calls this responsibility of the creature "human fraternity itself" (*OTB* 116). Nonmortal beings—fairies, elves, gods, Enlightenment subjects—have nothing to do with Levinasian ethics, which is grounded, first of all, in corporality, in an immediate exposure, "such that irritability, susceptibility or exposedness to wounds and outrage characterizes its passivity, more passive still than the passivity of affects" (*OTB* 108).[11]

Body is the site of proximity, where "the subject is reached or touched without the mediation of the logos," Levinas writes (121). There is no logic or representational power that could catch up to this immediate (as in nonmediated) contact, which amounts to "an unconditional *Yes* . . . a *Yes* older than naive spontaneity" ("Substitution" 93; see also *OTB* 121). Proximity leaves *any* creature somewhat stupid—transcendentally stupid, as Ronell puts it—ultimately deficient, flawed, wanting, at least by Enlightenment standards, and there is no way to examine this stupidity "apart from the subject accredited by the Enlightenment" (*S* 19). Corporeality is the ungrounding ground of Levinasian ethics, which would seem to bode well for Bobby.

But that is not the case, at least not from Levinas's perspective. In a late interview, for example, he defines creatureliness as "pure being," emphasizing that "the human" is defined by its capacity to break with its animal impulses:

[W]hat I want to emphasize is that the human breaks with pure being, which is always a persistence in being. This is my principal thesis. A being is something that is attached to being, to its own being. That is Darwin's idea. The being of animals is a struggle for life. A struggle for life without ethics. It is a question of might. . . . However, with the appearance of the human—and this is my entire philosophy—there is something more important than my life, and that is the life of the other. That is unreasonable. Man is an unreasonable animal. ("Paradox" 172)

So in contradiction to the entire history of Western philosophy (save Heidegger), Levinas proposes that man is *not* the "rational animal." It is obviously of some consequence whether "the life of the other"—the life that is more important to "the human" than that human's own life—refers to *any* other or only to another *human* other, but more on that below. For now, let's stick to the "break" that grounds Levinas's "entire philosophy." He has announced it before. Indeed, some twenty years prior to this interview, Levinas proposes in *Totality and Infinity* that the "gap between the animal and the human"—even, presumably, between the canine and the idiot—comes down to this: whereas the animal lives complacently *in itself*, the specifically human animal is "capable of living for the Other and of *being* on the basis of the Other who is exterior to him" (149).[12] Being-for-the-other, according to Levinas, is a strictly human predicament, but it is not a function of logical reasoning. Self-sacrificing generosity is not logical; at least from a Darwinian perspective, it makes no sense. The sacrificial readiness that breaks with "pure being" is attributable neither to practical reason nor to "pure reason," as Kant would have it, but to a responsibility prior to freedom that any idiot would have in spades—but that for some reason (it's still not clear why) not a single nonhuman animal would have *at all*.

"Noted for his graciousness and courtesy," Prince Myshkin simultaneously demonstrates a certain "social defenselessness," Ronell notes. He "caves without cowering, folds or bows according to an exigency that disrupts any priority of self"; indeed, "the profusion of courtesies offers up a sense of destitution that he embodies before the other." When the prince is "laughed at," he laughs along with his persecutors, admitting that he would have done the same thing in their place. "Precisely," Ronell adds. "Without the intention or means of dispossessing his addressees, he is in their place, always, without exception." To the extent that he puts himself in the place of the other, Ronell proposes, "the Idiot signals an exemplary instance of Kantian ethicity," though the ethical duty is hyperbolized almost immediately by the detection of an even more radical passivity than the subjection to "pure reason":

> Despite it all, Myshkin, even in the ultimate scene of blank stupor, is maintained as the guarantor of unbreachable responsibility. Caressing the murderer in an effort to soothe him, Myshkin displays what it means to be responsible for the other, devoted to the other, even unconsciously, without "doing": it is an action without doing, an ethically maintained passivity. He slips into the other's anguish. Putting the self in place of another necessarily implies, for the modern subject, a rupture in identity, a self-departure or significant interruption; however, the Idiot's manner of consistently extenuating himself before the other points to something else. His place has been designated from the start as being open to displacement, marked as it is by the apparent contingency of random encounter. . . . [H]e keeps himself insistently out of place, with no place of his own, always at once host to the other and also, oddly, retaining the bearing of docile guest. (205)

Both host and hostage to the other, the prince is not so much free to offer up his place as he is originarily displaced; despite his wealth and station, he enjoys no home base but instead "exists" in the mode of giving way. The substitution attributed to Myshkin does not come down to ability or aptitude or will but to a fundamental homelessness and vulnerability, an *inability* simply to be in himself or for himself. And Bobby? According to Levinas's category distinction, whereas the prince's soothing caresses indicate that he has slipped "into the other's anguish," the pooch's "barking in delight" can only indicate that he is, in himself, delighted.

Prince Myshkin embraces his irreparable deficiency without hesitation or limitation, demonstrating an exorbitant responsibility without freedom and unconstrained by empirical guilt or capacity. Ever poised for the sacrifice, Myshkin answers to anyone—"Here I am"—and apologizes to everyone: "Being an idiot means always having to say you're sorry," Ronell writes (215). "A sorry being," he apologizes even to those who persecute him, absorbing injury and assuming responsibility, because, "having no understanding," he could *not* have been responsible, could *not* have acted responsibly:

> The logic is awry: he is the cause because, in the end, there's no possible way for him to have been the cause—he can't help it, he didn't understand, he was almost an idiot. Because he cannot take responsibility as a conscious, sufficient subject, because he cannot be present to a task the failure of which he stands accused, he is responsible for it all. The idiot has to apologize for everything because there is nothing for which he is not responsible. The judgment has

already been made prior to any act, and it orders the idiot to live by the purity of an irreversible prejudice. Precisely because I, as an idiot, cannot be a fully responsible being, precisely because my consciousness is punctured, I must and do take full responsibility. I take responsibility for the darkness, the lapse, the fever, and the delirium. This is why, always and ever, "I am sorry." (216)

It is because "he cannot take responsibility as a conscious, sufficient subject" that he must take *full* responsibility for everything and for everyone. Responsibility precedes empirical evidence of guilt: he is responsible (even) for not being able to be responsible.

Significantly, however, the entire weight of the idiot's ethical liability hinges, Ronell points out, on the opening provided by the "almost":

> In order to say he is sorry, [Myshkin] has had to refer to himself as someone who was *almost* an idiot, which modifies the accusers' sentence. The "almost" is what engages the absolute; it is only because he was almost an idiot that he assumes absolute responsibility. If he had been a total idiot, as we now freely say, he would have been home free as concerns the assumption of ethical liability. The rhetorical force that renders him a responsible subject lies within the "almost"—the crevice or opening that allows for consciousness and decision. (217)

It's because he was *almost* an idiot that "there can be no refuge, no ducking out as concerns the reach and breach of ethicity," Ronell writes. "It is because he posits himself as having been almost an idiot that he can—he must—take total responsibility" (217). This "almost" marks the gap between a mere creature defined by react-ability and a thinking creature defined by response-ability. The specifically ethical relation requires some sliver of "consciousness and decision": you at least have to *know* you're not measuring up. And that already requires that you be able to grasp *that* there is an infinite demand, that it is addressed to "you," and that no one can respond in your place.[13]

It seems that, for Levinas, what separates the "thinking creatures" from the mere creatures is this *conscious* inability to ignore the obligation, this *conscious* inability to be unresponsive, indifferent, spontaneous. In other words, Levinas's line in the sand, a line that holds even if the thinking creature should turn out to be "in a certain sense an idiot," is drawn at the capacity to *experience* the rhetorical imperative. Without the experience of the obligation, there can be no ethics but only the mechanistic deployment of programming. Levinas *presumes* that this experience is uniquely human, so Bobby is not, for him, the last Kantian in Nazi Germany; he is, rather, a crude imitation, a "cherished dog" *aping* the last Kantian. "There is a proto-ethical moment in his gestures," Matthew Calarco writes, "but no ethics or politics proper" (58). Or, as David Clark puts it, "although he looks like a Kantian and sounds like a Kantian, and has a humanizing effect on the prisoners that is explicitly called Kantian, he is *not* Kantian. How could he be? '[T]he dog is a dog. Literally a dog!'" (88). Levinas does insist that "there is a transcendence in the animal!" (152); however, that transcendence involves not the animal's singularity of expression, *kath 'auto,* but his or her capacity to testify to "the freedom and singularity of the human" (Calarco 58)—which itself depends upon the presumption of this scandalously indivisible line between the mere creature and the thinking creature.

Let me say that I'm not convinced that the experience of the rhetorical imperative (*as* an imperative) is unique to human creatures. It's not clear to me that Bobby's delighted barking demonstrates an "animal complacency in oneself" or that his barking and wagging are any more reducible to "signifiers without a signified" than any other speech act. No anthropomorphizing is required, I don't think, to suspect that this homeless creature's determination to show up for the prisoners—both to greet them warmly in the morning and to welcome them back enthusiastically in the evening—may indicate that he is "capable of living for the Other and of *being* on the basis of the Other who is exterior to him" (*TI* 149). As Peter Atterton observes, "Bobby's 'friendly barking' is in response to the encounter with the Other who is Levinas himself in this instance" (57). Why insist—and with such certitude, basing an "entire philosophy" on it—that no nonhuman animals consciously *assume* a responsibility to the Other, not even "to their offspring or to humans they guard or guide," Llewelyn adds (*Middle* 57)? Why is it necessary that the conscious assumption of this responsibility prior to freedom, of this obligation to "the life of the other," be absolutely unique to the so-called human animal?

Instances of domestic and wild animals performing what appear to be spectacular (contrary both to instinct and to logic) acts of self-sacrificing generosity are well documented: a grown leopard protecting an infant baboon it just orphaned, a crow providing food and protection for a feral kitten, an elephant holding vigil 24/7 for a beloved dog recovering from surgery, a chimpanzee trying to help an injured bird fly away, a rescued Greyhound taking it upon herself to welcome and nurture every wounded mammal admitted to a wildlife sanctuary, and so on. Accounts of all sorts of so-called lower animals saving humans, often at their own peril, are as numerous. As George A. Kennedy noted in "A Hoot in the Dark: The Evolution of General Rhetoric," a seminal essay that should also have been pathbreaking, "biologists frequently describe some animals as demonstrating 'altruism,' meaning a concern for others expressed through protecting them at their own risk, grooming them, or assisting them in gaining food" (11). Evidence of animal "altruism"—not only in primates but also in rats, birds, dogs, elephants, dolphins, and so on—abounds in biology, psychology, ethology, zoology, and primatology.[14] It's hardly contestable today, even if the term "altruism" is a somewhat misleading descriptor for this response-ability that Levinas describes as a "persecution," an unrelenting obligation to respond to the call of the Other.

So what's at stake in this move to shut animals "away in a class," to deprive "them of expression," and to condemn "them to being 'signifiers without a signified'"? What is at stake, in Clark's words, "in Levinas's desire to seal Bobby up in the prison of his species, lest he say more or do more than what is anthropocentrically allotted him"? "For what is Bobby doing," Clark continues, "when, by Levinas's own account, he so gaily greets the prisoners and recognizes them as 'other,' that is, as 'men'? More: what is 'language' if it is not the wagging of a tail, and 'ethics' if it is not the ability to greet one [an]other and to dwell together *as* others?" (90–91).

Le Visage du Chien

You might imagine that even if Levinas cannot accept Bobby as an ethical subject obeying the rhetorical imperative, the infinite obligation to respond, he will at the very least grant that an ethical subject would be responsible to and for Bobby. Given Levinas's insistence that my responsibility to the other is radically nonreciprocal, he should at least grant that "the life of the other," which is more important to "the human" than that human's own life, could be a nonhuman other—a "cherished dog," for example. But that does not appear to be the case, either (and just to be clear: if Bobby cannot be an Other in Levinas's scheme of things, neither can he be a "third party"). There is no indication that Levinas, the thinker par excellence of the address as such, receives Bobby's greeting *as* an address, as an address that requires a response or that calls one to one's responsibility. There is no indication, that is, that Bobby's own vulnerability and destitution provoke in Levinas an interruption of self and an obligation to respond, a sense of responsibility to this displaced creature who is ultimately "chased away" from the partial shelter of a "wild patch" inside the camp.[15] Why not? Because—and here begins the circular reasoning—Bobby's "face" is not *human*, because it is at the very most a secondary face, a face that shows up only analogously, as a weak reflection of the human face.

For Levinas, there are "things," which require linguistic cover to have any significance at all, and then there is "the face of the Other," which expresses its own significance, *kath 'auto*, by shedding all representational form and therefore calling me and my sense of spontaneity and self-sufficiency into question. This is pretty much an either/or for Levinas, he offers no other possibility, so nonhuman animals will have to line up with the rocks or with the faces.[16] In a 1986 interview, graduate students from the University of Warwick asked Levinas, straight up, which is it? "But is there something distinctive about the human face which, for example, sets it apart from that of an animal?" And Levinas equivocates:

> One cannot entirely refuse the face of an animal. It is via the face that one understands, for example, a dog. Yet the priority here is not found in the animal, but in the human face. We understand the animal, the face of an animal, in accordance with *Dasein*. The phenomenon of the face is not in its purest form in the dog. In the dog, in the animal, there are other phenomena. For example, the force of nature is pure vitality. It is more this which characterizes the dog. But it also has a face. (169)

Levinas here adopts a Heideggerian middle ground, situating "the animal" between the stone and man.[17] So Bobby, for example, appears to line up with the faces, but only after a distinction is made between primary and secondary faces, and only after the face has suddenly, inexplicably, become a "phenomenon." The face is what primarily characterizes "the human," but it is only secondarily what characterizes "the animal," which therefore only *sort of* has a face, a face which cannot be "entirely" refused. What primarily characterizes "the animal" is not its face but its animality, its "pure being" or "pure vitality," from which "the human" by definition breaks. But if, in my encounter with the face of the Other, what calls to me and commands me is precisely that other's corporeal exposedness and inassimilable otherness—its finitude—why would this call be less compelling coming in from so-called pure corporeality? If what calls to me in the other's face is not a power or capability—not the power to speak or the capacity to think—but precisely a not being able to not suffer, a vulnerability and destitution, a "possibility without power," as Derrida puts it

(*Animal* 28), then wouldn't this call come in all the more intensely from what Levinas insists on calling a "pure vitality"? Apparently not: "The absolutely foreign alone can instruct me. And the absolutely foreign can only be man," Levinas writes (TI 73).

The interviewers try again: "According to your analysis, the commandment 'Thou shalt not kill' is revealed by the human face; but is the commandment not also expressed in the face of an animal? Can an animal be considered as the other that must be welcomed? Or is it necessary to possess the possibility of speech to be a 'face' in the ethical sense?" And this time Levinas's response is even more puzzling because now, contrary to everything he has said since *Totality and Infinity*, he situates the face in a rhetoric of rights: "I cannot say at what moment you have the right to be called 'face'" (171). He then reinforces the previous ambiguity: "The human face is completely different and only afterwards do we discover the face of an animal. I don't know if a snake has a face. I can't answer that question. A more specific analysis is needed" (172). Proposing that what attracts us to a dog is perhaps "his child-like character," Levinas again shifts the relation with the animal out of ethical territory. The interviewers respond astutely by sharpening the focus of their question, which is also our question: "If animals do not have faces in an ethical sense, do we have obligations towards them? And if so, where do they come from?" Levinas responds:

> It is clear that, without considering animals as human beings, the ethical extends to all living beings. We do not want to make an animal suffer needlessly and so on. But the prototype of this is human ethics. Vegetarianism, for example, arises from the transference to animals of the idea of suffering. The animal suffers. It is because we, as human, know what suffering is that we can have this obligation. (172)

So the face of a nonhuman animal does not itself issue to me the invitation to respond nor the command "you shall not kill"; it is only by analogy, by an identification that comes down to an anthropomorphism, that one can experience responsibility toward a nonhuman animal. This is problematic on so many levels that it is difficult to catch enough traction to respond. Everything Levinas has said up to this point about the face describes it as that which interrupts any possibility for identification or analogy. So if "the animal" has a face by a certain analogical movement grounded in the encounter with the face of "the human," then the animal does not have a face in Levinas's sense of the term; in fact, the *human* does not have a face in Levinas's sense of the term. Either the clean opposition Levinas is pushing between "the animal" and "the human" is bogus or else—or else: Levinas's entire ethics of the face is bogus. My aim is to suggest the former.

It would be one thing if Levinas were simply contradicting himself here, but it's not that simple. Indeed, in "The Ethical Importance of Being Human," Pat J. Gehrke argues that "Levinas is more than consistent to be skeptical about the face of the dog or the snake and to claim that all ethical responsibilities for the nonhuman other emerge only as resultant of the uniquely human ethics that is before all being" (435). Though I can't do it justice here, Gehrke's argument runs something like this: for Levinas "only in the other human can a trace of the Infinite Otherness shatter being-for-itself" (433); "the human" is for Levinas "separated and bound in a fraternity of alterity before there is any organizing principle, idea, or shared quality that would create the species or the genus" (434); and so "the only *esse* of the human is responsibility, and this essence precedes all ontological characteristics. Responsibility is prior even to consciousness and being," Gehrke continues, "but it is the hallmark of human being" (435). In this short essay, Gehrke manages to articulate the internal coherence of Levinas's particular style of humanism. And yet, a nagging question remains: Why then is it not within the realm of possibility, no way no how, to describe an animal, any animal not classified as *Homo sapiens*—say, Bobby—as "human" in Levinas's sense? If "the human" precedes "all ontological characteristics" and so any possibility of genus-species analytics, why is it out of the question that an existent later classified as a different species might indeed be "separated and bound in a fraternity [or sorority?] of alterity" that precedes and exceeds that classification? There is no internal contradiction here precisely because the category of "the human" is, despite it all, restricted to *Homo sapiens* from the start. Gehrke is surely correct that a humanist perspective rules Levinas's philosophy from the ground up; his anthropocentric blindspot is the size of a Mack truck. But then again, whose isn't?

If there is any legitimacy to what Levinas calls "face," and if "the animal" has a face *at all*, even a little bit, then it could not have been acquired secondarily by analogy to whatever it is that Levinas calls "the human," itself based, top to bottom, on a simple opposition to "the animal." Clark proposes, for example, that "Bobby's face cannot be entirely refused, not because there is something residually 'human' or 'prehuman' about it, but precisely because of its nonhuman excess, because that face, screened though it is through Levinas's axiomatic discourse, constitutes a 'yes' that is not a 'yes,' a 'yes,' belonging uniquely to the animal, to *this* animal, and given freely to the human prisoners" (91). That is, Bobby's "yes," which is not the *word* "yes," comes in, as Derrida says with a different animal in mind, from the "wholly other, more other than any other, which *they* call an animal" (*Animal* 11). Neither inertly thing-like nor complacently in himself, Bobby *faces* those "exterior" to him, greets them, in short *regards* them: both acknowledges and demonstrates concern for them. And yet, even when Levinas offers an account of Bobby in "The Name of a Dog," he takes no account of the fact that *this* animal addresses him, responds to him, and therefore calls to him, obligating him.

The Pooch and the Pussycat

In *The Animal That Therefore I Am,* Derrida proposes that there are "two types of discourse, two positions of knowledge, two grand forms of theoretical or philosophical treatise regarding the animal." The first type, with which we are all familiar, is "signed by people who have no doubt seen, observed, analyzed, reflected on the animal, but who have never been *seen* by the animal. Their gaze has never intersected with that of an animal directed at them." Or else, if they had been "seen furtively by the animal one day, they took no (thematic, theoretical, or philosophical) account of it" (13). That is, the disturbance of the encounter, of an animal other *looking back,* did not register *as* a disturbance for these thinkers. Levinas: "Someone rang, and there is no one at the door: did anyone ring?" ("Phenomenon" 66). The thinkers of this first type of discourse on "the animal" either have never been disturbed by *being seen* by an animal or else they did not wish to "retain" the disturbance. "They neither wanted nor had the capacity to draw any systematic consequence," Derrida writes, "from the fact that an animal could, facing them, look at them, clothed or naked, and in a word, without a word, *address* them . . . from down there, from a wholly other origin" (13). For such an "experience"—if we can call it that—would surely have "obliged them to recognize, at the moment of address," Derrida proposes, "that this was their affair, their lookout [*que cela les regardait*]" (14). And it was maybe Levinas's affair most of all, or it is at least tempting to think so, since he is the one who assumed responsibility for producing so moving and concrete a rhetoric of the saying, of the address as such.

The second type of discourse on the animal, Derrida says, would be signed by poets or prophets "who admit to taking upon themselves the address that an animal addresses to them"; however, he knows of "no *statutory representation*" of this second type. It is instead his intention to offer one, to follow the traces of this "wholly other they call 'animal'" (14).[18] To this end, Derrida describes an encounter with "the absolute other," an encounter that takes place every morning when his "little cat"—not a figural cat but "a real cat, truly, believe me, a little cat" (6)—follows him into the bathroom to request breakfast but then "demands to leave said bathroom as soon as it (or she) sees me naked, ready for everything and resolved to make her wait" (13). Derrida's insistence that "it is a real cat" and not a conceptual generality is meant to "mark its unsubstitutable singularity," the fact that he is trying to talk, obviously in figures and concepts, about a mortal being that cannot be reduced to a figure or concept:

> When it responds to its name (whatever "respond" means, and that will be our question), it doesn't do so as the exemplar of a species called "cat," even less so of an "animal" genus or kingdom. It is true that I identify it as a male or female cat. But even before that identification, it comes to me as this irreplaceable living being that one day enters my space, into this place where it can encounter me, see me, even see me naked. (9)

When Derrida describes this living being as "a real cat," he is citing chapter eleven from Lewis Carroll's *Through the Looking Glass*, which consists of a single sentence: "And it really *was* a kitten, after all." Or, as a French translation puts it: "and, after all, it really was a little black pussycat" (*Animal* 7). So when Derrida wants to point to an "irreplaceable living being," to that which exceeds language's awesome powers of representation—he cites the language of another, in this case a poet who is no longer living or responding. And, if I may now cite Ronell, "this is by no means an atypical gesture" (*CW* 29).[19] All signifying utterances are defined by this power of repetition in alterity, by their capacity to be ripped from one context and remixed or repurposed in another: a sign that could only be used once would not be a sign. Speech is essentially repeatable, as Derrida never stops repeating, and even what is said only once, only here and only now, is made possible by its repeatability, which is to say by its impurity. There is not first of all an intentional subject saying what she means and meaning what she says in the present, and then the rush of impurities, deviations, and delays brought on by writing. The speaking subject is already an effect of iterability and so of repeatability—that is, of a kind of imitation or simulation. If "monkey talk" involves speaking from "behind the bars of quotation marks," then that is one more thing that humans share with monkeys. Signifiers point to other signifiers and not to signifieds; after Derrida, few understand the implications of that better than Levinas, which makes the dichotomy that he marks over and over in "The Name of a Dog" all the more puzzling. And all the more disappointing.

Though we can't be certain, Derrida tells us, that he is not perversely inscribing his "whole talk within a reading of Lewis Carroll" (7), he nonetheless insists that "my real cat is not Alice's little cat," is not the cat "who speaks in *Alice in Wonderland*" (8, 7). Why? Because Derrida is "not about to conclude, upon wakening, as Alice did, that one cannot speak with a cat on the pretext that it doesn't reply or that it always replies the same thing. Everything that I am about to entrust to you," he writes, "no doubt comes back to asking you to *respond* to me, you, to me, reply to me concerning what it is to *respond*. If you can. The said question of the said animal in its entirety comes down to knowing not whether the animal speaks but whether one can know what *respond* means. And how to distinguish a response from a reaction" (8).

In chapter twelve of *Through the Looking Glass,* Alice complains that whatever you say to kittens, their reply is always the same: they purr. They don't help you out by purring for "yes" and mewing for "no," or by following any other sort of rule. Because they always purr, you can never be sure whether a kitten's purr means "yes" or "no." "But how *can* you talk with a person," Alice asks, "if they always say the same thing?" According to her (and to Descartes), you're wasting your time speaking to an animal because it doesn't really reply—"not really, not ever," Derrida adds. But "isn't Alice's credulity rather incredible? She seems, at this moment at least, to believe that one can in fact discern and decide between a human *yes* and *no*. She seems confident that when it comes to man it is possible to guess whether yes or no," even after "the Cheshire Cat had told her, in the course of a scene that deserves a long meditation: 'We're all mad here. I'm mad. You're mad'" (9). Alice behaves as if the specifically human response were fully intentional and reasonable, an authentic response distinct from reaction or instinct or an unplumbable psychodrama—as if these distinctions were obvious and clear; in any case, as if "I" would be in a position to discern among them, and as if that capacity were the key to communication, to response-ability.

A space of madness, depropriation, trauma, the language relation involves an interruption in cognition: in *le visage d'autrui*, "I" lose my sense of mastery and control. When I am "feeling disarmed before a small mute living being," Derrida proposes (18), I might try to *regain* my sense of spontaneity by turning away. But that would leave me "faced with a cat that continues to see me, to watch me leave when I turn my back on it, a cat that, from that moment on, because I no longer see it seeing me still, from behind, I therefore risk forget-ting" (11). Or I could "turn away" precisely by projecting, anthropomorphiz-ing, "overinterpreting what the cat might thus be saying to me, in its own way, what it might be suggesting or simply signifying in a language of mute traces, that is to say, without words." I might, "in a word," assign "to it words it has no need of" (18). Both options temporarily rescue me, perhaps, from an impos-sible encounter with the absolute other, from the madness of this *rhetorical* re-lation that affects and persuades me without granting me power or mastery.

Bobby is a "wandering dog," a stray animal, previously unfamiliar to Levi-nas, but he is simultaneously all too familiar, all too thematizable and appropri-able—or reappropriable. According to Levinas's own account, his encounter with Bobby does not interrupt his sense of spontaneity, is not an "experience" of expropriation, but instead *confirms* his identity, his humanity, which is based on its clean and indivisible opposition to what he, even after meeting Bobby, continues to call "the animal." Either this small refugee is not other enough to be an Other for Levinas, to disturb his powers of cognition, or else Levinas does not "retain" this disturbance, does not want (or is not able) to "take it up." Conversely, Derrida encounters his own "little cat," the pampered companion who is not even a neighbor, who lives *with* him and greets him every morning in the bathroom, as the "wholly other, like the every other that is every (bit) other found in such intolerable proximity that I do not as yet feel I am justified or qualified to call it my fellow, even less my brother" (12).

What happens in this daily bathroom encounter: not simply that one naked animal sees another naked animal but that the one sees the other *seeing* him naked, seeing his nakedness. The other animal *looks back*, regards Derrida, from a point of view unknown to him, from "the point of view of the absolute other" (11). And Derrida cannot not take it up:

> Nothing can ever rob me of the certainty that what we have here is an exis-tence that refuses to be conceptualized [*rebelled à tout concept*]. And a mortal existence, for from the moment that it has a name, its name survives it. It signs its potential disappearance. Mine also, and that disappearance, from this mo-ment to that, *fort/da*, is announced each time that, with or without nakedness, one of us leaves the room. (9)

What is exposed to Derrida in the instant that he sees this "little cat" looking at him, seeing him naked, is *her* nakedness, her exposedness—that is, her mor-tality, her inability *not* to suffer. Here, in the face to face, Derrida is addressed by another mortal, not a human mortal but an absolutely other sort of mortal, who responds to her name, who responds, that is, to the call of an other.[20]

Alluding to Levinas's insistence that as long as you are seeing the color of the eyes, you are not encountering the "face" of the other, Derrida gives us a glimpse of a more radically Levinasian ethics than Levinas himself is willing to inscribe:

> What does this bottomless gaze offer to my sight [donne à voir]? What does it "say" to me, demonstrating quite simply the naked truth of every gaze, when that truth *allows me to see and to be seen* through the eyes of the other, in the *seeing* and not just *seen* eyes of the other? I am here thinking of those seeing eyes, those eyes of a seer whose color must at the same time be *seen* and *forgotten*. (12)

Face-to-face with a "little cat," Derrida is not assured of his own identity but instead comes to question the "abyssal limit" of what is called "the human":

> As with every bottomless gaze, as with the eyes of the other, the gaze called "animal" offers to my sight the abyssal limit of the human: the inhuman or the ahuman, the ends of man, that is to say, the bordercrossing from which vantage man dares to announce himself to himself, thereby calling himself by that name that he believes he gives himself. And in these moments of nakedness, as regards the animal, everything can happen to me, I am like a child ready for the apocalypse. (12)

In the face of this "small, mute, living being," Derrida *loses* his humanity, loses the very concept of "the human." The transcendence of this animal, its expression, throws into question not only Derrida's own sense of identity and spontaneity but the putatively solid *border* between "the human" and "the animal," which grounds the history of philosophy from Plato to Levinas, grounds Judeo-Christian religions, grounds Western culture itself.[21]

There is, of course, no longer any interest in debating whether there *is* a kind of "discontinuity, rupture, or even abyss between those who call themselves men and what so-called men, those who name themselves men, call the animal." That discussion is over, Derrida insists, "closed in advance." Anyone who would try to argue otherwise "would have to be more asinine than any beast. . . . Even the animals know that (ask Abraham's ass or ram or the living beasts that Abel offers to God: they know what is about to happen to them when men say

'Here I am' to God")," Derrida writes. The discussion only becomes interesting again, and valuable, when the focus is not on whether there is "a limit that
produces discontinuity," but rather on "what a limit becomes once it is abyssal,
once the frontier no longer forms a single indivisible line but more than one
internally divided line; once, as a result, it can no longer be traced, objectified,
or counted as single and indivisible. What are the edges of a limit that grows
and multiplies by feeding on an abyss?" (30–31). The discussion only becomes
significant again, in other words, when it begins with the recognition that:

> [B]eyond the edge of the *so-called* human, beyond it but by no means on a
> single opposing side, rather than "The Animal" or "Animal Life" there is already
> a heterogeneous multiplicity of the living, or more precisely (since to say "the
> living" is already to say too much or not enough), a multiplicity of organiza-
> tions of relations between living and dead, relations of organization or lack of
> organization among realms that are more and more difficult to dissociate by
> means of the figures of the organic and inorganic, of life and/or death. (31)

These relations are both intertwined and abyssal and so "can never be totally
objectified," leaving no "room for any simple exteriority of one term with respect to another" (31).

But such a recognition would mean, first of all, that it would no longer be
possible to refer to "the animal" in the singular, as if this "catch-all concept" designated every living nonhuman thing, from a blind protozoon to an orangutan.
But humans would keep doing it anyway, Derrida predicts, and when one did,
he would be uttering "an asinanity [*bêtise*]," which itself would confirm "not
only the animality that he is disavowing but his complicit, continued, and organized involvement in a veritable war of the species" (31). It is no accident that it
is at the very moment when Levinas is pushed by his interviewers to the point
of having to differentiate between a dog and a snake that he suddenly becomes
incapable of responding: "I don't know if a snake has a face. I can't answer that
question." He offers a response that is "an admission of nonresponse," Derrida
writes, "an admission that he is incapable of responding *to* this very question
and of answering *for* this question on the animal, concerning the face of the
animal."[22]

> But this response in the form of a nonresponse is human. Quite human, all too
> human. No animal at all, Levinas implies, would admit in the same way to the
> incapacity to answer what is in sum the question of responding: for to have a

face is to be able to respond or answer, by means of the "Here I am," before the other and for the other.... And in responding that he can't respond, Levinas says, "Here I am"; he responds, but by admitting that he can't respond to the question of knowing what a face is, namely, of knowing what responding is, and he can thus no longer answer for his whole discourse on the face. (108–9)

The question to which Levinas responds that he cannot respond, the one for which he cannot in the end *be* response-able, is the one on which his "entire philosophy" rests: what does it mean to respond? "For declaring that he doesn't know where the right to be called a 'face' begins," Derrida continues, "means confessing that one doesn't know at bottom what a face is, what the word means, what governs its usage, and that means confessing that one didn't say what responding means" (109). To be unable to respond to this fundamental question puts *into* question "the whole legitimacy of [Levinas's] discourse and ethics of the 'face' of the other." Specifically, it calls into question the conditions designed, clearly and cleanly, to separate the responders from the reactors.

Toward a Nonhuman(ist) Rhetorical Inquiry

Still, what else has Derrida done but reconfirm the legitimacy of Levinasian ethics by problematizing these conditions? What he learns in the face of the "wholly other," in this case his "little cat," is that there is no solid and indivisible line between "the human" and "the animal," which means that there is no such thing as "the human" or "the animal" as such. So though it may indeed be the case that "the absolutely foreign alone can instruct me," it could not be the case that "the absolutely foreign can only be man" (*TI* 73). The anthropocentric presumptions apparent in Levinas's texts and interviews do not sink the ship of Levinasian ethics, which nonetheless stands in need of certain deconstructive correctives that Levinas himself would never have approved and that may well have "apocalyptic" implications. Obviously, we have only just begun the "more specific analysis" that Levinas, to his credit, invites.[23] And it could be significant for rhetorical studies if—following after Derrida, who is following after the animals—scholars in the field would begin to question this distinction, this taken-for-granted border between the authentic response and the mere reaction. This all too simple dichotomy is one basis on which rhetorical studies, too, draws its boundaries and establishes its alibis.

If the imperative to respond is situated, as Levinas says, *prior* to consciousness—prior to freedom or will or the cultural norms of politesse—then how is it possible to distinguish the conscious assumption of the response clearly and definitively from instinct or mere reaction? And how certain is it that "mere" is an acceptable or justifiable qualifier here? If the line between response and reaction cannot be "traced, objectified, or counted as single and indivisible," if it, too, feeds on an abyss, what kind of (apocalyptic) implications does that have in the field for our rhetorics of agency and solidarity, publics and counterpublics? If it is fair to suggest that the saying of the face at the very least *involves* persuasion without a rhetorician, and that the response at the very least *involves* a preconscious and so precognitive (re)action, then is it still possible to contend that at the center of the "rhetorical situation" there stands a knowing, speaking, responding subject who understands her- or himself and the other (at least whether the other replies with a "yes" or a "no") and communicates that understanding, sometimes with eloquence and grace? Is it still possible, that is, to contend that the prince demonstrates rhetorical agency but not the pooch? Or is it not time, past time, for rhetorical scholars to push beyond the (merely) epistemological concerns that have for so long circumscribed our theories of persuasion toward the examination of a "nearly existential" affectability, persuadability, responsivity? That push would require that we reconsider both the role and the scope of "affect" in the language relation, which would in turn require us to reconsider what this "language relation" involves and who or what might be engaged in it.

Notes

Introduction: A Rhetoric of Responsibility

1. The term "community" remains for many reasons problematic. Jacques Derrida, for one, couldn't allow himself to use "community" or to endorse its use, even in the deconstructive works of his student and dear friend Jean-Luc Nancy. See, for example, *The Politics of Friendship*, where he suggests that it may be necessary to dump the too fraternal motifs of "community, appurtenance or sharing, whatever the sign assigned to them. Affirmed, negated or neutralized, these 'communitarian,' or 'communal' values always risk bringing the brother back" (298). Nonetheless, Derrida does concede that "perhaps this risk must be assumed in order to keep the question of the 'who' from being politically enframed by the schema of being-common or being-in-common, even when it is neutralized, in a question of identity (individual, subjective, ethnic, national, state, etc.)" (298–99). Nancy, too, admitted in an interview that he didn't "like to use the term community without certain precautions," and that he was "against any interiority of community." This is why he prefers to speak of being-in-common or being-with, but they have their own problems. ("Thought as a Gap" 6). We will therefore use the terms "community," "belonging," and "solidarity" with extreme caution here, and with a vigilance against the humanist, androcentric, and anthropocentric histories with which they are associated.

2. In *Speaking for the Polis*, Takis Poulakos argues that for Isocrates the logos was the "maker of unity and guide to unification—a force which brings people together under a common end and a shared set of values, which shapes their self-understanding as agents of their own destiny through their participation in political deliberation" (5). Twenty-five hundred years later, rhetoric continues to be credited not only with the power to shape self-understanding but also to create communal sensibility by unifying separate selves across common purposes and values. In the preface to his edited volume, *Rhetoric and Community*, J. Michael Hogan defines community as a "repository of shared purpose, values, and traditions" (xii). He notes that his collection is designed to explore the ways in which "rhetoric defines, rallies, polarizes, or marginalizes specific communities," and to map "the discursive routes that lead communities either to constructive unity or to fragmentation, even bloodshed" (xv). In *Addressing Postmodernity*, Barbara Biesecker states up front that her book is rhetorical insofar as it "insists on, indeed argues strongly on behalf of, the power of persuasive discourse to constitute audiences out of individuals, to transform singularities into collectives, to fashion a 'we' out of a plurality of 'I's,' and to move them to collective action" (1). Obviously, Burke's rhetor hails his or her audience into existence, pulling together a community of listeners by prompting them to identify with (and to identify themselves across) a common interest, value, or desire. It is in this way, as Carolyn Miller puts it, that the problem of the one and the many finds "a rhetorical solution." Rhetoric's task, she says is "to construct one out of many, over and over again" (91). In *Rhetoric and Poetics in Antiquity*, Jeffrey Walker

explicates Aristotle's description of the role of epideictic's audience in order to propose that it is epideictic that "shapes and cultivates the basic codes of value and belief by which a society or culture lives; it shapes the ideologies and imageries with which, and by which, the individual members of a community identify themselves" (9–10). Similarly, Michael Halloran and Gregory Clark propose that epideictic does not "*argue* the ideas or ideals that bind people into a community so much as it *displays* them to a witnessing public" (141). And in his *Rhetorical Landscapes in America*, Clark notes with Burke that epideictic persuades people to attitude before it persuades them to action, arguing that "when individuals identify themselves with a particular enactment of a belief or a commitment that symbolizes the common ground of their community, they engage privately in the public ritual of rhetorical interaction that Burke called *identification*" (20). And so on.

3. See, most specifically and extensively, Victor J. Vitanza's *Negation, Subjectivity, and the History of Rhetoric*, which, by the way, is an exemplary treatise on relationality, as well. In his introduction to Hogan's collection, Roderick Hart also examines the ways in which the rhetoric of hate operates in communities to create a common enemy and therefore solidify communal bonds. "For each community in existence," Hart writes, "there is also an uncommunity, an assembly of the befouled and besotted who have heard the Word and rejected it" (xxv). Burke famously explicated rhetoric's capacity to produce the "underside" of community in his chillingly methodical unpacking of Hitler's *Mein Kampf*. Elsewhere, Burke offers racism and temporary wartime alliances as examples of "identification by antithesis," suggesting that "union by some opposition held in common" is "the most urgent form of congregation by segregation." Indeed, Burke continues, "one's notion of his [*sic*] personal *identity* may involve identification not just with mankind or the world in general, but by some kind of congregation that also implies some related norms of differentiation or segregation" ("The Rhetorical Situation" 268).

4. Biesecker noted almost twenty years ago in her response to Bitzer and Vatz that rhetoric would have no power at all among "already constituted subjects . . . whose identity is fixed prior to the rhetorical event itself" ("Rethinking the Rhetorical Situation" 110–11). Still, Biesecker's line of argument remains solidly within the arena of thematization and representation, concluding that "every 'fixed' identity is the provisional and practical outcome of *symbolic engagement* between speaker and audience" (112; my emphasis). Bradford Vivian's illuminating work, *Being Made Strange*, is a more recent attempt to rethink the standard presumption that rhetoric is the "instrument by which the intentions of individual human agents are carried out" (13). Vivian's conception of a "rhetoric beyond representation," while breaking spectacularly with the privilege of the intentional subject, does however remain in certain significant ways bound to the arena of representation more broadly, taking affect to be a product of symbolic interactions (105), whether conscious or unconscious. This present work will attempt to expose another level of affective operation, one that precedes and exceeds symbolic intervention.

5. See, for example, *The Experience of Freedom*, 72.

6. In his seminar on "The Body" in Saas-Fee, Switzerland, in August of 2001, Nancy offered an intense deconstruction of the notion that "body" is a discrete container for being-there, or worse, for "selfhood."

7. Heidegger's description of Dasein's "individuation" is explicated in chapter four.

8. Gilles Deleuze's use of the term "haecceity" is very similar to Nancy's use of "singularity"—both designate nonpersonal, "event-type individuations . . . where there's no subject" (*Ne-*

gotiations 115), where a proper name indicates a relational force *taking place* in the finite here and now. Deleuze and Guattari, in *A Thousand Plateaus*, describe haecceities as individuations consisting "entirely of relations of movement and rest between molecules or particles, capacities to affect and to be affected." Indeed, a storm system, "a season, a winter, a summer, an hour," they observe, "have a perfect individuality lacking nothing, even though this individuality is different from a thing or a subject" (261). Haecceities, pure events that provoke and undergo change with every "encounter," are capable, Deleuze says, "of ousting the verb 'to be' and its attributes" (141), capable of nudging notions of fixed, immanent being into the between-us space of finite becomings—where everything is happening.

9. Alain Badiou contends that the task of philosophy today is to think beyond finitude—the finitude of bodies and the finitude of situations—proposing that finitude does indeed designate "a discrete form":

> In a word: it is essential to break with the omnipresent motif of finitude. Its origins both critical and hermeneutical, as well regarded by the phenomenologists as by the positivists, the motif of finitude is the discrete form via which thought yields in advance, accepting the modest role it is enjoined to play, in all circumstances, by contemporary nihilism in all its ferocity. (*Infinite Thought* 122)

And again from the same text, though he refers to this "new axiom" in several of his works:

> In fact, a lot of philosophers say precisely that, that situations are finite, such is the theme of the essential finitude of the human being. I think it's necessary to work against that kind of conviction. The consequences of the fact that situations are infinite—we don't know them very well. It's a new axiom. It constitutes a rupture to say that situations are infinite and that human life is infinite and that we are infinite. It's a new axiom and we have to explore its consequences. It is more interesting and more attuned to the necessity of the times than declaring that we are finite and all is finite, we are mortal beings, being-for-death, and so on. We are being-for-the-infinite. (137)

After Derrida, I'm not sure thinking the boundlessness of contexts still constitutes a "new axiom" or a rupture in philosophical thought. Badiou dismisses Heidegger and, by extension, post-Heideggerian thinkers of finitude by ignoring finitude's *intrinsic* infinity, reinstating a pre-Heideggerian dichotomy in order to flip its site of privilege, to celebrate the infinite *as opposed* to the finite, immortality *as opposed* to mortality. But infinite *différance* is itself finite, Ronell reminds us. And the unconscious, the trace, the lapse, the "meanwhile," the Other (in both Lacanian and Levinasian iterations): also infinitely finite (*Finitude's Score* 5). With all due respect to Badiou, post-Heideggerian thinking of finitude *is* the "secularisation of infinity" ("Being by Numbers" 87); it is also, pace Joan Copjec, the dissolution of any fantasy of a "beyond" (28). There is no transcendence *of* finitude—there is instead a kind of finite transcendence, infinite imminence, which is to say: the radical impossibility of immanence. So one need neither overestimate the value of the matheme (Badiou) nor reduce body to "the seat of sex" (Copjec) to secularize infinity and challenge the immanentism inherent in "the biological definition of life" (Copjec 25).

10. Diane Perpich suggests that "[r]hetorically, the face is an image that represents the inadequacy of every image for representing alterity. That is, it represents the impossibility of its own representation and so the problems begin" (103). How to mediate a trace of the immediate

without reducing the uncontainable to the containable? That is one of Levinas's most persistent questions. As Perpich notes, Levinas disagrees with Derrida's early critique in "Violence and Metaphysics" that for any ethical response at all to occur, the other must "*appear* for an ego (in general)" (123). Levinas responds, on the contrary, that "[t]o comprehend a person is already to speak with him" ("Is Ontology" 6; see also Perpich 110). That is, the response is always already an effect of the structure of the address as such, which is at the very least coexistent with the comprehension of an appearance. In his later works on Levinas, Derrida agrees. In *Giving an Account of Oneself*, Judith Butler also takes up this Levinasian insight.

11. In contradistinction to the entire history of philosophy, Levinas posits ethics—rather than ontology or epistemology—as first philosophy, as the basis, that is, for all subsequent thought. Ethics, for him, designates a relation to alterity irreducible to comprehension, a relation that precedes the subsumption of the other within a graspable theme or concept. But inasmuch as this "relation" conforms to a call-and-response structure, it is already rhetorical, a *rhetorical imperative*.

12. Ronell's *Crack Wars*, for example, operates simultaneously as literary analysis, philosophical inquiry, psychoanalytic examination, and biting cultural and political critique. The sections entitled "EB on Ice," "The Doctor's Report," and "Cold Turkey" are themselves independent literary works ranging from science fiction to a sort of street theater. And this collision of frames is inevitable, Ronell says, because if the work were to perform itself strictly "in the genre of the philosophical essay, psychoanalytic interpretation, or political analysis—it would be expected to make certain kinds of assertions which obey a whole grammar of procedure and certitudes." Any one of these methods of inquiry, she acknowledges, "would have secured the project within a tolerably reliable frame." However, each one already presumes a level of understanding that is, for her, *in*tolerable: "[I]t's too soon to say with certainty that one has fully understood how to conduct the study of addiction and, in particular, how it may bear upon drugs. To understand in such a way would be to stop reading, to close the book, as it were, or even to throw the book at someone" (49–50).

1. Identification

1. There was no clean break, no moment at which Burke suddenly turned against Freud. What I hope to demonstrate here, rather, is that according to the subtle registers of the Freudian ambivalence machine, Burke's love harbored within it a desire to take out his teacher, to take his place, to replace him and his theory of identity. "Ambivalent from the very first," identification in Freud is simultaneously loving and rivalrous, a *devouring* affection. It's not only that identification involves inclusion by virtue of exclusion, congregation by virtue of segregation; it is also that identification by definition involves seizing the other's place, ousting the other from the position that "I," having devoured the other, now presume to occupy. According to Freud, wherever there is identification, there is already and intrinsically *war*.

2. For another approach to this issue, see Mark H. Wright's very fine and very early essay, "Burkean and Freudian Theories of Identification." Burke was obviously under the influence of other thinkers as well (Marx, for example). And in her fascinating essay "Language as Sensuous Action," Debra Hawhee makes a strong case for Sir Richard Paget's influence on Burke's theory of identification.

3. Burke zooms in on the productive tension between fusion and division in his analysis

of "the principle of courtship in rhetoric," which he defines as the "use of suasive devices for the transcending of social estrangement" (*RM* 208). The principle of courtship maintains and perpetuates itself, he says, thanks to the unending "mystery" sparked by identification's inability finally to accomplish itself, to achieve complete unity. The "precondition of all appeal," Burke writes, is the "purely technical pattern" in which the speaker shapes "his speech as to 'commune with' the spoken-to." And the irreducible distance between existents, the "standoffishness," as he puts it, "is necessary to the form, because without it the appeal could not be maintained. For if union is complete," he writes, "what incentive can there be for appeal? Rhetorically, there can be courtship only insofar as there is division" (271). This drive to keep the appeal or the "courtship" alive, Burke says, is a "motivational ingredient in any rhetoric," and the "standoffishness" through which it operates is a purely formal or technical "self-interference" that is inherent in language itself (*RM* 269): "There is *implicit in language itself*, the act of persuasion; and *implicit in the perpetuation of persuasion* (in persuasion made universal, pure, hence paradigmatic or found) *there is the need for interference*. For a persuasion that succeeds, dies" (274). The "ultimate rhetorical grounds for the tabus of courtship," Burke writes, resides in the conditions of "standoffishness" (274), in the principle of interference that deflects the goal, preventing the persuasion, the identification, from finally accomplishing itself. "When the plea is answered," Burke writes, "you have gone from persuasion into something else" (274).

4. We can all name affiliations that seem to define who we are, as well as certain loose affiliations that we could take or leave. Most of us are also aware that we are identified by affiliations that are less palatable, less direct, and/or less conscious to us than the ones we specifically choose, and Burke zeroes in on those as well:

> The fact that an activity is capable of reduction to intrinsic, autonomous principles does not argue that it is free from identification with other orders of motivation extrinsic to it. . . . Any specialized activity participates in a larger unit of action. "Identification" is a word for the autonomous activity's place in this wider context, a place with which the agent may be unconcerned. The shepherd, *qua* shepherd, acts for the good of the sheep, to protect them from discomfiture and harm. But he may be "identified" with a project that is raising the sheep for market. (*RM* 27).

Burke's point is that even these indirect identifications are available for critique; they are critiquable—and so perhaps resistible—precisely because they are products of representation.

5. Heidegger illuminates the subject of representation in his discussion of Descartes and representation in *Nietzsche*, IV, chapter 16.

6. Burke scholars rarely challenge his claim that the "centrality" of the nervous system is intrinsically divisive. "Estrangement," Biesecker writes, "is a biological, indeed ontological, fact; it is inscribed in the nature of the human being proper" (46). Robert Wess concurs: "Prior to the identifications and divisions of rhetoric, there is the biological division of one central nervous system from another" (204–5). And so on.

7. Biesecker argues quite compellingly that part three of Burke's *Rhetoric* offers an "ontology of the social," an attempt to ground the ultimate condition for sociality in the predicament of the human organism.

8. Burke most fully explicates what he calls the "ultimate" ground of the individual in the *Rhetoric*:

"Man" arises out of an extrahuman ground. His source is, as you prefer, "natural," or "divine," or (with Spinoza) both. In any case, the scene out of which he emerges is *ultimate*. And in this respect it must be "super-personal," quite as it must be "super-verbal." For it contains the principle of personality, quite as it contains the principle of verbalizing. The distinction between personal and impersonal, like that between verbal and nonverbal, is scientific, pragmatic, and thus is justified when our concerns are pragmatic. But from the standpoint of ultimate speculation, there must be an *order* here: First, there is "nature" in the less-than-personal sense; next, there is the "personal" distinguished from such impersonal nature as an idea of something is distinguished from the thing. But ultimately there must be nature in the "over-all" sense; and nature in this sense must be "superpersonal," since it embraces both "personality" and "impersonality" (289).

This "ultimate" ground, in other words, is an extra-personal and extra-linguistic *nature*, which already contains the potential for both language and personality—and so for identification (290). It is out of this not-yet-human ground of biological estrangement (motion pole), that "man" arises as the linguistically enabled agent/actor whose essence it is to "transcend" this estrangement.

9. In the *Rhetoric* Burke also notes that there may be no such thing as "'personality' in the human realm. And when you get through dissolving personality into the stream of consciousness, or into dissociated subpersonalities, or into 'conditioned reflexes,' or into appearances of substance that derive purely from such extrensic factors as status and role, there may not seem to be any intrinsic core left" (290). Still, Burke never stops positing the biological *as* this core, not of individual personality but of *separate* personalities, which themselves may be completely constructed, products of identification, ideology, and so on. Division is the ontological condition for identification, according to him, and so for rhetorical exchange, for sociality itself.

10. A quick biology refresher: sensory or afferent neurons send impulses from the sense organs (the exposed receptors) to the brain and spinal cord; motor or efferent neurons carry impulses from the brain and spinal cord to muscles and glands (the effectors); and interneurons, located only within the central nervous system, *connect* sensory and motor neurons, carrying impulses between them.

11. For a fascinating review of recent research on mirror neurons and resonance mechanisms, see Rizzolatti, Fadiga, Fogassi, and Gallese, especially 252–53.

12. See, for example, the 1977, 1983, 1989, 1994, and 1997 studies by Meltzoff and Moore.

13. By positing an essence of the organism, in other words, Burke deflects the more radical implications of originary exposedness. If an organism is always already exposed, affected—open to the other's affection—then there is no essence of that organism, no way even to pose the ontological question: what is it? And yet, Burke's own unfolding of the paradox of substance had already suggested this, which makes his position on the body, "the original economic plant," all the more puzzling.

14. In *Les complexes familiaux dans la formation de l'individu* (originally written in 1938 for *L'Encyclopédie française* VII), Lacan addressed this direct and immediate identification, acknowledging that it must precede even the specular representation of the "mirror stage." Mikkel Borch-Jacobsen notes that this insight "should have ruined the whole *theory* of the imaginary in advance" (*Lacan* 69).

15. This process involves what Freud called "reality testing." For a brilliant discussion of this phenomenon and its implications, see "Prototype 3" in Avital Ronell's *The Test Drive*, 64–71.

16. Freud also approaches this problem in his concept of melancholia, about which I'll venture only a few preliminary remarks. Early on, Freud described melancholia as the pathological result of an inability to mourn: whereas successful mourning names a normal process whereby libidinal cathexes are eventually withdrawn from a lost love object and reinvested in another, melancholia involves an incorporation of the object, so that libido, rather than finding a substitute, "withdraws into the ego" and the object-cathexis is replaced by an identification—a process Freud describes as "a *regression* to narcissism." The "shadow of the object" falls upon the ego, as Freud puts it, which swallows but cannot or will not digest the foreign body; ego becomes a little tomb for the dearly departed, who refuses finally to depart ("Mourning and Melancholia" 249). Later, however, in *The Ego and the Id*, Freud confesses that he had failed to "appreciate the full significance of this process," which he now recognizes as "common" and "typical" rather than pathological (28). Here, he describes the melancholic structure as both the condition for the work of mourning and crucial to the formation of ego's character:

> It may be that by this introjection, which is a kind of regression to the mechanism of the oral phase, the ego makes it easier for the object to be given up or renders that process possible. It may be that this identification is the sole condition under which the id can give up its objects. At any rate the process, especially in the early phases of development, is a very frequent one, and it makes it possible to suppose that the character of the ego is a precipitate of abandoned object-cathexes and that it contains the history of those object-choices. (29)

Ego turns out to be a kind of crypt for lost or abandoned objects, where they are preserved through incorporation and so never quite lost or abandoned enough.

Laurence Rickels and Avital Ronell—two *other* American readers of Freud—follow Abraham and Torok, as well as Derrida, in exploring this inability to let go under the name "cryptonymy." "The *primal* precondition of every so-called self-relation," Rickels observes in *The Case of California*, is that "it must always take a detour via the dead other" (5). "Even the most ancient theories of ghosts see the specter," he continues in *Aberrations of Mourning*, "as a dead person who has been improperly buried" (4). And in this case, the "dead people" (the unmournable) are improperly buried in the ego, the "character" of which turns out to be the prototypical horror flick and thriller—not just *The Night of the Living Dead* but also *When a Stranger Calls*, the tale of an outside that affects from within, and of an inside that affects itself on the outside. I think, for instance, of Ronell's famous reading of Emma Bovary, whose self-relation detours through the double-incorporation of a dead [m]other "on which Emma continues symbolically to feed," and a dead [br]other who "remote controls her" (*Crack Wars* 118). According to Freud, the contamination is primary: ego is *constituted* through and by its identifications. Indeed, in "Mourning and Melancholia" when Freud describes the shift from object-relation to identification as a "regression," he suggests that the object-relation was *already* identificatory, already a narcissistic object choice. If the loss of the object provokes an identification, in other words, it's due, apparently, to the profoundly identificatory nature of the relation to the object (see also Borch-Jacobsen, *Freudian Subject* 185).

17. In *Group Psychology*, suggestion becomes a synonym for identification: "The other members of the group, whose ego ideal would not, apart from this, have become embodied in his person without correction, are then carried away with the rest by 'suggestion,' that is to say, by means of identification" (79).

18. In the 1990s, the ethical and political implications of the predicament of suggestibility were exposed more generally when the tragic "science" of Recovered Memory Therapy (RMT)—a.k.a. False Memory Syndrome—which ignored all Freud's warnings, made international headlines. In an RMT session, the therapist uses various suggestive techniques (hypnosis, guided imagery, and so on) to "assist" the patient in imaging/figuring/piecing together what are presumed to be the repressed traumatic memories triggering current psychogenic illnesses (bulimia, anorexia, and so on). Between the late 1980s and early 1990s, and to the utter bewilderment of their families of origin, hundreds of thousands of RMT patients in the United States and Canada suddenly "remembered" horrific incidents of childhood abuse, which were typically sexual and often also involved ritualistic and/or satanic elements. These "memories" almost always turned out to have originated in fantasy (in nightmares, horror flicks, novels), something Freud had already taught us. (Burke was also alert to the possibility that fantasy can be experienced as reality: "the symbolic consummations in forgotten or vaguely remembered dreams might serve as motivational incentives [as sources of guilt, and the like]. The dreams might secretly have the effect of profoundly experienced actualities" [*Language* 69].) Yet, for almost a decade grown children hauled their aged parents into court en masse to answer for these suddenly "remembered" crimes, and they often won.

19. For an exhilarating examination of the way that Freud's argument self-destructs, see both versions of Borch-Jacobsen's "The Primal Band," in *The Freudian Subject* (127–239) and *The Emotional Tie* (1–14).

20. But see Borch-Jacobsen's stunning rereading of the *Totem and Taboo* myth as an ethics of finitude in the second chapter of *The Emotional Tie*, "The Freudian Subject: From Politics to Ethics," 15–35.

21. As I suggested above, Freud proposes that this originary disidentification takes place not only beside the dead body of a loved one but also, for example, in the separation of birth or when the breast won't stay put. That is, it takes place wherever narcissistic appropriation is interrupted, wherever an inassimilable surplus announces itself. Levinas proposes something slightly different: that this interruption takes place in the language relation, whenever a "you" and an "I" engage in "conversation" (*entre-tien*).

22. Jenny Edbauer Rice's examination of the affective force in the second President Bush's incomprehensible orations would be one example of a rhetorical analysis that does not presume that identification is compensatory to division. Samuel McCormick's presentation at the USC Conference on Rhetorical Theory in October 2009, "Toward the Rhetoric of Everyday Life," offered a similar glimpse into the material force of Bush's damn near incomprehensible yet still somehow effectively affective bumblings.

2. Figuration

1. In "Being, Time, and Definition: Toward a Semiotics of Figural Rhetoric," Carol Poster proposes that "the division of figures into figures of thought and figures of speech . . . implies a philosophy of rhetoric that divides substance from ornament and thought from speech" (124). I have no desire to embrace such distinctions but rather to point up that "face," for both de Man and Levinas, dissolves them.

2. Heidegger's student Ernesto Grassi also famously focuses on the generative power of the

trope, locating metaphor at the "root of our human world" (33). Timothy Crusius's excellent new introduction to Grassi's *Rhetoric as Philosophy* crystalizes the significance of his work: rhetoric as figuration is the basis not only for philosophy, which is huge, but for all thought.

3. We'll get to the others, but here's Lacan: "The symbol manifests itself first of all as the murder of the thing, and this death constitutes in the subject the eternalization of his desire" ("The Function and Field of Speech and Language in Psychoanalysis" 104).

4. For a compelling reading of the voice-ghosts connection from a somewhat different angle, see Joshua Gunn's *Modern Occult Rhetoric: Mass Media and the Drama of Secrecy in the Twentieth Century*. And for an inquiry into the haunted history of rhetoric, see Michelle Ballif's "Historiography as Hauntology: Paranormal Investigations into the History of Rhetoric."

5. Judith Butler discusses the relation between the figure of the face and the process of humanization somewhat differently in her explication of Levinas in *Precarious Life*, pp. 131–51.

6. I'm referring to the four-fold that Heidegger discusses in "The Origin of the Work of Art."

7. "To the extent that language is figure (or metaphor, or prosopopoeia) it is indeed not the thing itself but the representation, the picture of the thing and, as such, it is silent, mute as pictures are mute. Language, as trope, is always privative" (*RR* 80).

8. Lacan makes a similar distinction in the early seminars between the "ego" who (mutely) sees him or herself in the other/mirror and the "subject" who speaks, the subject of enunciation.

9. See also de Man: "As soon as we understand the rhetorical function of prosopopoeia as positing voice or face by means of language, we also understand that what we are deprived of is not life but the shape and sense of a world accessible only in the privative way of understanding. Death is a displaced name for a linguistic predicament, and the restoration of mortality by autobiography (the prosopopoeia of the voice and the name) deprives and disfigures to the precise extent that it restores" (*RR* 81).

10. Blanchot reminds us that Narcissus did *not* recognize himself.

11. In a seminar in Saas-Fee, Switzerland, in 2002, Avital Ronell noted that Rousseau constituted/invented the notion of solitude, the interiority of a solitary self, in the Fifth Walk of his *Reveries of the Solitary Walker*. On the island of Saint-Pierre in the middle of the Lake of Bienne, he says, he experienced what he describes as "precious *far niente*"—idleness in the sense of letting go and letting be—which allowed for a kind of self-gathering that had nothing to do with world or world building. On the water in a small boat, drifting, he detaches from theocracy; he is alone: no passion, no disturbance, no mitsein. But significantly, Ronell points out, this self-gathering moment, this institution of the figure of the self-sufficient self ("self-sufficient like God," Rousseau writes [89]), is founded *on the water*. It is therefore without foundation, groundless, inessential.

12. In *The Infinite Conversation* Blanchot questions the distinction Levinas wants to maintain between the ethical relation with *Autrui* (though he won't grant it a capital) and the exposedness to indeterminate being (the *il y a*). We'll discuss this distinction in chapter four.

13. I want to emphasize that face is irreducible both to the front of the head and to figural operations. In *Otherwise than Being*, Levinas often turns to the skin as a figure for the ephiphany of the face—that is, as a figure for the dissolution of figure. The skin, he says, is an already exposed surface that, in the ephiphany, breaks through, once again giving us the experience of a "denud-

ing of denuding" (49). Furthermore, by the later work, face seems no longer to require physical presence. He opens *Proper Names* with an acknowledgment that there are also certain writers, Blanchot included, "whose *saying* signifies a face" (4). And throughout *Otherwise than Being*, he performs what he calls the "reduction of the said to the Saying," producing a text whose saying, we could also say, "signifies a face."

14. Levinas is not consistent with his capitalization, but he does consistently maintain the *autre/autrui* distinction.

15. Let me note, too, that Levinas's neologism is "formed with the *il* (he) or *ille*"—not with the *elle*. Though he insists that illeity would precede any notion or marking of sexual difference, it is tellingly impossible to propose "*elleity*" as a synonym for *illeity*. So though I would like just now to have written "a s/he-ness," Levinas, to my endless frustration, does not allow for it.

16. Derrida questions Levinas's (and Heidegger's) anthropocentrism in several places. In "Eating Well," for example, he writes: "The subject (in Levinas's sense) and the *Dasein* are 'men' in a world where sacrifice is possible and where it is not forbidden to make an attempt on life in general, but only on the life of a man, of other kin, on the other as *Dasein*" (113). There is no denying that Levinas focuses his ethical philosophy on the human, and we will address his particular brand of humanism in the P. S.

17. "According to certain supercilious grammarians," Blanchot continues, refusing the capital, the term is limited to the objective case: "*autrui* should never be used in the first person. I can approach *autrui*, *autrui* cannot approach me. *Autrui* is thus the Other when the other is not a subject" (*IC* 70). *Autrui* is of the Outside, in Blanchot's terms, irreducible to the phenomenal world and to the tropological field that puts it into play. Neither object nor subject, *Autrui* is the one without horizon: "the unidentifiable, the I-less, the presence of the inaccessible" (*IC* 70).

18. I'm equivocating here because typically one thinks of an "experience" as something a self-present subject *has*, but Levinas redescribes experience or "pure experience" as a brush with exteriority, with alterity, with what is completely irreducible to me and so with what takes "me" out, with precisely what interrupts my sense of self-presence and self-coincidence. To encounter something for which I am prepared, something I am preprogrammed to assimilate or appropriate, then, would not amount to an experience in Levinas's book.

19. Let me say once again that I am struggling here and throughout with Levinas's insistance on the masculine pronoun "il," which is no accident or oversight but attests to the exclusion of the "elle" from his conception of the ethical relation.

20. Kant names two modes of sublime experience: mathematical and dynamic. The former arises when one encounters something so vast (the concept of eternity, Egyptian pyramids, the Alps, a peaceful ocean) that it exceeds the grasp of reason and overwhelms the powers of comprehension. The latter arises when one encounters something so powerful (an erupting volcano, hurricane Katrina, a raging ocean or tsunami) that one fears for life and limb. "To call the ocean sublime," Kant writes, "we must regard it as poets do, merely by what strikes the eye; if it is at rest, as a clear mirror of water only bounded by the heaven; if it is restless, as an abyss threatening to overwhelm everything" (*Critique of Judgment* 82). The idea of the infinite that arises in the face of the Other is an instance of the mathematical sublime. For, the Other's resistance to my powers of comprehension is nonviolent, without force.

21. See also *Ethics and Infinity*, 57: "The face speaks. It speaks, it is in this that it renders possible and begins all discourse."

22. We should perhaps pause here to examine the term "conversation" (*entre-tien*) in Levinas's work, especially since it has invited charges of phonocentrism. He certainly privileges oral discourse, frequently citing Plato's Socrates in order to echo his denunciation of writing and to affirm the ability of the speaker to remain present (*kath' auto*) to his or her speech, to come to its assistance. Yet, as Blanchot notes in *The Infinite Conversation*, there is some ambiguity here, both because for Levinas the speaker is *not* self-present to him- or herself, is not a speaking *consciousness*, and because in "conversation," my interlocutor is not in any way equal to me, is not even on the same plane as myself. What seems at times in Levinas's work to slip into a description of tranquil humanist dialogue between two constituted entities is complicated by the fact that for him conversation with the other is effected by a "cuvature" of intersubjective space that prevents any equalizing or leveling, that prevents the possibility, as Blanchot puts it, of any "common denominator between the Self and *Autrui*" (57). Not even the common denominator of "subjectivity" will cut it since neither the "I" nor the other is capable of speaking in the first person, of "assisting" speech as a self-sufficient subject. Now, I have no intention of defending Levinas against the charge of phonocentrism here—in *Totality and Infinity* anyway, it is possible that the charges could stick. However, I do want to point out, alongside Blanchot, that even in *Totality and Infinity* this case is extremely complicated in a way that, for example, it is not complicated in Gadamer's texts. I also want to note that in his later work it becomes even more difficult to nail Levinas on this charge, when the saying of the face may come through in/as writing, as text.

23. In its first turn, then, the speech that takes place in *le visage d'Autrui* lines up to some extent with what Lacan calls "full" or "true speech," speech that says nothing but the nothing at the level of the said, but that engages in the saying of it as "a symbolic gift of speech" in order to fulfill the relational "pact" ("Function and Field" 79).

24. The world of "things" is naked, too, Levinas acknowledges, inasmuch as things or objects are completely opaque. Having no light of their own, they require interpretation (adornment), a borrowed light: "To disclose a thing is to clarify it by forms," Levinas writes, "to find for it a place in the whole by apperceiving its functions or its beauty." The work of science and art, he suggests, is to disclose by clothing, to take us beyond the mere perception of things by adorning them in signification. But the face is not a thing, so conversation "is entirely different," Levinas says, "it consists in entering into a relationship with a nudity disengaged from every form, but having meaning by itself, *kath' auto*, signifying before we have projected light upon it, appearing not as a privation on the ground of an ambivalence of values . . . but as an always positive value. Such a nudity is the face" (*TI* 74). When I face the other—the sensible, visible, identifiable other—the Other *looks back*: "the eyes break through the mask," Levinas writes, "the language of the eyes, impossible to dissemble. The eye does not shine; it speaks" (*TI* 66). Conversation, first of all, is the relation with the face, but the nakedness of the face is beyond my power and possibility; I cannot clothe and so clarify it by giving it form because it has already broken through all form, signifying itself not across some recognizable generality but by/as itself (*kath' auto*), in excess of generalizable form and without reference to a system. Nothing, no possession or attribute or concept links me to the face of the Other—to *Autrui*—who, in exceeding my power, calls me into question.

25. Already in 1953, in "Freedom and Command," Levinas had described the face-to-face relation as a kind of persuasion before speech, "a relationship of command without tyranny, which is not yet an obedience to an impersonal law [of reason], but is the indispensable condi-

tion for the institution of such a law" (18). And in his most mature work, *Otherwise than Being*, he describes the saying of the face as "an overflowing of the said itself by a rhetoric which is not only a linguistic mirage, but a surplus of meaning of which consciousness all by itself would be incapable" (*OTB* 152).

3. Hermeneutics

1. As Mailloux notes in "Re-Marking Slave Bodies," two exemplary instances of this argument against "rhetorical hermeneutics" are offered by Arabella Lyon and Rosa Eberly. Mailloux counters that rhetorical hermeneutics "does try to provide strategies for participating in disciplinary debates over the nature of interpretation, foundationalist theory, and the relation of history and politics to both," and further that it is possible to "use rhetorical hermeneutics to analyze cultural and political matters beyond the academy" (100, 102).

2. The most noteworthy exception is Michelle Ballif, who challenged this link in "Writing the Third Sophistic Cyborg: Periphrasis on an [In]Tense Rhetoric" and in *Rhetoric, Sophistry, and the Woman with the Rhetorical Figure*, as well as on various conference panels that she, Mailloux, and I have organized. And though Victor J. Vitanza has not directly challenged Mailloux's articulation of this position, he has been arguing for the ethical significance of a nonhermeneutic rhetoric in everything he's written since "Critical Sub/Versions."

3. From Schleirmacher's *Hermeneutik und Kritik*: "The correlation of hermeneutics and rhetoric consists in the fact that every act of understanding is the reversal of an act of speech, for the thought that was at the basis of the spoken discourse must enter into consciousness" (qt. in Hamacher 70).

4. There are other ways to define "hermeneutics," and if time and space permitted, we could tease through the ways that hermeneutics *also* remains irreducible to this formula of production/ interpretation. In the dialogue on language that opens *On the Way to Language*, Heidegger says he regrets having used the expression "hermeneutics" in *Being and Time* because he was trying to suggest something much "broader" than "interpretation," something that is "in keeping with that vastness that springs from originary being. In *Being and Time*," he writes, "hermeneutics means neither the theory of the art of interpretation nor interpretation itself, but rather the attempt first of all to define the nature of interpretation on hermenetuic grounds" (1982, 11). As Heidegger explicitly states in *Being and Time*, what he means by hermeneutics implies "no circle at all" (7), no prejudgment structure—it is therefore irreducible to what Schliermacher calls "the art of understanding." However, the constant misreading prompts Heidegger, after *Being and Time*, to ditch the term hermeneutics altogether and to adopt instead the "more primordial" term "*hermeneuein*," leaving it untranslated to evoke something other than the appropriation of meaning:

> The expression "hermeneutic" derives from the Greek verb *hermeneuein*. That verb is related to the noun *hermeneus*, which is referable to the name of the god Hermes by a playful thinking that is more compelling than the rigor of science. Hermes is the divine messenger. He brings the message of destiny; *hermeneuein* is that exposition which brings tidings because it can listen to a message. Such exposition becomes an interpretation of what has been said earlier by the poets who, according to Socrates in Plato's *Ion* (534e), *hermenes eisin ton theon*—"are interpreters of the gods. . . . All this makes it clear that hermeneutics means not just the interpretation but, even before it, the bearing of message and tidings." (*OWTL*, 29)

So *hermeneuein* is not simply the announce*ment* but also the announc*ing* of the "divine message," a saying which gives not only a signified meaning but also a greeting, an address that communicates, before anything else, *that* the other speaks to me: an exposition of exposedness. In "Sharing Voices," Jean-Luc Nancy offers an interpretation of interpretation as *hermeneuein*, a "hermeneutics" that does not exclude "the possibility that meaning will be *given* purely and simply—in all the rigor of the idea of a *gift*, which fits neither anticipation nor premonition" (215).

5. In "Freedom and Command," Levinas again describes rhetoric as violence, proposing that it approaches the other "from an indirect angle," which is already violence, already murder (19; see also Jill Robbins, 17–18).

6. Hyde's insistence, contra Levinas, that the saying is not without eloquence demonstrates one of the ways in which he reduces the saying to the said. Quoting Wilbur S. Howel, Hyde writes:

> [T]he true nature of [the orator's art] "is made up of the methods which reflection and experience have evolved to make a discourse such as to establish the truth and to arouse a love for it in the hearts of [human beings]. Things which strike and arouse the heart . . . eloquence is just that." And if one appreciates "the heart" in a strictly Jewish way—as the capacity of conscience—then rhetorical eloquence deserves to be praised as something that, as in the case of YHWH, can serve the purpose of opening others to a truth that needs to be acknowledged for the good of all concerned. (110–11)

And he concludes that the saying itself, the silent "saying of the face" in Levinas's complex terminology, is also "not without eloquence" but is a "magnificent and moving discourse that reveals such an awe-inspiring truth that witnesses cannot help but be awestruck" (111). By contrast, Levinas describes the saying as a "rhetoric without eloquence" because the saying, which is not simply absorbed by the work of figuration, resists and withdraws from the movement of appropriation. The said of any saying may be "eloquent" or "truly moving," but the saying itself interrupts the semantic power of the trope, opening a relation with nonappropriable otherness. As such, the saying involves affect—"I" am exposed to the other's affection/alteration—which may also trigger what Heidegger would call the "mood" of anxiety. But it could not, in and of itself, arouse emotion, nor could it offer a consciously graspable "truth." Whereas Hyde's discussion of the saying gets collapsed, for pragmatic purposes, into a discussion of the said, I'm trying to maintain the double movement (the "plural speech," as Blanchot calls it) of the saying *and* the said, to resist the hermeneutic impulse to reduce the former to the latter.

7. One anonymous reviewer for an early version of this chapter wrote: "given my critical biases, I am much more attracted to non-fiction than fiction when it comes to demonstrating any 'truth' about the nature of rhetoric and hermeneutics." The problem is that this particular bias—for nonfiction over fiction, for pragmatics over poetics—is precisely what silences any rhetoric of the saying. Not because the saying doesn't take place in "real life," but because its resistance to (re)presentation makes it an easy sacrifice in the rush to interpret, granting the immediate reduction of the saying to the said, of the ethical to the pragmatic. I turn to a fictional address here both because it is the example that Mailloux provides for us and because literature has taught us that fiction often demonstrates remarkable powers of exposition. "The singular staging of the imaginary—'literature' in the widest sense," Ronell writes, "has a tradition of uncovering

abiding structures of crime and ethicity with crucial integrity; one need only think of what Hegel drew from *Antigone* or Freud from *Oedipus Rex*" (*CW* 11). I would not, of course, presume to compare *Star Trek: The Next Generation* to *Antigone*, but I am suggesting that "literature in the widest sense" has the capacity to expose both the radical singularity of experience and its traumatic interruption in ways that what we conventionally call "nonfiction" cannot.

8. In *Dictations: On Haunted Writing*, Ronell figures writing as a mode of conversation, of conversation with the departed, dead or alive.

9. It is, again, in this sense that Levinas can say that subjectivity is always already ethical. The ethical relation is not first of all something an ego accomplishes; rather, as a language relation, as a function of the address, it is what makes it possible for me to say "I" to begin with. There is no "I" that is not at the service of a "you."

10. I'm echoing and following the lead of Ronell here, who suggests in "Trauma TV" that testimonial video "at times produces the Ethical Scream which television has massively interrupted" (311).

11. See also *The Gift of Death*, where Derrida speaks of:

> [T]he gift that is not a present, the gift of something that remains inaccessible, unpresentable, and as a consequence secret. The event of this gift would link the essence without essence of the gift to secrecy. For one might say that a gift that could be recognized as such in the light of day, a gift destined for recognition, would immediately annul itself. The gift is the secret itself, if the secret itself can be told. Secrecy is the last word of the gift which is the last word of the secret. (29–30)

12. Avital Ronell pointed out this connection to me, and I thank/think her for it.

13. Blanchot situates the dislocation of the "I think" not so much in the thinking but in the speaking: "What is strange in the Cartesian certitude 'I think, therefore I am,' is that it only presented itself by speaking, and that speech, precisely caused it to disappear, suspending the *ego* of the *cogito*, consigning thought to anonymity without any subject—to the intimacy of exteriority" (1995, 54).

14. More from Levinas: "As a 'pure knowledge' langauge consists in the relationship with a being that in a certain sense is not by relation to me, or, if one likes, that is in a relationship with me only inasmuch as he is wholly by relation to himself, *kath' auto*, a being that stands beyond every attibute" (*TI* 74).

15. In "Reality and Its Shadow," Levinas calls the incessant and interminable nature of *l'entre-temps* "something inhuman and monstrous," the time not of death but of dying, an endless interval that "cannot give itself the other shore" (11). In art, this is also the time of irresponsibility for Levinas; but in the interhuman relation, it is the time of the encounter.

16. Inasmuch as conversation involves both the saying and the said, it involves both the experience of depropriation and of appropriation—this is why Blanchot describes conversation with the other as a "plural speech" (*IC* 80–82).

17. This line is quoted by Hamacher (15) and Ronell (*S* 161), both of whom are citing Schlegel's *Fragmente zur Poesie und Literatur*, in *Kritische Friedrich-Schlegel-Ausgabe*, ed. Ernst Behler, Jean-Jacques Anstett, and Hans Eichner (Paderborn: Schöningh, 1958), 16.I: 69, "Zur Philologie," II no. 95: "Es gibt einen hermeneutischen Imperativ."

18. See, for example, John Muckelbauer's smart response to an earlier version of this chapter, where he describes "Davis's project" as being "committed to developing a practical style of

engagement with the other (whomever or whatever that might be) that doesn't simply treat the other as someone to be colonized, appropriated, and translated into something reassuring and comforting for me." While I would, of course, support such an ethics of practical engagement, what I am arguing for here is much more modest, and/but at the same time, for some, much more difficult to affirm: that however one responds to the other, one has already answered to an obligation, an always prior rhetorical imperative to which one can *only* respond. There is no spontaneous agency; there is response-ability. There is the said—yes, of course; it is the content of the response, which rhetorical studies and writing studies have admirably and exclusively taken up. But there is first of all the address, the condition for any said, and I am urging the fields of rhetorical studies and writing studies to develop rhetorics that attend to it, to develop rhetorics of the saying.

4. Agency

1. Joshua Gunn and I were in the same workgroup, and—to be fair—he remembers more diversity in the discussion than I do. Certainly the "agency" position papers demonstrate much more diversity than Geisler's report indicates. And the plenary presentation by Karlyn Kohrs Campbell, also in our workgroup, pointed up the diverse potentiality of approaches: "The term 'agency' is polysemic and ambiguous, a term that can refer to invention, strategies, authorship, institutional power, identity, subjectivity, practices, and subject positions" (1).

2. At the University of South Carolina's Conference on Rhetorical Theory in October 2008, Lenore Langsdorf (whose panel consisted of herself, Michael Hyde, Jeffery Nealon, and Stuart Murray) suggested that rhetoric would do well to ditch the notion of the "agent" and focus on "agency," the action or production of some effect. Her well-taken point, also articulated by Lundberg and Gunn, is that the so-called agent is an effect of agency (rather than the other way around) and of a complex relational dynamic. Levinas suggests something similar but with a twist: that the "agent" is not (only) nonspontaneous because s/he is an effect of dynamic relations, of ecstatic structuring, but because s/he is the effect of an always prior *assignation*, a pre-originary rhetorical imperative.

3. If Levinas is perhaps too easily patched into discourses on ethics, Heidegger is perhaps too easily dismissed from them. The under-interrogated presumption—by Levinas(ians) and others—that the Heideggerian corpus evades ethics, that Heidegger successfully dodged and ducked ethical articulation, does not necessarily hold up under serious scrutiny. Indeed, in a 2001 essay published in *La Pensée Dérobée*, Jean-Luc Nancy pulled up the still covert dossier on Heideggerian ethics, which he calls an *originary* ethics. And Hyde should be commended for offering, against the grain of Levinas's (and Levinasians') texts, the meticulous explication of an ethical layer in *Being and Time*.

4. Levinas is referring to Plato's idea of the Good not as equal to but as the *source* of both knowledge and truth. In his famous simile, Plato suggests that if the sun shines on the visible world as the source of that visibility, then the Good shines on the intelligible world as the source of intelligibility. What Levinas holds on to is the notion that "the Good" cannot in and of itself be known but instead names the *source* of any knowing, and that its "rays" "penetrate" the subject (the subject is its effect and not its cause) before it has the chance to choose. See, for example, Plato's *Republic*, 507–9. The Good in Levinas, as it turns out, "shines on" consciousness not from the heavens but from the lowly realm of the "interhuman" relation.

5. Dasein's ecstatic structuring leaves it open to hearing a call from its future, Heidegger says,

so that Dasein "always exists in just such a manner that its 'not-yet' belongs to it" (243). Dasein's uniquely circular existential structuring grants it "the possibility of existing as a whole potentiality for being," and Heidegger differentiates it from other circular structurings. Ultimately, he lands on a tentative analogy to unripe fruit: "The 'not-yet' has already been included in the very Being of the fruit, not as some random characteristic, but as something constitutive. Correspondingly, as long as any Dasein is, it too *is already its "not-yet"* (243–44). However, Heidegger hastens to add that Dasein is no fruit: "with ripeness the fruit *fulfills* itself," whereas with death, Dasein loses its "specific possibilities." That is, "even unfulfilled Dasein ends," and indeed, "for the most part, Dasein ends in unfulfilment, or else by having disintegrated and been used up" (244). This is why, as Derrida points out in *Aporias,* death for Dasein always comes too soon, "why life will always have been too short" (26).

6. For Heidegger, "ready-to-hand" indicates one's everyday relation with things in the world, which is not one of reflective contemplation but of use and employment within the context of Dasein's being-in-the-world. When one hammers one does not contemplate the hammer *as such* but simply and rather automatically *uses* it, relating to it as a piece of equipment to be purposefully manipulated. However, when a tool breaks, it is torn from the intricate relational fabric that constitutes Dasein's being-in-the-world and shows up *as such*; it is no longer simply readyto-hand but "present-at-hand." When anxiety strikes, Dasein is itself ripped from its relational context, showing up for itself as such, presenting itself to itself for contemplation.

7. Still, let me reiterate that Dasein's resolute choice is a resolute *repetition*. Once individualized, Dasein is free, and free to affirm its freedom in the resolute decision to repeat itself, to hand down to itself again the very possibilities that have already been disclosed, the very world into which it had been thrown. So Dasein's resolute choice is already conditioned by its being-with, by all its prior influences and affections. "The factical possibility that comes down to Dasein is, of course, a possibility that has been defined historically," Fynsk explains, "and thus we encounter again a mode of being-with insofar as the possibility of existence that has been is that of a Dasein that 'has been there'" (*Heidegger* 46). Radically individuated Dasein returns to the world and to others, this time in an authentic way, prepared—and here, perhaps, is an inspiration for Hyde's approach—to "choose its hero." But this hero is no one new, Heidegger assures us:

> Repeating is handing down explicitly—that is to say, going back into the possibilities of the Dasein that has-been-there. The authentic repetition of a possibility of existence that has been—the possibility that Dasein may choose its hero—is grounded existentially in anticipatory resoluteness; for it is in resoluteness that one first chooses the choice which makes one free for the struggle of loyally following in the footsteps of that which can be repeated. (385)

The hero Dasein chooses in anticipatory resoluteness is a Dasein that has been there already.

Heidegger refers to the "hero" twice in *Being and Time*, and both times it signifies a model that Dasein chooses to follow or (in the other instance) not to follow: "Everydayness is determinative for Dasein even when it has not chosen the 'they' for its 'hero'" (371). Fynsk notes that "Dasein does not choose its hero in the sense that the hero's existence is one possibility among others that might be selected (Dasein's 'choices,' in this sense of the word, are given to it); rather, 'choice' is to be understood here in the sense of affirmation or 'resolving upon.' Dasein's choice . . . originates in its primordial, free-resolving, which opens it to the possibility of 'loyally following' the existence that has been (this, a redoubling of the resolution-choice in the sense of an active affirmation)" (47). *Amor Fati.* Whereas inauthentic Dasein may choose the "they" for its hero unthinkingly, by default, authentic Dasein resolutely chooses a Dasein that has been there for its hero, an already existing model, "loyally following in the footsteps of that which can be repeated."

8. "I can die for the other in a situation where my death gives him a little longer to live," Derrida explains. "I can save someone by throwing myself in the water or fire in order to temporarily snatch him from the jaws of death, I can give her my heart in the literal or figurative sense. . . . But I cannot die in her place" (*Gift of Death* 42–43).

9. Heidegger makes the point many times, so we'll settle here for a sampling: "Thus death reveals itself as that *possibility which is one's ownmost, which is non-relational, and which is not to be outstripped*" (251); "Anticipation discloses to existence that its uttermost possibility lies in giving itself up, and thus it shatters all one's tenaciousness to whatever existence one has reached" (264); "Death does not just 'belong' to one's own Dasein in an undifferentiated way; death *lays claim* to it as an *individual* Dasein. The non-relational character of death, as understood in anticipation, individualizes Dasein down to itself" (263). And so on.

10. See, for example, *Being and Time*:

> When we are talking ontically we sometimes use the expression 'understanding something' with the signification of "being able to manage something," "being a match for it," "being competent to do something." In understanding, as an existentiale, that which we have such competence over is not a "what" but being as existing. The kind of Being which Dasein has, as potentiality-for-Being, lies existentially in understanding. Dasein is not something present-at-hand which possesses its competence for something by way of an extra; it is primarily Being-possible. (143)

And so on. Werner Hamacher comments: "Understanding thus means to be able" (27).

11. In *Aporias* Derrida suggests something very different but similarly disastruous for the existential analysis Heidegger performs in *Being and Time*:

> If death, the most proper possibility of *Dasein*, is the possibility of its impossibility, death becomes the most improper possibility and the most ex-propriating, the most inauthenticating one. From the most originary inside of its possibility, the proper of *Dasein* becomes from then on contaminated, parasited, and divided by the most improper . . . the *Enteignis* [expropriation] always inhabited *Eigentlichkeit* [Authenticity] before even being named there. (77–78)

12. Though they are not simply conflatable, it may be helpful to think of the *il y a* along the lines of what Lacan calls the Real.

13. In *The Inoperative Community*, Nancy notes that though he "can be in solidarity with Levinas's distaste for certain accents, shall we say, of dereliction in Heidegger's discourse," he nonetheless cannot buy the idea of existence without existents, of the *es gibt* as a "generality" (105).

14. Levinas reminds us that "different forms of the night [can] occur right in the daytime. Illuminated objects can appear to us as though in twilight shapes. Like the unreal, inverted city we find after an exhausting trip, things and beings strike us as though they no longer composed a

world, and were swimming in the chaos of their existence" (*EE* 54). Here he could be describing anyone's return from, say, RSA or MLA or NCA or CCCC.

15. "To kill, like to die," Levinas writes, "is to seek an escape from being, to go where freedom and negation operate. Horror is the event of being which returns in the heart of this negation, as though nothing had happened. 'And that,' says Macbeth, 'is more strange than the crime itself'" (*EE* 56). Indeed, "specters, ghosts, sorceresses are not only a tribute Shakespeare pays to his time," Levinas writes, "or vestiges of the original material he composed with; they allow him to move constantly toward this limit between being and nothingness where being insinuates itself even in nothingness, like bubbles of the earth ('the Earth hath bubbles'). Hamlet recoils before the 'not to be,'" Levinas explains, "because he has a foreboding of the return of being ('to dye, to sleepe, perchance to Dreame')" (*EE* 57). Levinas proposes that "the apparition of Banquo's ghost is also a decisive experience of the 'no exit' from existence, its phantom return through the fissures through which one has driven it. 'The times have been, that when the Brains were out, the man would dye, and there an end; But now they rise again . . . and push us from our stools. This is more strange than such a murther is'" (*EE* 57).

16. Suicide, Blanchot observes, operates on an enormous faith in the dialectic, which is "entirely founded upon the possibility of death, upon the use of death as power." But what we learn from suicide, he says, what we learn and "ceaselessly forget," is that:

> he who has been all the way to the end of the desire of death, he who opens, as Heidegger said, *the possibility of impossibility*—or again, he who believes himself to be master of unmastery—lets himself get caught in a sort of trap and halts eternally (halts, obviously, just an instant) at the point where, ceasing to be a subject, losing his stubborn liberty, and becoming other than himself, he comes up against death as that which doesn't happen or as that which reverses itself (betraying, as though demented, the mendacity of the dialectic by bringing it to its conclusion)—reverses the possibility of impossibility into the *impossibility of every possibility*. (*WD* 70)

17. It seems worth mentioning that the clear and indivisible distinction Heidegger maintains between Dasein as properly mortal and "the animal" as a merely living thing hinges on Dasein's capacity to experience death as such, "death as death," as Heidegger puts it in *On the Way to Language*: "Mortals are they who can experience death as death. Animals cannot do so. But animals cannot speak either. The essential relation between death and language flashes before us, but remains still unthought" (107). This unthought relation between language and death has been taken up at length by both Derrida (*Aporias*) and Giorgio Agamben (*Language and Death*), so I won't dwell on it here. Still, let me note in passing, because Levinas certainly isn't going to, that this purportedly clean distinction between Dasein and all other living things fails to hold once it is no longer presumed that *mortals* are capable of experiencing death *as such,* that the call of conscience could grant that capacity—once it is no longer presumed that Dasein, unlike every other living thing (according to Heidegger), is capable of *properly dying*. It's not just that animals have no relation to death "as such," Derrida reminds us, but that "neither does man, that is precisely the point!" (*Aporias* 76).

18. In this work, the other "par excellence"—which Levinas says does not amount to "another me, an alter ego known by sympathy"—turns out to be "the feminine," and the enormity of Levinas's gender trouble begins right there, in the potentially androcentric presumption (*EE* 86).

Luce Irigaray, Tina Chanter, Jacques Derrida, and many, many others have already gotten him for this, so we don't have to. But let me just say that fourteen years later in *Totality and Infinity*, "the feminine" alterity is ambiguous, both the opening to alterity itself and the opening to *Eros*, the relation between lovers. Levinas calls the latter "the very contrary of the social relation," especially in that it "excludes the third party," closing itself off and remaining "supremely non-public" (*TI* 264–65). The figure of the two is not a figure for the *ethical* relation in Levinas, which always already involves "the third party." As the opening to *Eros*, Levinas proposes, "the feminine is the other refractory to society, member of a dual society, a society without language" (*TI* 265).

19. In *Adieu*, Derrida rereads *Totality and Infinity* otherwise, as "an immense treaties of hospitality"—both "on" hospitality and "as" hospitality, as an exegesis or argument that *performs* hospitality—that situates the "welcoming of the other" already as a response. "[T]he welcoming *of* the other (objective genitive) will already be a response: the *yes to* the other will already be responding to the welcoming *of* the other (subjective genitive), to the *yes* of the other" (21–23).

20. The central chapter of *Otherwise than Being* is "Substitution," which first appeared in October 1968 in the *Revue Philosophique de Louvain* 66 (no. 91): 487–508.

21. If we must speak of God here—if we must—then we'd have to slap that label not on the addressor position, a slot that remains empty in Levinas's account, but on the address as such, which becomes an "address" only after the fact, in the response. In any case, for Levinas one lands on this impossible signifier, "God," a posteriori when struggling to make sense of the epiphany of the face: "This tie to the other (*autrui*), which does not reduce itself to the representation of the Other (*autrui*) but rather to his invocation, where invocation is not preceded by comprehension, we call religion. The essence of discourse is prayer" ("*L'essence du discours est prière*") ("Is Ontology" 7).

22. In his first and perhaps most famous work on Levinas, "Violence and Metaphysics," Derrida proposes that any ethics at all would first of all require the "*recognition*" and "letting-be" of an "other." Here's Derrida:

> Thought, or at least the precomprehension of Being—conditions . . . the *recognition* of the essence of the existent (for example someone, existent as other, as other self, etc.). It conditions the respect for the other, as what it is: other. Without this acknowledgment, which is not a knowledge, or let us say without this "letting-be" of an existent (Other) as something existing outside me in the essence of what it is (first in its alterity), no ethics would be possible. (137–38)

But Levinas insists again fourteen years later in *Otherwise than Being*—more carefully this time—that the ethical relation precedes and is the condition for both thought and Being. Prior to the apparition of a self capable of the "precomprehension of Being," there is the response to an underivable provocation, which posits both self and other as substantives.

23. Let me repeat that Levinas is trying to describe a preoriginary obligation to respond, an obligation that precedes representation and thematization. This obligation is not a function of symbolic meaning but is instead the condition for any symbolic exchange whatsoever. So though one could always refute the preoriginariness of this obligation, to *critique* it through any possible interpretive frame (be it psychoanalytic, Marxist, feminist, postcolonial, and so on) makes about as much sense as critiquing a natural disaster—a tsunami or a tornado. However frustrating one might find his androcentric and anthropocentric language, however misleading one might find

his critique of Heidegger, however creepy one might find his references to "the Good" in Plato (or to "God," no matter how deconstructed), Levinas cannot be fairly dismissed for missing the violence inherent in symbolic relations. Levinas, a survivor of the Shoah whose extended family was murdered by Nazis, understands the violence inherent in symbolicity. This violence is what prompts his inquiry.

24. Judith Butler descibes the depropriating experience this way:

> To be addressed carries with it a trauma, resonates with the traumatic, and yet this trauma can be experienced only belatedly through a *second* occurrence. Another word comes our way, a blow, an address or naming that suddenly, inexplicably slaughters, even as one lives on, strangely, as this slaughtered being, speaking away. (*Giving* 84)

25. Derrida notes that "Levinas not only reproaches Heidegger for the fact that Dasein is argued from the privileged position of its own death . . . but because it gives itself death as a simple annihilation, a passage to nonbeing, which amounts to inscribing the gift of death as a being-towards-death within the horizon of the question of being." What Levinas is trying to indicate is something else altogether:

> On the other hand the death of the other—or for the other—that which institutes our self and our responsibility, would correspond to a more originary experience than the comprehension or precomprehension of the sense of being. . . . What is most ancient would here be the other, the possibility of dying *of* the other or *for* the other. Such a death is not given in the first instance as annihilation. It institutes responsibility as a *putting-oneself-to-death* or *offering-one's-death*, that is *one's life*, in the ethical dimension of sacrifice. (*Gift of Death*, 48)

5. Judgment

1. I will address Levinas's anthropocentrism in the P. S. that follows.

2. The famous scene from Burke's *Philosophy of Literary Form*:

> Imagine that you enter a parlor. You come late. When you arrive, others have long preceded you, and they are engaged in a heated discussion, a discussion too heated for them to pause and tell you exactly what it is about. In fact, the discussion had already begun long before any of them got there, so that no one present is qualified to retrace for you all the steps that had gone before. You listen for a while, until you decide that you have caught the tenor of the argument; then you put in your oar. Someone answers; you answer him; another comes to your defense; another aligns himself against you, to either the embarrassment or gratification of your opponent, depending upon the quality of your ally's assistance. However, the discussion is interminable. The hour grows late, you must depart. And you do depart, with the discussion still vigorously in progress. (110–11)

3. For a fine discussion of the ways in which Badiou and Levinas overlap, on the other hand, see Michael Bernard-Donals' excellent essay "'Difficult Freedom': Levinas, Language, and Politics."

4. The "public sphere" designates those realms of social life in which nongovernmental opinion formation takes place. Quite a lot of important and compelling work has been done at the intersection of rhetorical studies and public sphere studies. I'm thinking of the exemplary (yet

extremely diverse) work produced by, say, Michael Warner, Melissa Deem, Rosa Eberly, Patricia Roberts-Miller, and Gerard A. Hauser, for example, all of which productively critiques, expands, and/or transforms Habermas's notion of the public sphere from a rhetorical perspective. Here, we will not be challenging the notion of publics and counterpublics but redescribing their conditions of possibility.

5. Derrida: "interruption of ethical immediacy is itself immediate. The third does not wait; its illeity calls from as early as the epiphany of the face in the face to face" (A 32). There are two "thirdnesses" operating here, so let me unpack this: Though both the third party and the "thirdness" of illeity approach in the "face" of the neighbor, Levinas carefully distinguishes between the two. Whereas the third party (the "stranger" or "foreigner") comes to interrupt ethical immediacy, instituting the necessity for justice and so for equality, reciprocity—law and politics—illeity's thirdness is a third-person-ness irreducible to the "I-thou" relation, a radical irreversibility (nonreciprocity) *in* the relation with *le visage d'Autrui*. Illeity, in other words, amounts to the irreducible other*ness* in the other, the Other in the other. The nailing down of terms, however, only deepens the complexity of relations and responsibilities, since there is also "illeity, *in the third person*," Levinas tells us (*OTB* 150, my emphasis). Indeed, a few pages later—if you can tolerate the androcentric assault—he writes: "The other is from the first a brother of all the other men. The neighbor that obsesses me is already a face, both comparable and incomparable, a unique face and in relationship with other faces, which are visible in the concern for justice" (*OTB* 158). *In* the epiphany of the face (of the neighbor), illeity's "third person-ness" points to the early arrival of the third party, of all the other others—illeity signals a "singular plurality in the heart of singularity," Derrida writes (A 33). And/but there is also illeity *in* the third party, the Other in all the others; illeity in the other is not simply a trace of the infinite in the finite, as Michael Marder puts it, but "the figure of the Other in the Other, infinity in infinity" (para 13). These are the formulations that make Badiou crazy.

6. For an interesting examination of this fundamental hospitality within the frame of digital rhetorics, see James Brown's exceptional dissertation, "Hospitable Texts."

7. More from *The Telephone Book:*

> And yet, you're saying yes, almost automatically, suddenly, sometimes irreversibly. Your picking up means that the call has come through. It means more: you're its beneficiary, rising to meet its demand, to pay a debt. You don't know who's calling or what you are going to be called upon to do, and still, you are lending your ear, giving something up, receiving an order. It is a question of answerability. (2)

8. Before the beginning, "infinity will already have been pre-originarily welcomed," Derrida writes. "Welcomed in anarchy. This responsible response is surely a *yes*, but a *yes to* preceded by a *yes of* the other" (A 23).

9. As Derrida puts it, "the welcome cannot be derived, no more than the face can, and there is no face without welcome" (A 25).

10. In *Giving an Account of Oneself*, Butler articulates a similar point in slightly differently terms: moral judgment "unbeholden to the ethics implied by the structure of address, tends toward violence" (63).

11. Two of Derrida's lectures are collected in *Of Hospitality*. A handful of the later seminars on hospitality were published in *Acts of Religion*.

12. Michael Warner describes public formation not simply as an effect of "conversation" (this time with a Habermasian rather than a Levinasian inflection) but also as the product of fluctuating modes of attention that require only the most minimal uptake: "It is even possible for us to understand someone sleeping through a ballet performance as a member of that ballet's public," Warner writes, "because most contemporary ballet performances are organized as voluntary events, open to anyone willing to attend or, in most cases, to pay to attend. The act of attention involved in showing up is enough to create an addressable public. Some kind of active uptake, however somnolent, is indispensible" (88). Levinas would suggest that even this barely attendant attention, this "somnolent" attention, is already a *function* of infinite responsibility.

13. The Kantian terminology is not quite accurate, and in *Philosophy in a Time of Terror*, Derrida offers three reasons that hospitality in the unconditional sense is not exactly reducible to a regulative idea: 1) this language (against the grain of Kant's own descriptions) makes it seem as if unconditional hospitality were simply *possible*, something an "I" could accomplish if it tried hard enough, rather than the impossible; 2) unconditional hospitality cannot consist in simply applying a rule or norm—there is no decision and so no justice when the decision is not one; and 3) Kant's entire line of thought is suspect since it relies on two forms of sovereignty: self and God (Habermas 134).

14. Dobbs: "I support the Minuteman Project and the fine Americans who make it up in all they've accomplished, fully, relentlessly, and proudly" (Mediamatters.org).

15. Bernard-Donals notes that the displacement involved "is not just a conceptual or epistemological one; it is also, potentially, a physical one. When the individual engages the other, she resides in a kind of no-man's-land, in which she is both at home and in exile, neither completely apart from, nor completely a part of, the community or the location from which she speaks" (66).

16. It's perhaps necessary at this point to acknowledge Levinas's own refusal to acknowledge responsibility for Palestinian suffering. Levinas's troublingly unapologetic Zionism shows up mostly in his Talmudic writings—here, for example, is a passage from an essay in *Beyond the Verse* called "Cities of Refuge":

> What is promised in Jerusalem, on the other hand, is a humanity of the Torah. It will have been able to surmount the deep contradictions of cities of refuge: a new humanity that is better than a Temple. Our text, which began with cities of refuge, reminds us or teaches us that the longing for Zion, that Zionism, is not one more nationalism or particularism; nor is it a simple search for a place of refuge. It is the hope of a science of society, and of a society, which are wholly human. And this hope is to be found in Jerusalem, in the earthly Jerusalem, and not outside all places, in pious thoughts. (52)

Though Levinas "wanted to protect the thematic of election . . . from every nationalistic seduction," Derrida notes, he nonetheless maintained a bewilderingly consistent faith in "the election of an eternal people, safe from all 'nationalist' . . . temptation" (A 118). This unwavering faith (as well as the conviction that a "wholly human" society would be a good thing) operates to some extent as an alibi, a ground for Levinas's refusal to assume responsibility for the third party: in this case, both Palestinians and nonhuman others. But as Derrida points out, "all nationalisms like to think of themselves as universal in an exemplary fashion" (A 117). Wherever one presumes to deduce not simply a law and a politics but their specific content from infinite ethical responsibility, s/he has abdicated that responsibility. "Nothing could make us more irresponsible," Derrida writes; "nothing could be more totalitarian" (*A* 117). Among others, Judith Butler (*Giving an Account*, 94–96), Adam Newton (62–63), and Michael Bernard-Donals offer astute critiques of Levinas's refusal to respond responsibly to Palestinians, situating them neither as the Other nor as the third party but as "people who are wrong" (Levinas, "Ethics and Politics" 294). Butler zeroes in on what she describes as Levinas's "blatant racism," pointing us to another passage in *Difficult Freedom* in which Levinas declares Judaism and Christianity to be the "cultural and religious preconditions for ethical responsibility itself and warns against the 'rise of the countless masses of Asiatic and underdeveloped peoples [who] threaten the new-found authenticity' of Jewish universalism" (94).

17. The Rhetoric Society of America's conference theme in 2008 was "The Responsibilities of Rhetoric." I am, by contrast, analyzing the rhetorics of responsibility.

18. For a fuller explication of Derrida's vision for a new approach to international law, see *Specters of Marx*. When the IPW charged its Network of Cities of Asylum with welcoming the foreign writer under threat, it was calling on a long and vibrant tradition of municipal hospitality. A city's limits are marked by relatively static and measurable boundaries, giving it the legal status of a "territory," but these boundaries do not solely determine a city's identity, which is constantly rewritten according to its dynamic relation with its inhabitants. Cities are territorialized by their legislated borders, in other words, but they are also perpetually deterritorialized by their hospitable acts, the living history of welcoming from which a city's identity continuously emerges. The Book of Numbers figures God himself ordering Moses to establish the first six cities of refuge and to charge them with taking in and protecting those who involuntarily take a life from that victim's "blood avengers." Salmon reminds us, too, that "since the Middle Ages, cities, being more liberal in this regard than States, have very often welcomed people who had been banished, and protected those who were threatened. We have only to think of Dante, Rabelais, or Voltaire. . . . In the strict sense of the word [cities] have been urban adventures, products of hospitality" ("Parliament" 13).

19. See also, for example, Yvonne van der Heijden's description of the IPW in the Nieman Reports.

20. Derrida everywhere affirms the double-charge, insisting that, on the one hand, hospitality must wait for the other, "extend itself toward the other, extend toward the other the gifts, the site, the shelter and the cover; it must be ready to welcome [*Accueillir*], to host and shelter . . . ; it must prepare itself and adorn itself for the coming of the hôte; it must even develop itself into a culture of hospitality, multiply its signs of anticipation, construct and institute what one calls structures of welcoming [*les structures de l'accueil*], a welcoming apparatus [*les structures d'accueil*]" ("Hospitality" 361). "But *on the other hand*," he continues, in contradistinction to both Kant and Rusdie, "the opposite is . . . simultaneously and irrepressibly true: to be hospitable is . . . *to be ready to not be ready*, if such is possible, to let oneself be overtaken, to not even *let* oneself be overtaken, to be surprised, in a fashion almost violent, violated and raped [*violée*], stolen [*volée*] . . . precisely where one is not ready to receive—and not only *not yet ready* but *not ready, unprepared* in a mode that is not even that of the 'not yet.'" After all, "the awaited hôte (thus invited, anticipated, there where everything is ready to receive him) is not a hôte, not an other as hôte" (361).

Incidentally, in *Means Without Ends*, Giorgio Agamben argues, also alongside Arendt, that "the refugee is perhaps the only thinkable figure for the people of our time," and he, too, pins a certain hope on the city—or rather, on just one city: Jerusalem (16). Agamben proposes that Jerusalem could open itself to the claims of two national territories, becoming, "simultaneously and without any territorial partition," the capital of both Israel and Palestine. "The paradoxical condition of reciprocal . . . aterritoriality that would thus be implied," he says, "could be generalized as a model of new international relations"—a model in which two or more political communities would inhabit the same region, each in a "condition of exodus" from the other (24). Perforating and "topologically deforming" state spaces, cities would then become cities of the world, truly cosmopolitan sites that would bring each resident face-to-face with "the refugee that he or she is" (25–26). Derrida and Agamben's very different visions, then, are grounded in a similar hope: that the city might become a site of extensive hospitality that will radically "reorient the politics of the state."

21. According to Champlain College's documents:

> The dissolution of the International Parliament of Writers (IPW) produced two organizations in its place, one in North America and one in Europe. In 2003, Russell Banks, the last President of the IPW, along with Salman Rushdie and former IPW President Wole Soyinka, established Cities of Refuge North America, formerly called the North American Network of Cities of Asylum (NANCA). ICORN, the International Cities of Refuge Network, is based in Stavanger, Norway and has organized over twenty cities of asylum, or refuge, across Europe.

The North American Network of Cities of Asylum has taken in and protected nine endangered writers to date, according to this document.

22. ICORN's Web site announces flat out and with emphasis: "It is important to note that *ICORN is not a refugee organization.* Neither the network nor its individual cities have authority over the laws and regulations of any country. Therefore, the Administration Centre strongly discourages all applicants and candidates from relying on ICORN as their only option for refuge" ("About"). Its "Founding Charter," dated June 11, 2006, lists explicit criteria for determining which "applicant writers" will be "taken into the network" and become "Guest Writers":

> 1. "The applicant must be a writer," where "writer" includes "novelists, non-fiction writers, playwrights, poets, editors, translators, publishers, journalists and cartoonists" (2).
>
> 2. The applicant must be either: under an imminent threat of "being killed, abducted, physically attacked or 'disappearing'"; be "sentenced or at risk of being sentenced to a prison term by the authorities in his/her country as a direct consequence of his/her writing" (excluding legitimate cases of "inciting hatred or violence through their writing)"; or be "unable to express themselves freely through his/her writing for fear of persecution due to the probable actions of the government or other non-government entities of the country in which he/she habitually resides" (2).

P. S. on Humanism

1. I started to add "nor ghosts nor androids," but Levinas does deal with the specter all over the place, noting for example that taking out the other in a fit of violence does not get at the Other, which continues its haunting address via the bad conscience that once again affirms the

ethical imperative. He does not deal, however, with technological emissaries of the "nonliving," which for him are mere things. See note 16.

2. Obviously, we could still question Levinas's presumption that "home" requires a dyadic, hetero coupling—hetero, at least in its performativity, if not in its anatomical or psychical structuring.

3. The quote marks are to indicate that philosophy in general, and Heidegger very specifically, would not describe Bobby as "existing." Derrida takes Heidegger as an exemplary instance, demonstrating that according to him, the dog lives but does not have a *Dasein*, a being-there: "a dog does not exist," Heidegger writes in *The Fundamental Concepts of Metaphysics*, "but merely lives." Domestic animals *"'live' with us"* he continues, "but we do not live with them if living means: *being* in an animal kind of way. Yet we are with them nonetheless. But this being-with is not an existing-with" (210). Animals do not have language (the "as" structure) and so do not have "world"; they cannot therefore be said properly to "exist" or to "die," according to Heidegger. Derrida, of course, challenges this (*Animal* 158–59).

4. "For hunted, beaten, or slaughtered animals," Derrida reminds us, "we are also men, alas, whom they identify only too quickly, regrettably, as men" (*Animal* 114).

5. See Kant's *Universal Natural History and Theory of the Heavens*, for example, where he proposes: "[M]ost of the planets are certainly inhabited, and those that are not will be in the future. Now what sort of interconnections will be brought about among the different types of these inhabitants through the relationship between their place in the cosmic structure and the central point from which the warmth which gives life to everything extends outwards?" (147).

6. Kant's racism and sexism seem to be pretty much in line with his culture at the time. He clearly considered the male the head of household by default, and his passion to categorize leads him in 1775 to sketch out, "in connection with the natural causes of their origin," a racial taxonomy that implies the natural inferiority of nonwhites ("On the Different" 48); indeed, Kant elswhere flat out states that to be "quite black from head to foot" is to be "stupid" ("On National" 57). Still, this presumed natural inferiority did not *necessarily* indicate exclusion from the realm of moral agency, which for Kant appears to include all human beings without consideration of race or sex or social class.

7. In his very early critique of Levinas's anthropocentrism, John Llewelyn writes that according to Levinas, Bobby "is too stupid, *trop bête*. Bobby is without logos and that is why he is without ethics. Therefore he is without Kantian ethics; and so he is without Levinasian ethics, since the ethics of Emmanuel Levinas is analgous to the ethics of Immanuel Kant in that each is an ethics with a God within the limits of reason alone, but without a dog or any other beast, except indirectly, if we are to judge by reason alone" (51).

8. Kantian and Levinasian ethics are analgous only up to a certain point; they are not synonymous.

9. See Kant's *Metaphysical Principles of Virtue* (part II of the *Metaphysics of Morals*), p. 105.

10. "In order to be serious, and responsible," Derrida writes "at the risk of bringing back down to earth all the enchanted readers who, dreaming of reconciling Levinas's ethics with the animals, set about idolizing this dog, it is necessary to limit straight away the scope of this hymn to Bobby" (*Animal* 114).

11. First, let me repeat that God, in Levinas, names not a being but a function of the relation with an other mortal (*autrui*). And second, Levinas's insight obviously challenges the mind/

body dualism presumed in Enlightenment thought, the notion that a nonmaterial consciousness is *trapped* inside a material body. According to him, mind is always already an effect of material incarnation, which is itself an effect of proximity. Consciousness and reason are situated as functions of a creaturely receptivity and responsivity.

12. The Other is exterior to me to the extent that he or she gives me the "idea of infinity" and so remains absolutely inassimilable, resistant to my powers of comprehension. "The idea of infinity" could not come from me alone but "occurs in the relationship with the other. The idea of infinity is the social relationship" ("Philosophy" 55). I should note that Levinas is repeating here without reflection or discussion another Heideggerian presumption: that "the animal," captivated by its environment, is not capable of the ek-stasis, the "ex-sistance" ("exiting from itself") that is the essence of human being (*Fundamental* 365).

13. I'd like to distinguish clearly and cleanly between the "infinite demand" of the rhetorical imperative, a limitless obligation to respond that dictates no particular response, and the demand from the Infinite said to have ordered George W. Bush, for example, to launch a "preemptive war," or to have required Andrea Yates to drown her five small children in the bathtub. I'd like to. But frankly the distinction is not all that clear to me. The rhetorical imperative, as the condition for responsivity, comes through with no instruction manual—which is why Ronell continually warns against the insolence of uninterrogated response, against embracing the fiction of a static-free call.

14. See, for example, Edward O. Wilson, *Sociobiology*; Frans de Waal, *Good Natured* and "Food Sharing and Reciprocal Obligations Among Chimpanzees"; Jane Goodall, *Through a Window*; N. N. Ladygina-Kohts, *Infant Chimpanzees and Human Child*; R. M. Church, "Emotional Reactions of Rats to the Pain of Others"; Richard C. Connor and Kenneth S. Norris, "Are Dolphins Reciprocal Altruists?"; and S. Wechkin, J. H. Masserman, and W. Terris, "Shock to a Conspecific as an Aversion to Stimulus." I could easily go on.

15. Matthew Calarco points out that "*Bobby's life is also at stake in the camp*. He is not a pampered, Oedipal pet, but a nomad struggling to survive, living on 'in some wild patch of the prison" (58).

16. If time and space permitted, we'd need to deconstruct this distinction, too. For now, I point you to Jean-Luc Nancy's *The Sense of the World*, where he writes:

> A response that does not respond to a question is a response that is not the solution to a problem or the appeasement of an interrogation or the conclusion of a search. Instead, as we can see by the etymology of the word *response*, it is a given guarantee, a promise, an engagement. A given guarantee, a promise, an engaged *responsibility*. Some*one* is, first of all, less a being-present than an engaged presence—engaged perhaps first in nothing other than being-*here*, exposed *there*. In this sense, for example, a mere rock "responds" just as much as a man named Peter: there is being-exposed in a crowded world. (71)

See also Silvia Benso's excellent essay "Of Things Face-to-Face." Thanks to Pat Gehrke for pointing me to it.

17. See Heidegger's *Fundamental Concepts of Metaphysics*, where he argues that "the stone is worldless, the animal is poor in world, main is world-forming" (185). Here, in Levinas, the rock is without a face; the animal sort of, maybe, sometimes has a face; and the human has a face.

18. I should note that Nietzsche, both poet and prophet, was rendered incapable of tracing much of anything after witnessing the brutal beating of a horse on January 3, 1889, a trauma that

arguably involved an address from the nonhuman animal to Nietzsche's perfect and highly attuned little ears. Before that, Nietzsche had been pretty much the Dr. Doolittle of philosophy, if
not talking *to* then at least talking *through* the animals. Zarathustra, for instance, took not man but
the animals as his teachers as he searched for a path to the *Übermensch*. Kenneth Burke is highly
attuned to animals, as well. His *Permanence and Change: An Anatomy of Purpose* is so full of animals that Debra Hawhee calls it his "jungle book": "Lively, noisy, nonhuman animals dash, crawl,
and scurry across Burke's theories of human action, language as symbolic action, and dramatism"
("Kenneth Burke's Jungle Book" 2). Hawhee notes that Burke is "at his most Nietzschean" when
he compares the thinking processes of human and nonhuman animals and the privilege leans
slightly toward the animals: "if any ranking occurs in his discussion, it is of the seaming elegance
of fish-thought over the clotted complexity and stupid-making, disembodied abstractions of human thought" (4). However, there is no real sense in, say, *Thus Spoke Zarathustra* or *Permanence
and Change* that the author *had been addressed* by a nonhuman animal. Vicki Hearne, the poet
and animal trainer who wrote *Adam's Task* and *Bandit: Dossier of a Dangerous Dog*, should probably have been on Derrida's empty list, though. And Donna Haraway argues that that list would
be instantly populated if it were to include not only poets and prophets but scientists, such as
Jane Goodall, Gregory Bateson, Marc Bekoff, and Barabara Smuts (21). I would add Frans de
Waal to her list.

19. I admit that my reasons for bringing these two thinkers together here on the question
of "the animal" are not entirely scholarly, though I do introduce this gossip column with a nod
to Walter Benjamin and his understanding of the cognitive value of the anecdote. It's no secret
that Ronell often imposed her vegetarian views and anxieties at the Derrida table—we'll never
know just how much their frequent and animated conversations on the topic contributed to
Derrida's thinking on "carnophallogocentrism." In the summer of 2004, when he was quite ill, I
witnessed Ronell lift his spirits by sharing details from a report she had seen on penguin prosti-
tution. "Jacques," she began, leaning in, her eyes twinkling, "*here* is something for your work on
'the animal.'"

20. "No one can deny the suffering, fear, or panic, the terror or fright that can seize certain
animals and that we humans can witness," Derrida writes. Bentham's question in regard to the
animal, "Can they suffer?" is not, for Derrida, a question; rather, it "leaves no room for doubt."
And "that is why the experience that we have of it is not even indubitable; it precedes the indubitable, it is older than it" (28). Still, Derrida puts it differently: for him it is not "Can they suffer?"
but "Are they incapable of not suffering?"

21. There is another writer, arguably both poet and prophet, who "admit[s] to taking upon
[herself] the address that an animal addresses to [her]." In *The Passion According to G.H.*, Clarice
Lispector delivers an excruciating depiction of her protagonist's expropriating encounter with
a cockroach: in the "face" of the roach, G.H. loses her sense of "the human." After inadvertently
crushing it in the door of a wardrobe, she realizes that she has not killed it: it is half-crushed but
alive. "Alive and looking at me," she tells us. Her first thought is to finish the job: "I lifted my
arm up high, as if my entire body weight would come down on the wardrobe door along with
the blow from my arm." Pause for paragraph break, and then: "But it was then that I saw the
cockroach's face. It was aimed straight ahead, at the same level as my head and eyes. For an instant
I paused with my hand poised in the air. Then, gradually, I lowered it. But it was too late by a split
second: I had seen it" (47).

And *it* had seen *her*. That is, she had *seen it seeing her*. What follows this encounter with *le visage d'autrui* consists in an extreme "experience" of destabilization and *dehumanization*: "Listen, in the presence of the living cockroach, the worst discovery was that the world is not human, and that we are not human" (61). And then the apocolyptic affirmation: "Dehumanization is as painful as losing everything, as losing everything, my love" (66).

22. In a letter to Vaitier, analyzed by Derrida, Descrates argues that the question is not whether the animal-machine can react to what is said in its presence—obviously, it can—but whether it can respond to questions put to it. According to Descrates, the animal is a preprogrammed machine and so is incapable of responding to questions. "The question of response is thus that of the question," Derrida writes, "of the response as response to a question that, at one and the same time, would remain unprogrammable and leave to the other alone the freedom to respond, presuming that were possible. . . . The Cartesian animal, like its descendants [the Kantian, Heideggerian, Lacanian, and Levinasian animal] . . . would remain incapable of responding to true questioning" (*Animal* 84). That is the difference, then, between "the human" and "the animal": the human, presumably, *is* capable of responding to true questioning. But what's happening here, when the interviewers put the question to Levinas, point blank, is that he demonstrates a certain incapacity—he is responding, yes, but his response is *that* he is incapable of responding, of responding responsibly to this true questioning.

23. We are now perhaps in a better position to appreciate the guts and heart it would take for Levinas, late in the game and despite it all, to propose the necessity of a "more specific analysis" that could put his "entire philosophy" at risk. This proposition, Derrida notes, "is at the same time a responsible, courageous, and humble way to leave every chance to what is to come" (*Animal* 109).

Works Cited

Agamben, Giorgio. *Means Without End*. Trans. Vincenzo Binetti and Cesare Casarino. Minneapolis: University of Minnesota Press, 2000.

Arendt, Hannah. *The Origins of Totalitarianism*. London: George Allen and Unwin Ltd., 1967.

Aristotle. *The Nicomachean Ethics*. Trans. David Ross. Oxford: Oxford University Press, 1983.

Atterton, Peter. "Ethical Cynicism." In *Animal Philosophy: Essential Readings in Continental Thought*. Ed. Mathew Calarco and Peter Atterton. New York: Continuum, 2004. 51–61.

Badiou, Alain. "Being by Numbers." Interview with Lauren Sedofsky. *Artforum* (October 1994): 87.

———. *Ethics: An Essay on the Understanding of Evil*. New York: Verso, 2001.

———. *Infinite Thought: Truth and the Return to Philosophy*. New York: Continuum, 2005.

Ballif, Michelle. "Historiography as Hauntology: Paranormal Investigations into the History of Rhetoric." *Re/Theorizing Writing Histories of Rhetoric*. Ed. Michelle Ballif. Carbondale: Southern Illinois University Press, forthcoming.

———. *Seduction, Sophistry, and the Woman with the Rhetorical Figure*. Carbondale: Southern Illinois University Press, 2001.

———. "Writing the Third Sophistic Cyborg: Periphrasis on an [In]Tense Rhetoric." *Rhetoric Society Quarterly* 28.4 (Fall 1998): 51–72.

Bennington, Geoffrey. *Jacques Derrida*. Trans. Geoffrey Bennington. Chicago: University of Chicago Press, 1993.

Benso, Silvia. "Of Things Face-to-Face With Levinas Face-to-Face With Heidegger: Prolegomena to a Metaphysical Ethics of Things." *Philosophy Today* 40.1 (Spring 1996): 132–41.

Bernard-Donals, Michael. "'Difficult Freedom': Levinas, Language, and Politics." *diacritics* 35.3 (Fall 2005): 62–77.

Biesecker, Barbara. *Addressing Postmodernity: Kenneth Burke, Rhetoric, and a Theory of Social Change*. Tuscaloosa: University of Alabama Press, 1997.

Blakesley, David. *The Elements of Dramatism*. New York: Longman, 2002.

Blanchot, Maurice. *Friendship*. Trans. Elizabeth Rottenberg. Palo Alto: Stanford University Press, 1997.

———. *The Infinite Conversation*. Trans. Susan Hanson. Theory and History of Literature 82. Minneapolis: University of Minnesota Press, 1993.

———. *The Space of Literature*. Trans. Ann Smock. Lincoln: University of Nebraska Press, 1982.

———. *The Writing of the Disaster*. Trans. Ann Smock. Lincoln: University of Nebraska Press, 1995.

Borch-Jacobsen, Mikkel. *The Emotional Tie: Psychoanalysis, Mimesis, and Affect.* Trans. Douglas
    Brick. Palo Alto: Stanford University Press, 1992.

———. *The Freudian Subject.* Trans. Catherine Porter. Palo Alto: Stanford University Press,
    1988.

———. *Lacan: The Absolute Master.* Trans. Douglas Brick. Palo Alto: Stanford University Press,
    1991.

Brown, James. "Hospitable Texts." Dissertation, University of Texas at Austin, 2009.

Burke, Kenneth. *Attitudes Toward History.* 3rd ed. Berkeley: University of California Press,
    1984.

———. *Language as Symbolic Action: Essays on Life, Literature, and Method.* Berkeley: University
    of California Press, 1968.

———. "Methodological Repression and/or Strategies of Containment." *Critical Inquiry* 5.2
    (Winter 1978): 401–16.

———. *The Philosophy of Literary Form.* 3rd ed. Berkeley: University of California Press, 1974.

———. *A Rhetoric of Motives.* Berkeley: University of California Press, 1969.

Butler, Judith. *Giving an Account of Oneself.* New York: Fordham University Press, 2005.

———. *Precarious Life: The Powers of Mourning and Violence.* New York: Verso, 2004.

———. *The Psychic Life of Power: Theories in Subjection.* Palo Alto: Stanford University Press,
    1997.

Calarco, Matthew. *Zoographies: The Question of the Animal from Heidegger to Derrida.* New York:
    Columbia University Press, 2008.

Campbell, Karlyn Kohrs. "Agency: Promiscuous and Protean." *Communication and Critical/Cul-
    tural Studies* 2.1 (March 2005): 1–19.

Champlain College. "About Cities of Refuge." August 15, 2009. http://www.champlain.edu/In
    stitute-for-Global-Engagement.html.

Chanter, Tina. "Feminism and the Other." *The Provocation of Levinas: Rethinking the Other.* Ed.
    Robert Bernasconi and David Wood. New York: Routledge, 1988. 32–56.

Chase, Cynthia. *Decomposing Figures: Rhetorical Readings in the Romantic Tradition.* Baltimore:
    Johns Hopkins University Press, 1986.

Church, R. M. "Emotional Reactions of Rats to the Pain of Others." *Journal of Comparative and
    Physiological Psychology* 52 (1959):132–34.

Clark, David. "On Being 'The Last Kantian in Nazi Germany.'" *Animal Acts: Configuring the Hu-
    man in Western History.* Ed. Jennifer Ham and Matthew Senior. New York: Routledge, 1997.
    165–98.

Clark, Gregory. *Rhetorical Landscapes in America: Variations on a Theme from Kenneth Burke.* Co-
    lumbia: University of South Carolina Press, 2004.

Connor, Richard C., and Kenneth S. Norris. "Are Dolphins Reciprocal Altruists?" *American Nat-
    uralist* 119.3 (March 1982): 358–74.

Copjec, Joan. *Imagine There Is No Woman: Ethics and Sublimation.* Cambridge: MIT Press, 2002.

Critchley, Simon. "Deconstruction and Pragmatism—is Derrida a Private Ironist or a Public Lib-
    eral?" Critchley, *Deconstruction and Pragmatism* 19–40.

———. "Metaphysics in the Dark: A Response to Richard Rorty and Ernesto Laclau." *Ethics-*

Politics-Subjectivity: Essays on Derrida, Levinas and French Contemporary Thought. New York: Verso, 1999.

———. *Very Little, Almost Nothing: Death, Philosophy, and Literature*. New York: Routledge, 1997.

Critchley, Simon, Jacques Derrida, Ernesto Laclau, and Richard Rorty. *Deconstruction and Pragmatism*. Ed. Chantal Mouffe. New York: Routledge, 1997.

Crusius, Timothy. "Neither Trust Nor Suspicion: Kenneth Burke's Rhetoric and Hermeneutics." *Studies in the Literary Imagination* 28.2 (Fall 1995): 79–90.

Davis, Diane. "Addressing Alterity: Rhetoric, Hermeneutics, and the Non-Appropriative Relation." *Philosophy and Rhetoric* 38.3 (2005): 191–212.

———. "The Fifth Risk: A Response to John Muckelbauer's Response." *Philosophy and Rhetoric* 40.2 (2007): 248–56.

———. "Greetings: On Levinas and the Wagging Tail." *JAC*. Forthcoming, 2010.

Deem, Melissa. "Stranger Sociability, Public Hope, and the Limits of Political Transformation." *Quarterly Journal of Speech* 88.4 (November 2002): 444–54.

Deleuze, Gilles. *Negotiations*. Trans. Martin Joughin. New York: Columbia University Press, 1995.

Deleuze, Gilles, and Félix Guattari. *A Thousand Plateaus: Capitalism and Schizophrenia*. Trans. Brian Massumi. Minneapolis: University of Minnesota Press, 1987.

de Man, Paul. *Aesthetic Ideology*. Trans. Andrzej Warminski. Theory and History of Lit. 65. Minneapolis: University of Minnesota Press, 1997.

———. *The Resistance to Theory*. Theory and History of Lit. 33. Minneapolis: University of Minnesota Press, 1986.

———. *The Rhetoric of Romanticism*. New York: Columbia University Press, 1984.

Derrida, Jacques. *Adieu to Emmanuel Levinas*. Trans. Pascale-Anne Brault and Michael Naas. Palo Alto: Stanford University Press, 1999.

———. *The Animal That Therefore I Am*. Ed. Marie-Louise Mallet. Trans. David Wills. New York: Fordham University Press, 2008.

———. *Aporias*. Trans. Thomas Dutoit. Palo Alto: Stanford University Press, 1993.

———. "At this very moment in this work Here I am." Trans. Ruben Berezdivin. *Rereading Levinas*. Ed. Robert Bernasconi and Simon Critchley. Bloomington: Indiana University Press, 1991. 11–48.

———. *On Cosmopoliltanism and Forgiveness*. Trans. Mark Dooley and Michael Hughes. New York: Routledge, 2001.

———. "Eating Well: An Interview." Interview with Jean-Luc Nancy. Trans. Peter Connor and Avital Ronell. *Who Comes After the Subject?* Ed. Eduardo Cadava, Peter Connor, and Jean Luc-Nancy. New York: Routledge, 1991.

———. "The Force of Law: The 'Mystical Foundation of Authority.'" Trans. Mary Quaintance. *Deconstruction and the Possibility of Justice*. Ed. Drucilla Cornell, Michel Rosenfeld, and David Gray Carlson. New York: Routledge, 1992. 3–67.

———. "Generations of a City." *Open City: Alphabet City 6*. Ed. John Knechtel. Toronto: House of Anansi Press, 1998. 12–27.

———. *The Gift of Death*. Trans. David Wills. Chicago: University of Chicago Press, 1995.

——. *Given Time: I. Counterfeit Money.* Trans. Peggy Kamuf. Chicago: University of Chicago Press, 1992.

——. "Hospitality." *Acts of Religion.* Ed. Gil Anidjar. New York: Routledge, 2002. 358–420.

——. *Negotiations: Interventions and Interviews, 1971–2001.* Ed. and Trans. Elizabeth Rottenberg. Palo Alto: Stanford University Press, 2002.

——. *Paper Machine.* Trans. Rachel Bowlby. Palo Alto: Stanford University Press, 2005.

——. "On Reading Heidegger: An Outline of Remarks to the Essex Colloquium." *Research in Phenomenology* 17 (1987): 171–88.

——. "Remarks on Deconstruction and Pragmatism." Critchley, *Deconstruction and Pragmatism* 77–88.

——. "Violence and Metaphysics: An Essay on the Thought of Emmanuel Levinas." *Writing and Difference.* Trans. Alan Bass. Chicago: University of Chicago Press, 1978. 79–153.

Derrida, Jacques, and Anne Dufourmantelle. *Of Hospitality.* Trans. Rachel Bowlby. Palo Alto: Stanford University Press, 2000.

Dobbs, Lou. *War on the Middle Class: How the Government, Big Business, and Special Interest Groups Are Waging War on the American Dream and How to Fight Back.* New York: Viking, 2006.

Eberly, Rosa. *Citizen Critics: Literary Public Spheres.* Urbana: University of Illinois Press, 2000.

Edbauer, Jenny. "Executive Overspill: Affective Bodies, Intensity, and Bush-in-Relation." *Postmodern Culture* 15.1 (September 2004). http://muse.jhu.edu/journals/postmodern_culture/toc/pmc15.1.html

Freud, Sigmund. *An Autobiographical Study.* Ed. James Strachey. London: Hogarth Press and the Institute of Psychoanalysis, 1953–1974. Vol. 20 of *The Standard Edition of the Complete Psychological Works of Sigmund Freud* (hereafter: SE). 3–76.

——. *The Ego and the Id. SE* 19: 3–68.

——. *Group Psychology and the Analysis of the Ego. SE* 18: 67–145.

——. *Inhibitions, Symptoms, and Anxiety. SE* 20: 77–178.

——. "Mourning and Melancholia." *SE* 14: 237–60.

——. "An Outline of Psychoanalysis." *SE* 23: 141–208.

——. "Preface to the Translation of Bernheim's Suggestion." *SE* 1: 73–88.

——. "Psychical (or mental) Treatment." *SE* 7: 283–304.

——. "Thoughts for the Times on War and Death." *SE* 14: 275–301.

Fynsk, Christopher. *Heidegger: Thought and Historicity.* Ithaca: Cornell University Press, 1993.

——. "The Self and Its Witness: On Heidegger's *Being and Time.*" *Boundary* 2 10.3 (Spring 1982): 185–207.

Gehrke, Pat J. "The Ethical Importance of Being Human: God and Humanism in Levinas's Philosophy." *Philosophy Today* 50 (Winter, 2006): 428–36.

Goodall, Jane. *Through a Window: My Thirty Years with the Chimpanzees of Gombe.* Boston: Houghton Mifflin, 1990.

Habermas, Jürgen. "Pre-Political Foundations of the Democratic Constitutional State?" *Dialectics of Secularization: On Reason and Religion.* Trans. Brian McNeil. Ed. Florian Schuller. San Francisco: Ignatius Press, 2007. 19–48.

Habermas, Jürgen, Giovanna Borradori, and Jacques Derrida. *Philosophy in a Time of Terror: Dia-*

logues with Jürgen Habermas and Jacques Derrida. Ed. Giovanna Borradori. Chicago: University of Chicago Press, 2004.

Halloran, Michael S., and Gregory Clark. "National Park Landscapes and the Rhetorical Display of Civic Religion." *Rhetorics of Display*. Ed. Lawrence J. Prelli. Columbia: University of South Carolina Press, 2006.

Hamacher, Werner. *Premises: Essays on Philosophy and Literature from Kant to Celan*. Trans. Peter Fenves. Palo Alto: Stanford University Press, 1996.

Haraway, Donna. *When Species Meet*. Minneapolis: University of Minnesota Press, 2008.

Hart, Roderick P., and Suzanne M. Daughton. *Modern Rhetorical Criticism*, 3rd ed. Boston: Allyn & Bacon, 2005.

Hauser, Gerard A. *Vernacular Voices: The Rhetoric of Publics and Public Spheres*. Columbia: University of South Carolina Press, 1999.

Hawhee, Debra. "Kenneth Burke's Jungle Book." *Minnesota Review: The Feral Issue*, ns. 72–73. Forthcoming, 2010.

———. "Language as Sensuous Action: Sir Richard Paget, Kenneth Burke, and Gesture-Speech Theory." *Quarterly Journal of Speech* 92.4 (November 2006): 331–54.

Hegel, G. W. F. *Phenomenology of Spirit*. Trans. A. V. Miller. Oxford: Oxford University Press, 1977.

Heidegger, Martin. *Being and Time*. New York: Harper and Row, 1962.

———. *The Fundamental Concepts of Metaphysics: World, Finitude, Solitude*. Trans. William McNeil and Nicholas Walker. Bloomington: Indiana University Press, 1995.

———. "Language." *Poetry, Language, Thought*. Trans. Albert Hofstadter. New York: Harper and Row, 1971. 165–82.

———. *Nihilism*. Trans. Frank A. Capuzzi. San Francisco: Harper and Row, 1982. Vol. 4 of *Nietzsche*.

———. *On the Way to Language*. Trans. Peter D. Hertz. New York: Harper and Row, 1982.

———. *What is Called Thinking?* Trans. J. Glenn Gray. New York: Harper and Row, 1968.

Heijden, Yvonne van der. "International Network of Cities of Asylum." *Nieman Reports* Fall 2004. http://www.nieman.harvard.edu/reportsitem.aspx?id=100776.

Hogan, J. Michael, ed. *Rhetoric and Community: Studies in Unity and Fragmentation*. Columbia: University of South Carolina Press, 1998.

Hyde, Michael. *The Call of Conscience: Heidegger and Levinas, Rhetoric and the Euthanasia Debate*. Columbia: University of South Carolina Press, 2001.

———. *The Lifegiving Gift of Acknowledgment*. West Lafayette: Purdue University Press, 2005.

———. "The Rhetor as Hero and the Pursuit of Truth: The Case of 9/11." *Rhetoric and Public Affairs* 8.1 (2005): 1–30.

International Cities of Refuge Network. "About ICORN." 2009. August 15, 2009. http://www.icorn.org/history.php.

———. "Founding Charter." June 11, 2006. August 14, 2009. http://www.icorn.org/editor/filemanager/files/founding_documents/eng_thecharter.pdf.

Irigaray, Luce. "The Fecundity of the Caress." *Face to Face With Levinas*. Ed. Richard A. Cohen. New York: State University of New York Press, 1986. 231–356.

Jameson, Fredric. "The Symbolic Interference; or, Kenneth Burke and Ideological Analysis." *Critical Inquiry* 4.3 (Spring 1978): 507–23.

Jost, Walter, and Michael Hyde, eds. *Rhetoric and Hermeneutics in Our Time: A Reader*. New Haven: Yale University Press, 1997.

Kant, Immanuel. *Critique of Judgment*. Trans. John H. Bernard. New York: Cosimo Classics, 2007.

———. *The Metaphysics of Morals*. Trans. James Ellington. New York: Bobbs-Merril, 1964.

———. "On the Different Races of Man." *Race and the Enlightenment: A Reader*. Ed. Emmanuel Chukwudi Eze. Malden: Blackwell, 2000. 38–48.

———. *Perpetual Peace and Other Essays*. Trans. Ted Humphrey. Indianapolis: Hackett Publishing Co., 1983.

———. *Universal Natural History and Theory of the Heavens*. Trans. Ian Johnson. Arlington: Richer Resources, 2008.

Kennedy, George. "A Hoot in the Dark: The Evolution of General Rhetoric." *Philosophy and Rhetoric* 25.1 (1992): 1–21.

Kundera, Milan. *Immortality*. Trans. Peter Kussi. New York: Grove Weidenfeld, 1990.

Lacan, Jacques. *Les complexes familiaux dans la formation de l'individu*. *L'Encyclopédie française* VII (March 1938). Paris: Navarin éditeur, 1984. In *Autres écrits*. Paris: Le Seuil, 2001. 23–84.

———. "The Function and Field of Speech and Language in Psychoanalysis." *Écrits: A Selection*. Trans. Alan Sheridan. New York: W. W. Norton, 1977.

Laclau, Ernesto. "Deconstruction, Pragmatism, Hegemony." Critchley, *Deconstruction and Pragmatism*. 69–76.

Lacoue-Labarthe, Philippe. *Typography*. Ed. Christopher Fynsk. Palo Alto: Stanford University Press, 1989.

Lacoue-Labarthe, Philippe, and Jean-Luc Nancy. "La Panique Politique." *Retreating the Political*. Ed. Simon Sparks. New York: Routledge, 1997. 1–31.

———. "The Unconscious is Destructured Like an Affect." *Stanford Literature Review* 6.2 (Fall 1989): 191–209.

Ladygina-Kohts, N. N. *Infant Chimpanzee and Human Child: A Classic 1935 Comparative Study of Ape Emotions and Intelligence*. Ed. Frans de Waal. New York: Oxford University Press, 2002.

Leff, Michael. "Hermeneutical Rhetoric." Jost and Hyde, *Rhetoric and Hermeneutics in Our Time*. 196–214.

Leff, Michael, and Andrea A. Lunsford. "Afterwords: A Dialogue." *Rhetoric Society Quarterly* 34.3 (Summer 2004):55–67.

Levinas, Emmanuel. *Collected Philosophical Papers*. Trans. Alphonso Lingis. Pittsburgh: Duquesne University Press, 1998.

———. *Difficult Freedom: Essays on Judaism*. Trans. Seán Hand. Baltimore: Johns Hopkins University Press, 1990.

———. *Ethics and Infinity: Conversations with Philippe Nemo*. Trans. Richard A. Cohen. Pittsburgh: Duquesne University Press, 1985.

———. "Ethics and Politics." Trans. Jonathan Romney. *The Levinas Reader*. Ed. Sean Hand. Malden: Blackwell, 1989. 289–97.

———. "Everyday Language and Rhetoric Without Eloquence." *Outside the Subject*. Trans. Michael B. Smith. Palo Alto: Stanford University Press, 1994.

———. *Existence and Existents*. Trans. Alphonso Lingis. Pittsburgh: Duquesne University Press, 1978.

———. "Freedom and Command." *Collected Philosophical Papers*. 15–23.

———. *God, Death, and Time*. Trans. Bettina Bergo. Palo Alto: Stanford University Press, 2000.

———. *Is It Righteous to Be? Interviews with Emmanuel Levinas*. Ed. Jill Robbins. Palo Alto: Stanford University Press, 2001.

———. "Is Ontology Fundamental?" *Emmanuel Levinas: Basic Philosophical Writings*. Ed. Adriaan T. Peperzak, Simon Critchley, and Robert Bernasconi. Bloomington: Indiana University Press, 1996. 1–10.

———. "The Name of a Dog, or Natural Rights." *Difficult Freedom*. 151–53.

———. *Otherwise than Being: Or, Beyond Essence*. Trans. Alphonso Lingis. Pittsburgh: Duquesne University Press, 1998.

———. "The Paradox of Morality." An Interview with Emmanuel Levinas. *The Provocation of Levinas: Rethinking the Other*. Ed. Robert Bernasconi and David Wood. New York: Routledge, 1988. 168–80.

———. "Peace and Proximity." *Basic Philosophical Writings*. Ed. Adriaan T. Peperzak, Simon Critchley, and Robert Bernasconi. Bloomington: Indiana University Press, 1996. 161–69.

———. "Phenomenon and Enigma." *Collected Philosophical Papers*. 61–73.

———. *Proper Names*. Trans. Michael B. Smith. Palo Alto: Stanford University Press, 1996.

———. "Reality and Its Shadow." *Collected Philosophical Papers*. 1–13.

———. "Substitution." *Emmanuel Levinas: Basic Philosophical Writings*. Ed. Adriaan T. Peperzak, Simon Critchley, and Robert Bernasconi. Bloomington: Indiana University Press, 1996. 79–95.

———. *Time and the Other*. Trans. Richard A. Cohen. Pittsburgh: Duquesne University Press, 1987.

———. *Totality and Infinity: An Essay on Exteriority*. Trans. Alphonso Lingis. Pittsburgh: Duquesne University Press, 1961.

———. "The Trace of the Other." Trans. Alphonso Lingis. *Deconstruction in Context*. Ed. Mark C. Taylor. Chicago: University of Chicago Press, 1986. 345–59.

Lispector, Clarice. *The Passion According To G. H.* Trans. Ronald W. Sousa. Minneapolis: University of Minnesota Press, 1988.

Llewelyn, John. "Am I Obsessed By Bobby? (Humanism and the Other Animal)." *Re-Reading Levinas*. Ed. Robert Bernasconi and Simon Critchley. Bloomington: Indiana University Press, 1991. 234–45.

———. *The Middle Voice of Ecological Conscience: A Chiasmic Reading of Responsibility in the Neighborhood of Levinas, Heidegger, and Others*. New York: St. Martin's Press, 1991.

Lyotard, Jean-François. *The Differend: Phrases in Dispute*. Trans. Georges Van Den Abbeele. Theory and History of Lit. 46. Minnesota: University of Minnesota Press, 1988.

Lyotard, Jean-François, and Jean-Loup Thébaud. *Just Gaming*. Trans. Wlad Godzich. Theory and History of Lit. 20. Minneapolis: University of Minnesota Press, 1985.

Mailloux, Steven. *Disciplinary Identities: Rhetorical Paths of English, Speech, and Composition*. New York: Modern Language Association, 2006.

———. "Making Comparisons: First Contact, Ethnocentrism, and Cross-Cultural Communication." *Post-Nationalist American Studies*. Ed. John Carlos Rowe. Berkeley: University of California Press, 2000.

————. *Reception Histories: Rhetoric, Pragmatism, and American Cultural Politics*. Ithaca: Cornell University Press, 1998.

————. "Re-Marking Slave Bodies: Rhetoric as Production and Reception." *Philosophy and Rhetoric* 35.2 (2002): 96–119.

————. *Rhetorical Power*. Ithaca: Cornell University Press, 1989.

Marder, Michael. "Terror of the Ethical: On Levinas's *il y a*." *Postmodern Culture* 18.2 (2008). http://muse.jhu.edu/journals/postmodern_culture/vo18/18.2.marder.html.

Mediamatters.org. *Media Matters for America*. December 12, 2005. http://mediamatters.org/research/200512120004.

Meltzoff, Andrew N., and M. Keith Moore. "Explaining Facial Imitation: A Theoretical Model." *Early Development and Parenting* 6 (1997): 179–92.

————. "Imitation in Newborn Infants: Exploring the Range of Gestures Imitated and the Underlying Mechanisms." *Developmental Psychology* 25.6 (1989): 954–62.

————. "Imitation, Memory, and the Representation of Persons." *Infant Behavior and Development* 17 (1994): 83–99.

————. "Imitation of Facial and Manual Gestures by Human Neonates." *Science* 198 (1977): 74–78.

————. "Infant Intersubjectivity: Broadening the Dialogue to Include Imitation, Identity, and Intention." *Intersubjective Communication and Emotion in Early Ontogeny*. Ed. Stein Braten. New York: Cambridge University Press, 2006.

————. "Newborn Infants Imitate Adult Facial Gestures." *Child Development* 54 (1983): 702–9.

Miller, Carolyn R. "Rhetoric and Community: The Problem of the One and the Many." *Defining the New Rhetorics*. Ed. Theresa Enos and Stuart C. Brown. Sage Series in Written Communication 7. Newbury Park: Sage, 1993. 79–94.

Mohamad, Gunawan. *Conversations with Difference*. Trans. Jennifer Lindsay. Singapore: NUS Press, 2002.

Muckelbauer, John. "Rhetoric, Asignification, and the Other: A Response to Diane Davis." *Philosophy and Rhetoric* 40.2 (2007): 238–47.

Nancy, Jean-Luc. "Corpus." *Birth to Presence*. Trans. Brian Holmes. Palo Alto: Stanford University Press, 1993. 189–207.

————. *The Experience of Freedom*. Trans. Bridget McDonald. Palo Alto: Stanford University Press, 1993.

————. "Heidegger's 'Originary Ethics.'" *Heidegger and Practical Philosophy*. Ed. Francois Raffoul and David Pettigrew. New York: State University of New York Press, 2002. 65–86.

————. *The Inoperative Community*. Ed. Peter Connor. Trans. Peter Connor, Lisa Garbus, Michael Holland, and Simona Sawhney. Minneapolis: University of Minnesota Press, 1991.

————. "Of Being-in-Common." *Community at Loose Ends*. Ed. Miami Theory Collective. Minneapolis: University of Minnesota Press, 1991.

————. *The Sense of the World*. Trans. Jeffrey S. Librett. Minneapolis: University of Minnesota Press, 1997.

————. "Sharing Voices." *Transforming the Hermeneutic Context: From Nietzsche to Nancy*. Ed. Gayle L. Ormiston and Alan D. Schrift. Albany: State University of New York Press, 1990.

————. "Shattered Love." *The Inoperative Community*. 82–109.

———. "Thought as a Gap that Touches." Interview with Chantal Ponbriand. *Poiesis: A Journal of the Arts and Communication* 3 (2001): 6–13.

Nancy, Jean-Luc, and Philippe Lacoue-Labarthe. "La panique politique." *Retreating the Political.* Ed. Simon Sparks. New York: Routledge, 1997. 1–31.

Nealon, Jeffery. *Alterity Politics: Ethics and Performative Subjectivity.* Durham: Duke University Press, 1998.

Newton, Adam. *The Fence and the Neighbor: Emmanuel Levinas, Yeshayahu Leibowitz, and Israel Among the Nations.* Albany: State University of New York Press, 2001.

Nouvet, Claire. "An Impossible Response: The Disaster of Narcissus." *Yale French Studies: Literature and the Ethical Question* 79 (1991): 103–34.

Perpich, Diane. "Figurative Language and the 'Face' in Levinas's Philosophy." *Philosophy and Rhetoric* 38.2 (2005): 103–21.

Poster, Carol. "Being, Time, and Definition: Toward a Semiotics of Figural Rhetoric." *Philosophy and Rhetoric* 33.2 (2000): 116–36.

Poulakos, Takis. *Speaking for the Polis: Isocrates' Rhetorical Education.* Columbia: University of South Carolina Press, 1997.

Quandahl, Ellen. "More Lessons in How to Read: Burke, Freud, and the Resources of Symbolic Transformation," *College English* 63.5 (May 2001): 633–54.

Rickels, Laurence. *Aberrations of Mourning: Writing on German Crypts.* Detroit: Wayne State University Press, 1988.

———. *The Case of California.* Minneapolis: University of Minnesota Press, 2001.

Rizzolatti, Giacomo, Luciano Fadiga, Leonardo Fogassi, and Vittorio Gallese. "From Mirror Neurons to Imitation: Facts and Speculations." *The Imitative Mind: Development, Evolution, and Brain Bases.* Ed. Andrew N. Meltzoff and Wolfgang Prinz. Cambridge: Cambridge University Press, 2002. 247–66.

Robbins, Jill. *Altered Reading: Levinas and Literature.* Chicago: University of Chicago Press, 1999.

Roberts-Miller, Patricia. "Habermas' Rational-Critical Sphere and the Problem of Criteria." *The Role of Rhetoric in an Anti-Foundational World.* Ed. Michael Bernard-Donals and Richard Glejzer. New Haven: Yale University Press, 1998. 170–94.

Ronell, Avital. "Confessions of an Anacoluthon: Avital Ronell on Writing, Technology, Pedagogy, Politics." Interview with Diane Davis. *JAC* 20.2 (2000): 243–81.

———. *Crack Wars: Literature Addiction Mania.* Lincoln: University of Nebraska Press, 1992.

———. *Dictations: On Haunted Writing.* Lincoln and London: University of Nebraska Press, 1993.

———. "The Sacred Alien: Heidegger's Reading of Hölderlin's 'Andenken.'" *The ÜberReader.* 205–26.

———. *Stupidity.* Urbana: University of Illinois Press, 2002.

———. *The Telephone Book: Technology, Schizophrenia, Electric Speech.* Lincoln: University of Nebraska Press, 1989.

———. *The Test Drive.* Urbana: University of Illinois Press, 2005.

———. "Trauma TV: Twelve Steps Beyond the Pleasure Principle." *Finitude's Score: Essays for the End of the Millennium.* Lincoln: University of Nebraska Press, 1994. 305–27.

———. *The ÜberReader: Selected Works of Avital Ronell.* Ed. Diane Davis. Urbana: University of Illinois Press, 2008.

Rorty, Richard. *Achieving Our Country: Leftist Thought in Twentieth-Century America.* Cambridge: Harvard University Press, 1998.

———. "Remarks on Deconstruction and Pragmatism." Critchley, *Deconstruction and Pragmatism.* 13–18.

———. "Response to Ernesto Laclau." Critchley, *Deconstruction and Pragmatism.* 41–46.

Rushdie, Salman. "A Declaration of Independence." *Autodafe: The Journal of the International Parliament of Writers* 1 (2001): 92–93.

Salmon, Christian. "The Parliament of a 'Missing People.'" Trans. Betsy Wing. *Autodafe: The Journal of the International Parliament of Writers* 1 (2001): 9–15.

———. "Towards a Network of Cities of Asylum." Council of Europe. *Local Democracy: A Civic Project.* Strasbourg: Council of Europe Publishing, 1996. 133–36.

Selzer, Jack. *Kenneth Burke in Greenwich Village: Conversing with the Moderns, 1915–1931.* Madison: University of Wisconsin Press, 1996.

Shaviro, Steven. *Passion & Excess: Blanchot, Bataille, and Literary Theory.* Tallahassee: Florida State University Press, 1990.

Vitanza, Victor J. "Critical Sub/Versions of the Historiographies of Rhetorics; or the Rhetorics of the Histories of Rhetorics: Traditional, Revolutionary, and Sub/Versive." *PRE/TEXT* 8.1–2 (1987): 63–125.

———. *Negation, Subjectivity, and the History of Rhetoric.* Albany: State University of New York Press, 1997.

De Waal, Frans. "Food Sharing and Reciprocal Obligations Among Chimpanzees." *Journal of Human Evolution* 18 (1989): 433–59.

———. *Good Natured: The Origins of Right and Wrong in Humans and Other Animals.* Cambridge: Harvard University Press, 1997.

Warner, Michael. *Publics and Counterpublics.* New York: Zone Books, 2002.

Wechkin, S., J. H. Masserman, and W. Terris. "Shock to a Conspecific as an Averse Stimulus." *Psychonomic Science* 1 (1964): 47–48.

Wess, Robert. *Kenneth Burke: Rhetoric, Subjectivity, Postmodernism.* Cambridge: Cambridge University Press, 1996.

Wilson, Edward O. *Sociobiology: The New Synthesis.* Twenty-fifth Anniversary Ed. Cambridge: Belknap Press of Harvard University Press, 2000.

Wright, Mark H. "Burkean and Freudian Theories of Identification." *Communication Quarterly* 42.3 (Summer 1994): 301–10.

Index